CLAUDE JACQUES
in collaboration with René Dumont

ANGKOR

PHOTOGRAPHY BY LUC IONESCO,
JACQUELINE AND GUY NAFILYAN

PREFACE BY FEDERICO MAYOR,
Director-General of UNESCO

KÖNEMANN

Original title: Angkor
© 1990, Bordas S. A., Paris
Editor: Odile Berhemy
Proofreader: Tewfik Allal, Anne Cantal,
Marielle Veteau
Indexer: Pierre Valas
Typesetting: Daniel Leprince
Production: Francine Deligny

The passages relating to Khmer architecture, and in particular the technical descriptions of the main temples, are by René Dumont.

Illustrations:
page 2: Preah Khan. *Photo: Guy Nafilyan*
page 3: Angkor Thom, Terrace of the Elephants, detail.
Photo: Guy Nafiliyan
pages 6–7: Angkor park, a photograph taken by the SPOT Earth observation satellite. The map of Angkor is perfectly delineated here: clearly visible are first the Western Baray (1), almost entirely filled with water (the red point in the middle marks the location of the Western Mebon temple); Angkor Thom (2), which provides a useful indication of scale, since each of its sides is three kilometers long; Angkor Wat (3) and the smaller baray of the temple of Preah Khan (4), with the Neak Pean ensemble in the middle of the reservoir. In the area surrounding Angkor park, there are numerous other old ruins, generally identifiable by small rectangles of water (5). Above the modern road (6) from Siem-Reap to Sisophon (and beyond, to Bangkok) the old route (7) is clearly visible, leading from the northwest corner of the Western Baray.
SPOT image 269/323 produced for historical and archaeological research carried out at the Sorbonne by the École pratique des Hautes Études (Science historiques et philologiques). © CNES 1989, SPOT Image Distribution.

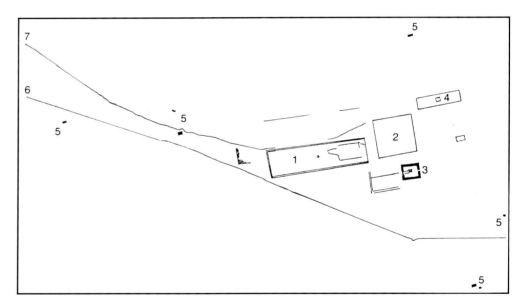

© 1999 for the English edition:
Könemann Verlagsgesellschaft mbH
Bonner Str. 126, D-50968 Cologne

Translation from German: Jane Carroll
Editor of the English language edition:
Chris Murray
Managing editor: Bettina Kaufmann
Project coordinator: Jackie Dobbyne
Typesetting: Goodfellow & Egan Ltd.,
Cambridge
Production Manager: Detlev Schaper
Assistant: Ursula Schümer
Printing and binding: Sing Cheong Printing Ltd.

Printed in Hong Kong, China

ISBN 3-8290-0504-0
10 9 8 7 6 5 4 3 2 1

PREFACE

Angkor is widely acknowledged to be one of the key works in our human heritage, yet most people know very little about it, and only the name of one small part of this vast site, Angkor Wat, has a familiar ring. Yet this area of ruins, covering more than 20,000 hectares, represents five centuries of the history and civilization of the Khmer people. Its more recent history is bound up with the discovery by Europeans of the wonders of East Asian civilizations and with a continuing dialogue between the cultures of East and West.

Claude Jacques, who knows Cambodia intimately, is renowned as an authority on Khmer inscriptions. His deep knowledge of Angkor is the result of his frequent visits to every corner of the site. Over many years he has painstakingly researched the significance of the texts engraved on stone, and this has enabled him to throw new light on Khmer history. The reader is drawn in first by the splendid photographs in this book, and then by Claude Jacques' enthusiasm as he describes vividly and precisely every aspect of the art and history of Angkor.

This book is a valuable guide for anyone "discovering" Angkor. The text and stunningly beautiful images combine to present a complete picture of the site, with its successive capital cities, its huge reservoirs, and its spectacular temple architecture, all so well analyzed by the architectural historian René Dumont. Detailed ground plans of the various temples are provided, and a series of plans, drawn by Guy Nafilyan, enable the reader to follow the fascinating story of Angkor over the centuries.

By demonstrating Angkor's priceless value to its readers, this book contributes greatly to the protection of the site, which has been so endangered by the political upheavals that have interrupted the vital restoration work that France and Cambodia were carrying out.

Now, new rescue work is being undertaken. All Cambodians, whatever their political color, acknowledge Angkor as the most potent symbol of their culture, and in the rest of the world there is a new understanding of it as one of the world's great heritage sites, a site that must at all costs be preserved. At the meeting of UNESCO's General Conference in 1989, the member states instructed the organization to take all measures necessary to coordinate international action to save these monuments.

And as Director-General of UNESCO, it is my fervent wish that Angkor, like such sites of universal importance as Abu Simbel in Egypt, Borobudur in Java, Indonesia, and Sana'a in Yemen, will be saved and made known to the whole world.

It is to be hoped that, through this book, Claude Jacques' passion for Angkor will be transmitted to others. Lying at the heart of this country, which has suffered so much violence, Angkor, historical capital of the Khmer nation, must become a place of meeting and mutual understanding for all those who care about humanity's cultural heritage.

Federico MAYOR
Director-General of UNESCO

CONTENTS

ANGKOR

FOREWORD

This book was first published in 1990. At the time Cambodia was beginning to recover from the succession of traumatic events it had suffered since 1970, but it was still not in a position to assume the heavy responsibility of looking after the many remarkable monuments at Angkor.

The few visitors returning to Angkor found that it had undergone a spectacular transformation as a result of the years of neglect. Nature had again claimed the site, and vegetation was growing luxuriantly everywhere, smothering the stones under a mass of greenery; it was like going back to the last century, when the site was first discovered by Westerners.

However, in the climate of bitter conflict that Cambodia had experienced and was still experiencing, the country's past—with Angkor as its most stunning manifestation—seems to have been one of the few factors capable of somehow reuniting the opposing factions. Clear evidence of this is the fact that Angkor Wat, the most beautiful of all the temples, was depicted on the flag of each of the warring groups.

Moreover, it seems to me remarkable that all the combatants demonstrated a respect for the Angkor monuments: right from the outbreak of hostilities, no fighting took place there, and no troops ever attacked researchers or tourists who found themselves stranded in the immense archaeological site. Although the buildings were damaged here and there by bullets, it's clear that these were isolated incidents. Particularly regrettable, however, was the damage at Angkor Wat, where, appallingly, a dozen of the wonderful *apsaras* (celestial dancers) carved on the walls were machine-gunned by delinquent soldiers, who in this case happened to be Khmers Rouges.

Sadly, there were also a few deliberate acts of vandalism in various sanctuaries, notably at Preah Khan, where numerous heads carved in high relief in the central temple were taken off with a chisel. Fortunately, the special heritage police who protect the site successfully eradicated this problem several years ago.

A more insidious problem has been the systematic theft of archaeological treasures. These thefts have occurred both in isolated temples and at Angkor itself, and even at the Angkor Conservation's depository. The stolen objects turn up in antique shops abroad, after having made an easy exit via Thailand. It seems that all the factions who had been present in the area were guilty. There is a glimmer of hope, however: several stolen objects that have been recovered by the Cambodian police are now back at Siem Reap, and a large number of sculptures, mostly Khmer, seized from antique dealers in Thailand, have been placed in a gallery at the National Museum in Bangkok.

When the war broke out in 1970, Bernard-Philippe Groslier, the last French conservator of the Angkor monuments, found it impossible to continue his restoration project. His main concern was to protect the work that had already been started, so that the monuments would suffer as little damage as possible while work was interrupted. The gallery at Angkor Wat that sheltered the long bas-relief depicting the "Churning of the Ocean of Milk" (one of the most famous scenes of Khmer mythology) was in danger of collapsing; it was therefore entirely dismantled and a straw canopy installed in its place to protect the bas-relief it covered. The task was far more difficult at the great temple of the Baphuon, where restoration, based on the method called anastylosis, had been started more than ten years earlier, but was still a long way off completion. Here conservation involved covering the retaining wall with laterite paving in order to prevent the sides of this temple mountain from collapsing; the paving has fulfilled its purpose perfectly to this day. Angkor Conservation possessed a large archaeological depository, so all the larger items were sent there and suitably protected, while the bronzes, ceramics and a number of small sandstone statues were sent to the National Museum at Phnom Penh, where they are still kept.

Buddha on a naga. The head has recently been stolen. Bayon style, end 12th century to beginning 13th century. Bayon, southeast corner tower of the second enclosure.
Photo: Guy Nafilyan

Temple guardians (*dvarapala*) and divinities. Bayon style, end 12th century to beginning 13th century. Preah Khan temple, central group.
Photo: Claude Jacques

The temple of Angkor Wat is one of the main national centers of Khmer Buddhism, and before the war large numbers of the faithful used to visit the Gallery of a Thousand Buddhas. Although many of the statues have disappeared, this gallery is still a much-frequented place of meditation.

Back in 1986, following the signing of an agreement between the Indian and the Khmer governments, the Archaeological Survey of India was asked to work on the most prestigious of the Angkor Wat monuments. Later, when the political situation became clearer, an international meeting was held in Tokyo, in January 1993, where it was decided to create the Comité International de Coordination pour la sauvegarde des monuments d'Angkor. The committee's secretariat-general, co-chaired by France and Japan, is run under the auspices of UNESCO. The committee meets in plenary session annually at Phnom Penh; in addition, technical meetings are held once or twice a year.

For its part, the Khmer government created in 1995 a body appropriately called APSARA (Autorité pour la Protection du Site et l'Aménagement de la Région d'Angkor), for the combined purpose of protecting the monuments and promoting the development of the region for the benefit of its inhabitants.

Today, a number of international teams are working at Angkor. Japanese researchers are carrying out excavations around the Prasat Suor Prat temples and in the great square at Angkor Thom, and they are also working on the restoration of the Bayon; another team from Japan is working in the temple of Banteay Kdei. American workers from the World Monuments Fund are focusing on the great temple of Preah Khan. An Indonesian team is restoring the entrance pavilions of the royal palace at Angkor Thom. German funds have financed some very fruitful research in the temple of Preah Ko in the Roluos group, and German archaeologists are working on the conservation of the *apsaras* of Angkor Wat.

Italy has carried out studies on the temple of Pre Rup, and China has just begun restoring the temple of Chau Say Tevoda. Finally, France has opted to complete the restoration work that was begun in the 1960s and interrupted by the war. This restoration concerns the great temple of the Baphuon, a huge project started in 1960; work on the Terrace of the Leper King has been completed and attention has now turned to the Terrace of the Elephants. In addition, important excavations are taking place in the royal palace and the Angkor Thom city complex, with results that are already proving to be very positive.

Meanwhile, teams of researchers are working in their respective countries on the findings from these on-site projects. With regard to the history of the sites, which is the main subject of this book, there is room here only for a rapid summary of the main new points that have emerged since the book was written in 1990.

Research carried out in the city of Indrapura—on the Roluos group, Preah Ko, and Bakong—has demonstrated in particular that the last-named temple, beneath the sandstone covering added by Indravarman I, had perfectly constructed laterite walls, which might date from the previous reign. Similarly, it's now possible to distinguish several stages in the construction of the temple of Preah Ko. It's clear that this period of Khmer history needs to be revised and that probably greater importance should be ascribed to the reign of Jayavarman III.

Moving to the late period of Angkor's history, it's now apparent that Jayavarman VII was not in fact the last of the great Khmer kings, as formerly believed: the wealth of the Khmer empire's capital city, even by the end of the 13th century, aroused the admiration of the Chinese visitor Zhou Daguan, and it seems that its prosperity did not end during that century. However, when the Khmer kings adopted Theravada (Lesser Vehicle) Buddhism, this spelled the end

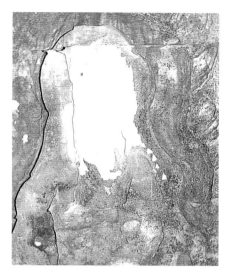

Head of divinity removed
with a chisel by vandals in
1988 or 1989.
In the temple of Preah Khan,
where this photograph was
taken in December 1989,
nearly 10 percent of the
divinities have suffered a
similar fate.
Preah Khan temple,
central group.
Photo: Claude Jacques

Kbal Spean.
Near the source of one of the
tributaries of the Siem Reap
river, in the heart of the
Angkor site, at Kbal Spean.
The river bed has been
engraved by ascetics with
linga and bas-reliefs, which
here represent the reclining
Vishnu. Mid-11th century.
Photo: Luc Ionesco, Top

of building great monuments in stone; construction was now in wood, on foundations that have been found in large numbers at Angkor Thom. Of course this wood, which might well have been richly carved and decorated, disappeared long ago. Unfortunately, there is little documentation in the form of monuments and inscriptions surviving from this final period of Angkor history, but the conclusion has to be that the decline of the city and the empire came rapidly. These final centuries, too, need to be looked at again; it will probably be found that the "Bayon style" lasted much longer than was previously thought, and that in a revised Khmer chronology works created in this style will appear until at least the end of the 13th century.

For various reasons, notably because of the prevailing political conditions, neither the Angkor group nor any of its individual monuments were included in UNESCO's list of world heritage sites, created in 1972. This obvious anomaly has now been corrected: Angkor was added to the list in December 1992.

The site of Angkor, with its extraordinary history and its stupendous artistic achievements, is now ready to welcome the many admirers that it so richly deserves.

Claude JACQUES

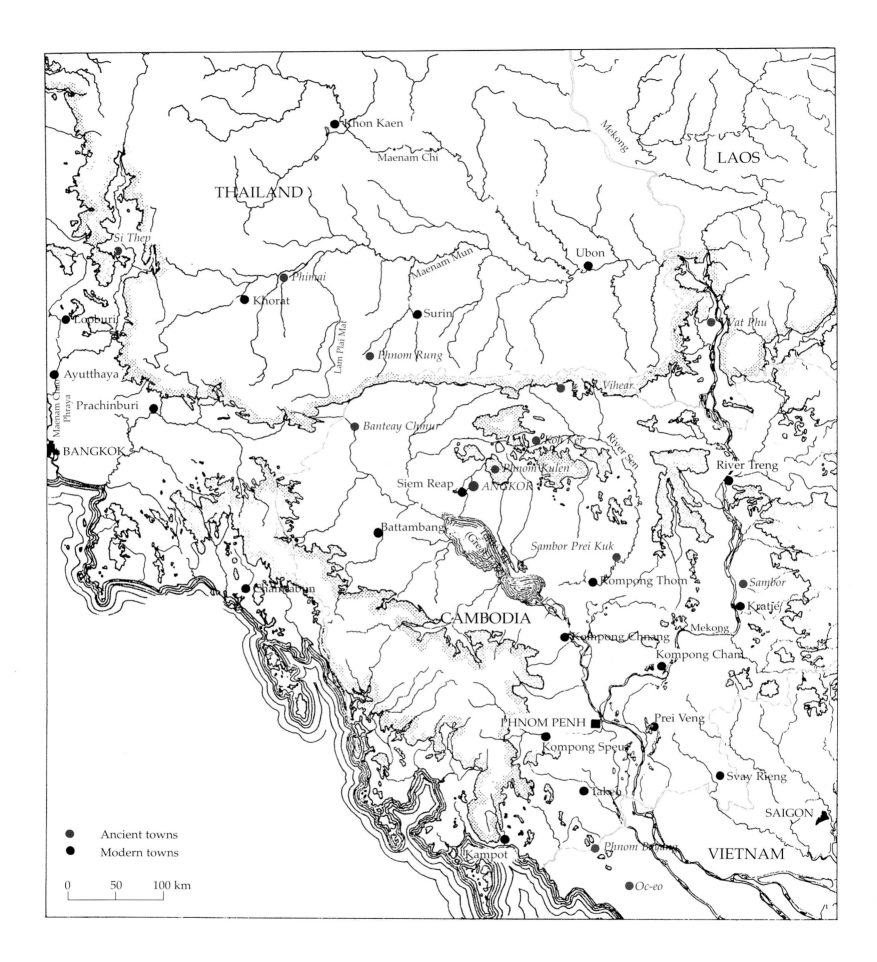

Map of Cambodia

Drawn by Françoise Lagarde

CHAPTER 1

Khmer Civilization

Khmer civilization remained essentially unchanged from the time when its major temples were built, between the 9th and 14th centuries, to the end of the 19th century. We can now read the story of that civilization in its surviving monuments and inscriptions.

The innumerable temples built to honor gods imported from India were meant to ensure prosperity in this world and happiness in the next. Local spirits watched over everyday life.

ngkor, like Rome, was not built in a day. Within what is now known as the Angkor park, which covers some 300 square kilometers, awestruck visitors encounter an intermingling of several centuries of history—from the 8th century at Prasat Ak Yum to the 14th century at Mangalartha, and even up to the 16th century, when the earliest "restoration" work at Angkor Wat was carried out by a Khmer king.

The name Angkor is a Khmer form of the Sanskrit word *nagara*, which means "city." It occurs in a number of modern Cambodian place names, such as Angkor Borei, which is south of Phnom Penh. In the Siem Reap area northeast of the Great Lake (Tonlé Sap) it is used in particular to denote the complexes of Angkor Wat, "the temple city," and of Angkor Thom, "the great city."

From the end of the 9th century there was a succession of at least seven capitals on various sites in Angkor park. Most of these cities were known by the same name, Yashodharapura, "the town of Him who brings glory," after the founder of the first of them, King Yashovarman I. There were also a number of upheavals, altering the landscape with the introduction of various construction projects, which, though often on a gigantic scale, were almost always ephemeral.

It was really only at the end of the 12th century, when the great king Jayavarman VII decided to enclose his new city within mighty walls, that the capital city became permanently located on one site. New religious

On the edge of the Tonlé Sap (the Great Lake). This scene, of countryside near Phnom Penh at the beginning of the 20th century, with an ox cart and houses built on stilts, must be very similar to what it would have been like in the Angkor period.
Photo: Dieulefils

monuments continued to be built within this enclosure until 1431, which is traditionally (but probably incorrectly) regarded as the date when Angkor was abandoned.

Our present knowledge of the history of this civilization, a history long forgotten by the Khmers themselves, has had to be reconstructed piece by piece; there are still many gaps that remain to be filled. This task of reconstruction has been carried out by researchers, mostly French, who since the end of the 19th century have been studying the temples and the inscriptions carved in stone.

No trace is left of any dwellings, even of royal palaces, other than at a few rare sites, where one or two scattered tiles have been found. The Khmers lived in wooden houses that disappeared long ago, so that their history, and a picture of their everyday life, have had to be rediscovered. This has happened mainly through clues offered by surviving expressions of their religion.

There are also other sources of information, which might be seen as more objective, the most notable being the *Chinese Dynastic Annals*. There is also an account of a journey to Ankor written by a Chinese envoy, Zhou Daguan, at the end of 13th century. The Chinese took an early interest in the people of the countries bordering their own, their aim being trade rather than conquest. These dynastic annals contain a large number of references to neighboring peoples and these are generally highly valued as sources of information, the assumption being that they are much more reliable and specific than indigenous documents. This commonly held view may need to be revised, however.

The Inscriptions

The earliest known indigenous inscriptions, carved in stone, the only material that resists the passage of time, date from the 5th and 6th centuries and are in Sanskrit. A short time later—one text bears a date of 612—the Khmer language appears in the inscriptions, but it has borrowed many words from Sanskrit, perhaps because all these inscribed texts are closely linked to Hinduism or Buddhism. Sanskrit arrived in the area along with Indian traders. When the Khmers—perhaps initially their kings—adopted the Indians' gods, they would also have used the language considered appropriate for addressing homage and prayers to these new deities.

Nearly 1,200 inscriptions in Sanskrit or Khmer have been found in the area covering the ancient land of the Khmers; most of them were translated and published by the French scholar George Cœdès, one of the outstanding figures in Khmer studies. These inscriptions were carved between the 6th and 14th centuries and most frequently were placed in sanctuaries. They are exclusively religious in nature, in that they relate either to religion or to the administration of the temples. Naturally there is an occasional reference to "civil" life, and these allusions, though they never form the main subject of the text, are valuable for the insight they afford into Khmer society. The inscriptions are the main source of the information that enables us to retrace, after a fashion, the ancient history of the Khmers. Given their nature, it is almost miraculous that they have revealed as much as they have: inscriptions left by other peoples in this part of the world, for example the Mons of Thailand, are far less rich in historical information.

It is important to understand why the ancient Khmers took the trouble to carve texts in stone, in Sanskrit or Khmer, or in both languages, sometimes with such care that the stones are real works of art. In particular, why did the Khmers bother to use Sanskrit, an Indian scholarly language that they probably rarely used outside their temples? Presumably because Sanskrit was the language of the Indian gods whom the Khmers honored and for whom they built these wonderful temples. The gods brought prosperity in this world and beatitude in the next: it was therefore advisable to treat them well, and to make sure, using the language they knew, that one was going to be clearly understood.

Sanskrit

Apart from a few rare exceptions, the Sanskrit inscriptions are in the form of poems, their sophistication varying according to the abilities of the author. These inscriptions were placed under the gaze of a particular god and seemingly were intended to attract that deity's attention to the person who had had the sanctuary built in his honor or, more often, who was offering him gifts. In most instances the poem appears to have been composed upon the death of the sanctuary's founder, the moment when the latter had greatest need of the god he had served.

In many cases the founder was a king, though there are also many temples built by dignitaries or by important families. Only the very wealthy could afford to perform such acts of piety, and these families were close to the

Stele at the hospital of King Jayavarman VII.
About 20 of these stelae have been discovered, with inscriptions setting out the rules governing the "hospitals" founded or reformed by Jayavarman VII at the end of the 12th century.
Stele at Sai Fong hospital (near Vientiane, Laos), side C.
Photo: EFEO

Left: An inscription at the Baksei Chamkrong temple. This poem here was specially composed for the two piers of the temple's tower. Because the stone had already begun to flake the scribe smoothed off the broken edges before engraving the text. Mid-10th century. North pier of the tower, Baksei Chamkrong. *Photo: Claude Jacques*

Right: Inscription at the Lolei temple. This inscription lists the temple servants working the fortnightly shift. North pier of the south tower (second row) (1.5 to 21), Lolei. *Photo: Guy Nafilyan*

throne; they were careful to include the name of the particular king they served, together with a short eulogy, a feature which has helped historians to date the inscriptions.

Of course, these documents are far from objective: they contain no unfavorable comments on the subject of the eulogy and, paradoxically, very few on any enemies he might possess, especially if these too happened to be kings. Monarchs, once consecrated, and even more so once cremated, were invested with a power that could be dangerous: it was as well not to provoke them.

The Khmer "archives"

The Khmer texts are altogether different. The overwhelming majority are in the form of inventories, listing the temple's possessions, such as land, livestock, servants, and furnishings. These lists cannot be regarded as exhaustive, because generally they include only gifts from a particular individual (often the founder celebrated in the Sanskrit poem, when there are

16

inscriptions in both languages). Nevertheless, they are a potential source of valuable information on the economy of the time, though as yet they have hardly been studied.

They are in fact more than simple lists. For example, there are numerous references to the prices paid for rice fields, and to the names of their owners; some even refer to disputes over these properties. These are the most interesting texts, because they give us a glimpse of everyday life.

One or two of these Khmer inscriptions record the history of a temple's possessions, with references to successive kings served by the family that owned the temple, thus also providing an historical sketch covering one or more centuries. In some texts there is evidence of temples jointly owning rice fields, and of one or several minor temples declaring themselves to be "co-partners" in another, more important, temple. The smaller temples made payments to a large one, and in return benefited from the latter's protection and prestige.

There are also endless lists of servants of both sexes (generally referred to as "slaves"), especially in the royal temples of the 9th and 10th centuries. These people, who worked both in the temple and in the rice fields, could not have been slaves in the true sense of the word because slaves were forbidden to enter a temple, which thereby would have been "defiled." It is hardly likely, therefore, that anyone would have carefully engraved the names of real slaves under the very eyes of the gods.

Other lists describe the temple furnishings, and particularly the ornaments that decorated the images and symbols of the gods, as well as other objects relating to worship. These references are of particular interest since all the objects themselves have completely disappeared.

The character of the inscriptions underwent various changes across the centuries. For example, there are numerous Sanskrit poems of great quality that date from the end of the 9th century and from the middle of the 10th century; there are also long lists of "slaves" from this period. There is a noticeably large quantity of royal decrees concerning the temples dating from about the end of the 10th century, while from the following century there are frequent references to temples belonging to family dynasties. Short inscriptions indicating the name of the god occupying a sanctuary scarcely ever appear before the 12th century. These varying trends are worth noting, but there is no reason to suppose that a custom indicated in an inscription carved in one era was not practiced in other periods as well.

Inscription with a plan at the north Prasat Khleang. There are many Khmer texts concerned with the boundaries of land acquired by the temples. This, however, is a unique example of a plan engraved on stone. The area is divided into six large plots: a river cuts through the northwest corner; in the middle of the northeast plot, squares indicate the site of a hamlet and of a sanctuary dedicated to the Hindu god Shiva; the rectangle in the center-west indicates another, more important, sanctuary dedicated to Shiva. The text states that the harvest from the surrounding plot is to be offered to the god. The harvest from the center-east plot is for Shikhareshvara, the god to whom the Preah Viehear temple is dedicated.
North Prasat Khleang, east façade; north pier of the south gate.
Photo: Jeanbor

Khmer literature

Khmer civilization, which produced so many wonderful works of architecture and sculpture, also seems to have generated a copious literature in many fields, as we can see from evidence in the carved inscriptions. However, nothing of the literature remains: a combination of climate and insects would have prevented long-term preservation of written texts. What is puzzling is why the works that filled the temple "libraries" were not copied by scribes down the centuries, as was the case elsewhere.

Fortunately we do have some idea of what the libraries might have contained. The Chinese envoy Zhou Daguan tells us at the end of the 13th century of some "writings in chalk on tanned skin," and certainly there also

Manuscripts.
Until quite recently, Cambodian documents were written either on specially prepared palm leaves that were engraved with a metal stylus, or on sheets of thick paper fastened together in an accordion shape, and written on in ink. Sometimes the paper was black and the ink white.
Below: Prepared palm leaves: *Chbap*, a treatise on ethics.
Right: Paper: a treatise on the science of divining.
Photo: Jeanbor

existed manuscripts written on specially prepared palm leaves. These were engraved with a metal stylus.

The carved inscriptions are full of allusions to classical Indian literature, to the great epics of the *Mahabharata* and the *Ramayana*. There are references to writings on ritual, on grammar, and on the *Dharmashastra* (treatises on the law governing the order of the world). Horoscopes reveal a sound knowledge of astronomy. All this proves that Khmer scholars must have possessed a vast culture of Indian origin, a culture also demonstrated in the bas-reliefs in the temples.

It is hard to believe that an important Khmer literature did not exist alongside the Sanskrit, yet there is scarcely any indication of it in the inscriptions. There are a few traces: some rare inscriptions in the Khmer language do give three actual extracts from royal chronicles. The first of these relates to the miraculous origins of a temple during the reign of Jayavarman III in the mid-9th century; the other two explain why two noble warriors of the second half of the 12th century were honored in the temple of Banteay Chmar after dying as heroes.

It is known that these chronicles were regularly updated and preserved by royal officials, as they were in fairly recent times. We know from inscriptions that the chronicles opened with entirely legendary chapters. If only we could read the original pages, and could discover whether they contain history or legend!

Khmer society

What the written sources do not give us is any idea of the daily life of the Khmer people. For that we must turn to the bas-reliefs of the Bayon temple, dating from the end of the 12th century, though even the few images we find here cannot help us to form a very clear understanding of the country's social structure. The grandeur of the monuments has led modern scholars to look for a parallel civilization as a possible model, and some thought this might be provided by the Egyptians, who were not too distant in either time or geography. The myth of the *Devaraja*, the "god-king," encouraged these scholars to imagine a theocratic society made up of a tiny minority of priests serving an all-powerful king, who ruled over a people in slavery.

The reality was surely very different. It is true that our knowledge of this civilization is almost entirely confined to its religious aspect, and that there are few clues to help us understand what daily life was like. Nevertheless, rather than letting ourselves be overwhelmed by the images we have of their religious life, we should try to imagine what their life was like outside the temples. It would not have been so very different from the way of life of the Khmer people in the 19th century, as described by Adhémard Leclère, a French colonial official in the northeast of the country and a wonderful observer of Khmer society and manners.

There has been a tendency to identify the rice fields described in the inscriptions with traces of ancient rice fields, and to assume therefore that the temples were virtually the only landowners. But common sense suggests

Scenes of everyday Khmer life shown on a bas-relief at the Bayon temple.
While a boat goes into battle in water swarming with fish, on one bank (at the bottom), there are people in their houses. On the left, they are getting ready to cook food on skewers. Nearby, a discussion is taking place; a man seems to be drinking through a straw or pipe; a fish trap in the shape of a basket, exactly like those used today, hangs from the ceiling. On the other bank (at the top) a man seems to be dancing to the music of a harp before an attentive audience. Bayon, bas-reliefs in the southern half of the outer south gallery.
Photo: Luc Ionesco, EFEO

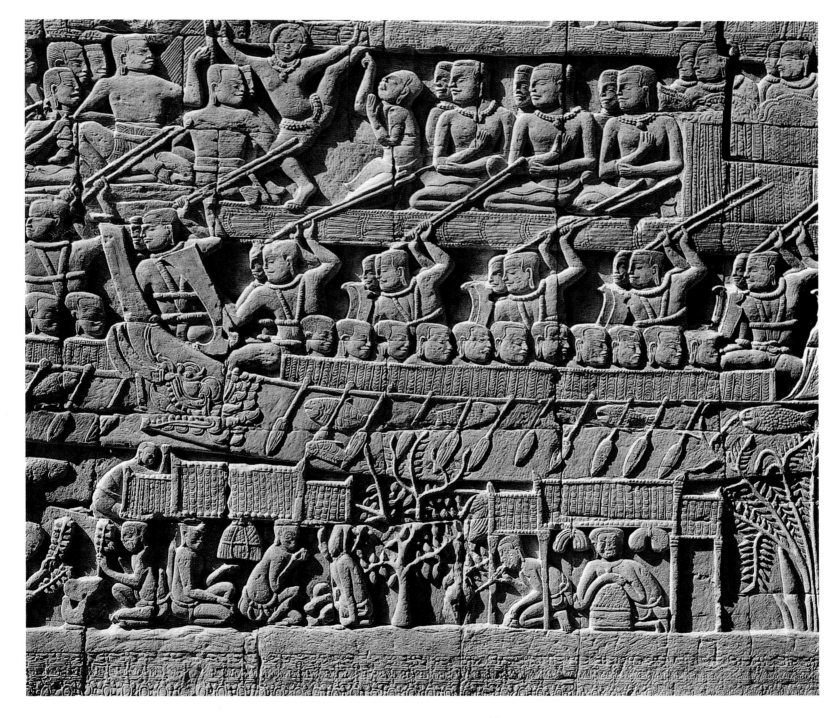

A scene of everyday Khmer life shown on a bas-relief at the Bayon temple: preparing a meal. The cooking pot stand, like the cooking pot itself, is ceramic. Bayon, bas-reliefs in the external gallery.
Photo: Luc Ionesco, EFEO

that, on the contrary, there would also have been lay owners of rice fields: at the very least, the people who sometimes donated rice fields to the temples.

The existence of great landowners, alongside a number of large temples, some of which owned vast areas of rice fields, appears clearly in texts from the end of the 12th century. This does not mean, however, that there were no small landowners in ancient Khmer society. In fact, it is reasonable to suppose that society then was essentially very similar to the society that existed until quite recently, and that a good deal of the land was divided up between the majority of the peasants.

We can deduce from the inscriptions that it was a highly structured society, to the extent that each man's name is generally preceded by a title or description indicating his station in life. However, the meaning of most of these terms, and where they placed people in the hierarchy, is now lost to us. The hierarchy was not rigidly fixed, in that the titles were conferred by the king, who would have been able to change them for others, if he so wished, and they were not automatically hereditary.

The king of kings could even create "kings" as a kind of honorary title. There are at least two known examples of high-ranking individuals, both of them religious tutors and advisers to the king, who received one of these titles: in the middle of the 11th century, Udayadityavarman II conferred on his *guru* Sadashiva the royal name of Jayendravarman; and, at the end of the 12th century, Jayavarman VII authorized his own *guru* to use the title Jayamangalarthadeva, and also specified that members of his family would

An unfinished bas-relief at the Bayon temple. Wild animals (a rhinoceros in the center?) in the forest. This unfinished bas-relief is interesting because it shows the way in which Khmer artists roughed out their subjects.
Bayon, bas-reliefs in the western half of the outer north gallery.
Photo: Luc Ionesco, EFEO

have the right to the title of "relative of the king." A relic of this usage was the royal title of *Samdech* that Prince Sihanouk bestowed as a special honor on Khmer top officials up until 1970.

The inscriptions also provide us with many names of functions concerning the royal court, the system of justice, and even local administration. However, they do not make up a coherent picture that could help us understand how the administration operated.

There were also the priests, who often describe themselves as Brahmins. In fact, the notion of caste, which is sometimes mentioned under its Indian name of *varna*, arises only in connection with the priests, and in cases where their particular duties appear to have been inherited. It does seem that some priests were part of a system of castes, some of which are occasionally referred to by name, though we do not know the details of this system. Jayavarman V created two of these Brahminical castes, and chose their members. Suryavarman I, following the unrest provoked by his accession to the throne, had no hesitation in confirming some Brahmins in their caste, while ruthlessly expelling others.

There is virtually no information about the common people other than the lists of "slaves" already mentioned. If, as I believe, these people were slaves only in relation to their god, the documents we possess give a picture of a Khmer peasant society closely linked to the life of the temple, as in more recent times it was linked to the life of the Buddhist pagoda. Once again, modern society enables us to envisage the ancient one.

There were also real slaves, however: they are sometimes enumerated (but never named) in inscriptions. Without doubt they were taken into slavery mainly from neighboring populations, in particular those who lived in remote mountainous areas and were regarded as barbarians.

A scene of Khmer religious life: two ascetics depicted on a pediment at the Bantea Chmar temple. One plays the harp, while the other reads a manuscript.
Photo: Luc Ionesco, EFEO

Family lines

The importance of family lines, which were matrilineal, is illustrated by several features of Khmer civilization, notably the fact that certain powerful families were the owners of temples, which were run by their representatives. It is likely that these temples housed, alongside the Indian gods, guardian ancestors who, when called upon, would pour out advice to their descendants through the voice of a medium, a custom practiced until quite recently.

The most high-ranking of these family lines, which naturally soon split into innumerable sub-divisions, may have included the successive kings, regarded as descendants of the legendary founder-monarchs: Kaundinya and his wife Soma on the one hand, Kambu and his wife Mera on the other. All four appear to be entirely mythical in origin and in fact to derive from two different legends.

All the Khmer kings claimed to be descendants of either Kaundinya and Soma or Kambu and Mera. Interestingly, the claim is not made for anyone else, as if this genealogical status, indispensable for acceding to the throne, granted no special prerogative in normal life. There was no strict rule regarding the succession of kings, who were simply chosen from within the royal family, except of course when a usurper seized the throne. Indeed, succession generally did take place in anarchic and even what could be considered dramatic circumstances.

The king and the royal dynasties

The two most important moments in a king's reign were his consecration, which made him both the supreme protector of his people and at the same time also a sacred personage, and his cremation, through which he became for ever one of the numerous divinities who watched over the kingdom. The consecration ceremony might have taken place several months after, or even before, the king actually took power, because it was necessary to wait for the astrologically propitious moment. It seems to have been carried out according to a solemn ritual based on the Indian model, and lasted several days. All kings were consecrated in this way, but a supreme king, "king of Khmer kings," was consecrated with another ceremony, which must have been one of remarkable splendor.

At their consecration, kings also received their "royal name," whose main feature, inherited from India, is the suffix -varman, which means "shield" or "protection." Thus Jayavarman means "he whose shield is victory," or "protected by victory." The original sense was quickly forgotten and the suffix simply indicated that the person bearing it had been consecrated a king.

The solemn cremation of a king also must have been based on an Indian ritual, though, at least for a king of kings, some purely Khmer elements were added. In particular, the deceased king received a posthumous name and from then on he was known by this name. In this way Yashovarman I became Paramashivaloka, "the king who has gone to the world of the supreme Shiva." Unlike the royal title the king bore in life, his posthumous name was used for him alone. The name appears only in the Khmer texts, whereas the Sanskrit poems continue to use the name the king had when alive.

The French scholar George Cœdès, in his account of the history of the Khmers and of the royal dynasties, failed to realize that often the lines of "legitimate" kings were interrupted, not because there was no heir, but because someone from another branch of the family had seized the throne, with varying degrees of violence. Of the 26 known supreme kings during the Angkor period, only eight were either the son or brother of the preceding ruler; and of these eight, at least one—the very founder of the first Angkor, Yashovarman I—ousted his father from power. Therefore the concept of legitimacy in royal succession was not greatly respected by pretenders to the throne, and there were numerous usurpers.

Jayavarman II, after having conquered several Khmer kingdoms, founded an empire by proclaiming himself chakravartin, "emperor of the world" or "universal monarch," during a special ceremony. He certainly intended that the empire he founded should survive him: for this purpose, not only did he have himself consecrated, but he also invented an opposite number for himself in the world of the gods, Devaraja. The traditional Khmer kings, who reigned over only one kingdom, certainly followed a rule of succession, but it is unlikely that they were happy to countenance one royal line in particular occupying the supreme throne for all time. This might have been the cause of the disturbances that sometimes accompanied the consecration of such a "king of kings."

Religion

Why did the indigenous peoples so easily adopt the gods the Indians brought with them when they moved into Southeast Asia? Presumably because they observed the effectiveness of new technologies introduced by the Indians and attributed this to the influence of the newcomers' deities. The Khmers, or the Chams, soon began placing these gods in their own temples. Given that the cosmology of the Indians' religion was probably very similar to that of the Khmers, the imported and the local deities would have sat quite easily together. The gods Shiva and Vishnu, as well as the Buddha, were particularly venerated, but the Hindu Shiva, regarded by Khmer kings over a long period as the supreme guardian of their empire, is the dominant figure. Most of the temples are dedicated to him, and in exchange he ensured the kingdom's prosperity.

The proliferation of religious sects that occurred in India was not mirrored among the Khmers. In this as in other spheres, the Khmers followed their first teachers and apparently did not try to probe deeper into or to challenge doctrines that may have seemed rather strange to them. Only one or two sects

Detail of a bas-relief at the Bayon temple: a scene of worship.
A dignitary of great importance—as indicated by the numerous parasols—prostrates himself before the god Vishnu, who is placed within a relatively simple shelter, with *apsaras* (celestial dancers) round him. In front of the sanctuary there is a small pool with lotuses growing in it. At the bottom right two Brahmin sages are engaged in discussion.
Bayon, bas-reliefs in the western half of the internal south gallery.
Photo: Claude Jacques

A bronze head of the Hindu god Shiva.
The art of Khmer bronze sculpture reached its peak in the second half of the 11th century. The eyebrows, the eyes, and the moustache were inlaid with metals and enamel, and the bronze was originally gilded. Bronze (32cm high; mid-11th century), found at Por Loboek (Siem Reap province), Angkor Conservation's depository.
Photo: Luc Ionesco, EFEO

Opposite, top
Shrine of a local deity.
These simple shrines are to be found scattered throughout the Khmer countryside. They are dedicated to the guardian spirits of the land, who are the object of the greatest care and attention—all the more so because they take stern revenge if they feel they have been ignored.
Oudong region.
Photo: Claude Jacques

Opposite, bottom
The Hindu god Vishnu reclining on the Cosmic Ocean.
This is probably the remains of the main idol from the Western Mebon temple, which was described by the Chinese envoy Zhou Daguan: "In the tower is a reclining Buddha in bronze, from whose navel water continually flows." This Buddha was in reality the god Vishnu and it is possible that the Chinese chronicler mistook the lotus at his navel for a spout of water.
Bronze (2.17m long, 1.44m high; mid-11th century), found near the Western Mebon temple.
Photo: Luc Ionesco, EFEO

are known within the cults of Shiva and Vishnu. Likewise, it is probable that Buddhism, which anyway was less widespread, did not split into numerous sects, although, alongside Mahayana Buddhism, which was the most commonly adopted form, there is evidence here and there of the existence of followers of a "primitive," or early, form of Buddhism.

The temples we see today give no more than a faint idea of the total number of sanctuaries that once existed. The surviving temples are all constructed of durable materials and must therefore have been built by the very wealthy; probably many more were built but have since disappeared. Nor would these have been the only kind of sanctuaries; others would have been built in non-durable materials by the less wealthy. We know from the inscriptions that sometimes it took years before it was possible to build in long-lasting materials a sanctuary in honor of a god; doubtless some plans were never realized for lack of money.

The Khmers never went so far as to abandon their own indigenous divinities, who ruled over the land and its riches, and who were human heroes turned into guardian spirits; in addition, each family line had its own protecting ancestors. There were also many evil spirits, which could, for example, be the cause of illness or death. All these various divinities were honored, but perhaps with a less elaborate form of worship than that accorded to the Indian gods.

Likewise, their sanctuaries must have been generally much simpler, and built of less durable materials, like those that house Khmer deities today. Not that these divinities were any less important to the Khmers—they probably feared them much more than they did the Indian gods, who were more distant. Local divinities could mete out immediate punishments when displeased and it seems likely therefore that they were treated with constant care.

However, no sanctuary remains, nor any description of the forms of worship that were practiced there (though it is possible that we simply do not recognize them as such). There are one or two references to these deities in the inscriptions, but there is no text actually dedicated to them. This is why we know so little about the most important local god, *Devaraja*, the "god who is king" or the "king of the gods," the spiritual counterpart of the Khmer "king of kings." Much has been written about this divinity, even though texts referring to him are particularly rare and provide little information. We shall return to him in the next chapter, when we consider the reign of Jayavarman II.

Some short inscriptions dating from the 12th century give the name of certain individuals who appear on the bas-reliefs of Angkor Wat, or of the gods who occupied the *cellae* of the temple complexes built at the end of the 12th century. Many of these inscriptions have been ground down and replaced with others, a fact that shows how idols came and went. Sometimes inscriptions give the name of the founder who paid for the statue, or even of the person who served as a model for it. This kind of information is also found at the base of bronze statues with, in some cases, the date when they were installed in a temple.

Life in the temples and the villages

What was life like in the temples and the villages? A number of inscriptions allow us to form an impression of what life in the villages must have been like, and they suggest that it was not so different from what it was in Cambodia in the 19th century. Long lists of "slaves," describing their duties, are engraved on the door posts of certain sanctuaries, such as Preah Ko and Lolei. This register of "slaves" (of the god), named on something like a roll of honor, is a clear indication that a large proportion of villagers took an active part in the life of the temple, just as those of modern times, differences apart, participate in the life of the Buddhist pagoda. It must be remembered that Hindu temples are not places of assembly as Christian churches generally are. They are the home of the god to whom they are dedicated, whose mission is to guard over the prosperity of the region, and whom the priests must serve as if he were a great lord.

Every morning, the god (in the form of a statue) was awoken, washed, dressed, and offered a meal; at midday he was again offered food, and once more in the evening, when he was prepared for his nightly rest. This was the daily duty of the priests in charge. At the same time, musicians were on hand to charm him, cooks to prepare his food; other attendants prepared the leaves on which his meals were presented, husked his rice, and made garlands of flowers for him. There were night guards for the temple, guards for its

At the Chau Say Tevoda temple: a death scene.
A man on the point of death is being assisted by a
divinity, represented as larger than he is, and is
already being mourned by attendants.
Fragment of a fallen pediment south of Chau Say
Tevoda. Mid-12th century.
Photo: Guy Nafilyan

Page 26
Khmer mythology: a three-headed naga spat out by a
makara.
Both of these mythical creatures, symbols of water, are
frequently represented on Khmer temples. Here, a sort
of pendant erupts from the mouth of the left-hand
naga at the Preah Palilay temple. End 12th century to
beginning 13th century.
Photo: Guy Nafilyan

treasures, guards for the various rooms. Peasants worked in the rice fields
that were owned by the god and provided the rice presented to him every
day of the year.

On feast days, when the population crowded into the temple, even more
attendants were required. All this was for a single god; much more was
needed in the big temples. There were six principal deities at Preah Ko, four
at Lolei, 109 at the temple mountain of Phnom Bakheng, as well as all the
numerous lesser divinities who also demanded attention.

As there were so many servants, they did not have to work full time in the
temple. For example, the northern sanctuary tower of Lolei lists 182
fortnightly servants, in addition to the priests. It is clear that, as a means of
demonstrating their faith, local inhabitants took turns in serving these gods,
who were in charge of ordering the world in general and theirs in particular.
Outside the temple, they attended to their everyday occupations.

Architecture

Page 27
Khmer mythology: a figure of kala, or kirtimukha, at
the temple of Preah Ko.
The function of such grimacing monsters was to
prevent evil spirits from entering the temples.
Sand and lime mixture on top of brick.
Temple of Preah Ko, north tower of the second tier.
End of 9th century.
Photo: Luc Ionesco, Top

Secular buildings and dwellings, whether palaces or the most humble
houses, would have been similar in style and materials to the houses still seen
today in Cambodia and in many areas of neighboring countries: built on
stilts, made entirely of wood, and roofed with thatch or tiles.

Systematic planning methods were applied to the construction of roads,
bridges and dikes, and the massive irrigation networks; all these, together
with the reservoirs and temples, formed large complexes; the population
lived in the area around them.

The reservoirs, called *baray*, the largest of which was 8 kilometers long and 2.2 kilometers wide, were conceived and constructed according to cosmological precepts that were part of the Khmer people's beliefs. But they also played a practical role, however, supplying water for everyday needs and for agriculture. Water management was fundamental.

The main testimony to the Khmer civilization is its temples, which survive in large numbers and in all sizes. The largest stand within enclosures over a kilometer in length and width. The walls of the city of Angkor Thom form a square whose sides measure three kilometers, and those of Preah Khan, in the province of Kompong Thom, measure four kilometers on each side, and stand within a triple enclosure of dikes and ditches.

Characteristics of Khmer architecture

The key characteristic of Khmer architecture is that it is cosmological: each temple is an image of the universe, a magical representation. If such a word as "icono-cosmic" existed, it would describe this architecture perfectly.

A Khmer temple is an *imago mundi*, an image of the world, as described in ancient treatises and depicted in bas-reliefs. The temples were not conceived as places of assembly in the way that Christian cathedrals and churches were (though they too, in their way, are an image of the universe). Khmer temple sanctuaries, which are in the form of towers, are very small: the *cella* (inner chamber) of the central sanctuary of Angkor Wat, which is one of the largest examples, measures only 4.6 by 4.7 meters, and the pedestal of its statue is almost as wide as the doorway, 1.6 meters.

Reached by precipitous flights of huge steps that climb the apparently endless succession of levels, the galleries of the temples hardly seem suited to religious processions. Some of these galleries are not even accessible in a normal way: at Ta Kev, the only way to enter them is by climbing in through the windows, because there is no door of any kind. Moreover, the windows were usually barred by rows of stone balusters.

Whether architectural (sanctuaries, enclosures, entrance pavilions, libraries, and various chambers) or decorative (lintels, columns, pediments, pilasters and so on), every element of a Khmer temple had its own symbolic function, and not just an aesthetic one. Unfortunately, the Khmer texts on this subject have been lost, many of them probably destroyed during the political tumult of recent years. Other traces of the past, preserved in the memories of the elderly, were also obliterated in the years of upheaval and bloodshed. All we can do now is refer to architectural treatises conserved and published in India.

There is a clear parallel to be drawn between the layout of the temples and the ancient concept of the cosmos as explained by George Cœdès, who wrote:

> In the Brahmanic concept of the world, there is a central continent, called Jambudvipa, at the heart of which rises the cosmic mountain, Meru, surrounded by the planets. Jambudvipa is encircled by six continents in the shape of concentric rings and by seven oceans, the seventh of which is bounded on the outside by a large stone wall. On the summit of Meru is the city of Brahma, the world of the gods, surrounded by the eight guardians of the points of the compass.

A religious scene depicted at the Bayon temple. The sacrifice of buffaloes was practiced until recently among the peoples of central Indochina.
Bayon, bas-reliefs in the southern half of the outer east gallery.
Photo: Luc Ionesco

The Kompong Kdei bridge over the river Chi Kreng. Ancient Khmer bridges built of stone (or, as here, of laterite) were not built with real vaults, and the corbeled archways used meant a large number of arches were necessary. As a result, the river had to be widened to compensate for displacement and allow the water to flow evenly. This bridge, built during the reign of Jayavarman VII, is still in use as part of the road between Siem Reap and Phnom Penh.
Spean Praptos, on the river Chi Kreng, at Kompong Kdei (60km south of Siem Reap).
Photo: Guy Nafilyan

The second most important characteristic of Khmer architecture, which in fact stems from the first, is the rigorous order of its composition. This applies as much to the simplest buildings as to the most elaborate monumental complexes.

This claim might seem surprising, especially to anyone who has seen the almost hallucinatory confusion of some of the major Khmer monuments. The strongest impression left by a visit to Angkor is of the monuments in the Bayon style from the time of Jayavarman VII, at the end of the 12th century and beginning of the 13th, because these are both the most numerous and also the most spectacular of the ruins. The style of this era, however, is untypical. Whatever its appearance, Khmer architecture is essentially regular and well ordered.

From the 7th-century Sambor Prei Kuk to the 12th-century Angkor Wat, all the temples are built in the same pattern: rectangular enclosures arranged concentrically in a precise order around a central sanctuary (or central group of sanctuaries). The position and dimensions of each component, and each set of components, are related to the center of the temple and the central sanctuary by a set of exact geometric rules.

This strict order of composition can also be seen in the hierarchy of the elements that make up the composition. The central *prasat* (sanctuary) dominates the whole in terms of height (though not always in the area of its ground plan), and all the various elements of the complex are distributed around it, according to their relative importance and volume, in such a way as to emphasize the significance of the *prasat* as the absolute center of the temple. The central sanctuary's pre-eminence is also underlined by the fact that it stands upon a terrace, and in many cases on a pyramid of terraces. The nature and arrangement of the temple's decoration is similarly subject to a hierarchical pattern: the decoration is richer and more abundant on the central sanctuary, which in some cases it completely covers, and becomes progressively less important the further it is from the center. This is most obvious at Banteay Srei: the surface areas of the three sanctuaries are richly decorated, with *dvarapala* carved on the central tower and *devata* on the north and south towers, while the antechamber to the sanctuary area is covered with a "tapestry" of tiles in alternating patterns. The libraries are richly decorated on their main western and eastern façades and their pediments are among the most beautiful examples of Khmer art, but their side walls are bare. There is progressively less decoration on the entrance pavilions and the annexes, down to the entrance pavilion of the fourth enclosure.

The two other main principles—or rather, systems—governing the composition of Khmer monuments are superimposition and concentricity. In addition, there are juxtaposition and symmetry, and a progressive reduction in size, down to the miniature.

Superimposition is clearly visible. The superstructure of every sanctuary consists of several levels stacked above the main body of the edifice, one on the other in ever-diminishing size. But the most striking feature of Khmer architecture, as distinct from other architectural styles of this type, is that of the "temple-mountain." While the sanctuary itself already represents an image of the cosmos, through the concentric superimposed universes of its superstructure, it in turn stands on a series of stepped tiers that provide a new representation of concentric superimposed worlds. The rules governing these constructions were probably derived from cosmological texts.

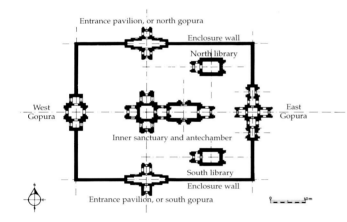

Typical layout of a Khmer monument with a single enclosure.
Based on the plan of Chau Say Tevoda drawn by Maurice Glaize (in *les Monuments du groupe d'Angkor*).

Concentric design features can be seen in the way the stories are super-imposed one on the other, but it is clearer still in the succession of concentric enclosures around the temple. It is possible, though, that the cosmological significance of two concentric enclosures is not the same as that of one tier superimposed on the other.

Juxtaposition is a feature that appears above all in multiple sanctuaries, and also in the positioning of annexes, but just as clearly in the arrangement of successive enclosures in a row, as at Prasat Thom, Koh Ker, or at Wat Phu and Preah Vihear.

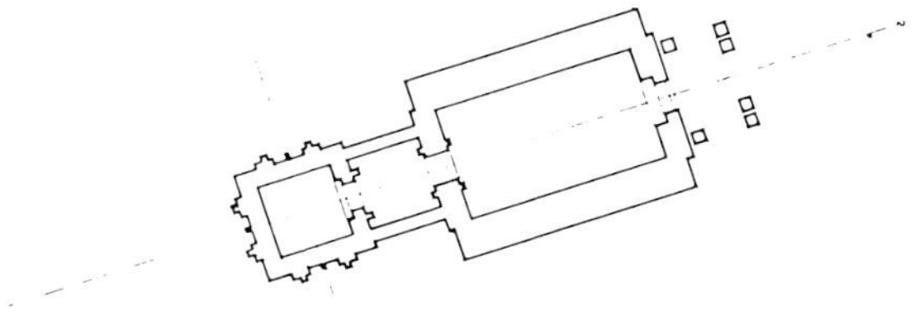

A gradual and proportionate reduction in size is first of all a function of superimposition and concentricity. Examples of this are the tiers of the superstructure set one above the other, and also the enclosures with their entrance pavilions, one within the other, getting smaller and smaller. But diminution is seen also in the miniature edifices perched at the corners of each tier in the guise of acroteria. There is also a remarkable example of diminution in the northern group of buildings at Sambor Prei Kuk. On the right-hand side of the central sanctuary's southern façade there is a "flying palace," a two-meter high tableau, sculpted in brick, representing a façade. Everything is there: a frame, columns, the lintel with its *makara*, pilasters, and pediment. At the top, in the tympanum of the pediment, there is a miniature of this façade itself, again carved in brick. So the temple is decorated with its own image, which in turn bears an image of itself, and so on.

This notion of the perpetual repetition of an image takes us to the very essence of Khmer art.

The juxtaposition of enclosures: the temple of Prasat Thom at Koh Ker.

The predominant arts in Khmer civilization

The French scholar Louis Bréhier wrote than in every civilization there is one art that is in the vanguard and that predominates over all the others. In the case of Classical Greece it was sculpture, in the Middle Ages it was architecture, in 17th-century Holland painting, and so on. In our day, it seems that it is the image, and especially the moving image, that predominates.

In the case of Khmer civilization, architecture was paramount. But Khmer sculpture, which is often of great beauty, was also very important. The statue of the god in a sanctuary is the essential element of the temple, and the temple surrounding the statue can be seen as a "statue" of the world.

Here, two facts are worth noting. First, monolithic temples, cut out of a single mass of stone, exist in India; and in Cambodia there are temples, dating from the final period of Khmer civilization, that were created from piles of stones out of which the elements of a temple were "carved." (The French scholar Henri Marchal used to say that the art of the Bayon temple was in fact "rock art," and though this is an exaggeration, there is some truth in it.) Second, inscriptions mention the date when statues were erected but never when the temples were inaugurated, nor when the foundation stones were laid. Yet it is known from the *shastra* (treatises) that very important ceremonies were held to mark the start of construction, as is demonstrated by the presence of tokens marking the event deposited under the actual foundations of the sanctuary, especially under the

31

pedestal of the main statue, or else at the top of the towers. In the latter case, tokens were inserted in recesses in a flat square slab. These recesses, some of them inscribed, contained precious stones or sometimes pieces of thin gold leaf, or even locks of hair or nail clippings from the donor of the sanctuary.

In some sanctuaries there was no statue in the center: instead the god was represented by his symbolic image, the *lingam,* or phallus, installed in a pedestal. Only the upper third of this phallus was visible: cylindrical and often having an egg-shaped top, this section of the *lingam* was consecrated to Shiva. The middle third, octagonal in shape, was consecrated to Vishnu; and the bottom third, square, was consecrated to Brahma. The two lower parts were concealed within the pedestal. The *lingam* passed through a stone slab that had a central hole and an overflow spout; this slab, called a *snaradroni,* represented the feminine symbol, the *yoni.*

Sculpture

The secondary sanctuaries (and sometimes also the main one) contained numerous statues in addition to the *lingam*: Shiva, Vishnu, very occasionally Brahma, frequently Ganesha, and Skanda, as well as many others, plus all the female deities, which are not always easy to identify. Then there were representations of monsters: Kala, Garuda, *makara,* and, above all, naga; together with those creatures guarding the entrances—*dvarapala* and lions— they all form an astonishing array of powerful images.

The bas-reliefs are of great importance. The technique appeared very early: the earliest examples known are the lintels and the "flying palaces" of Sambor Prei Kuk, dating from the 7th century, and those on the top tier of the Bakong pyramid. But it is in the 10th century that the first really beautiful sculpted scenes appear, on the pediments of the libraries at Banteay Srei. Less well known are the panel decorations on the walls of the Baphuon, almost all of them demolished or dislodged, and those of the Prasat Khna Seng Kev, hidden in a remote forest. There are sculpted scenes on pediments at Angkor Wat, Banteay Samre, and Beng Mealea, and huge mural bas-reliefs are to be seen above all at Angkor Wat, and also at the Bayon, and at Bantea Chmar.

Over the centuries, Khmer sculptural art seems to have gradually changed, moving from a fluid, naturalistic style to one of rigid and conventional forms. In the early period, the sculptors would have used models, probably imported small statues, but clearly they also observed the people around them. They reproduced the traditional poses portrayed in the Indian models, but at the same time—at any rate in the 6th and 7th centuries—they were also copying nature, the results being graceful and lifelike works. This close observation of real life is evident in the naturalness of the figures and in their gestures, and even more so in their garments, which are astonishingly realistic (as in the statue of Vishnu at Phnom Da, of Hari-Hara at Maha Rosei or at Prasat Andet or Sambor Prei Kuk, and that of "the Lady" at Koh Krieng). The various robes depicted on the statues of that early period could easily be made today with a cloth of the type used as everyday wear, a *sampot* or *krama.*

In time sculptors began copying existing statues (from memory), and their style became dry and hard. In the first half of the 10th century the statues are increasingly hieratic, and frontal in perspective, as in the style seen at Koh

A scene of Hindu mythology depicted at the Banteay Srei temple: the death of Kamsa.
Krishna prepares to kill his uncle, the cruel Kamsa, while turmoil reigns in the palace.
Banteay Srei, west pediment of the north library.
Third quarter of 10th century.
Photo: Luc Ionesco, EFEO

Ker, for example. It must be remembered, however, that this art was a form of magic and so the image had to respect a precise formula. The stylistic evolution was not without variations, however. Although the general trend was towards a harder, more rigid style, there were periods when a greater flexibility is apparent, no doubt due to the artists' own taste. There were also differences between one temple and another, with a leaning towards fluidity noticeable above all in the art of Banteay Srei and that of the Baphuon.

The style at Angkor Wat vacillates between the two tendencies. The sculptures in the round, although elegant and beautifully proportioned, tend towards a certain hardness; but you only have to walk along by the walls of the gopura, the libraries, and the galleries, to find graceful *devata*, beautifully robed and coiffured, in a great variety of poses. You have the feeling that the sculptors, constrained by rules of religious propriety when creating the statue of the god, gave free rein to their imagination when it came to decorating the temple walls with images of dancers of the royal ballet.

With the Bayon temple, a new stylistic development emerges. First, there was a great increase in both the number and size of the temples. The great profusion of images this entailed resulted in a lessening of artistic quality, presumably because there was no corresponding increase in the number of skilled artists. However, at the same time the demand arose for a new type of work, the portrait, and this did lead to an improvement in quality, as exemplified at Bayon by the famous spectacular towers with the giant faces, which must have been undertaken by the very best sculptors of the time. The Bayon style bas-reliefs introduce a new element by depicting, alongside turbulent battle scenes and representations of divine beings, scenes from everyday life. The walls of the Bayon are indeed "cinema in stone."

A Khmer mirror-bearing statuette.
Several of these objects have been found. It is difficult to say whether their function was sacred or secular.
Bronze, 30cm high. Angkor region, 12th century.
National Museum, Phnom Penh.
Photo: Luc Ionesco, EFEO

33

CHAPTER 2

The Pre-Angkor Period

Until the 9th century the land inhabited by the Khmers was divided into a multitude of small states. Occasionally, for the duration of a monarch's reign, they were brought together to form a small empire. The economy, which was based on agriculture, was not rich enough to support grand expansion plans and, apart from two groups at Sambor Prei Kuk, only a few relatively simple sanctuaries survive from this early period.

Then came the all-conquering king Jayavarman II, who founded the first real Khmer empire.

K hmer history is usually divided into three main periods: pre-Angkor, Angkor, and post-Angkor, with the dates of the middle period, when the center of power was located continuously at Angkor, deemed to be 802 to 1431—though such precision is probably mistaken. The early period was one of states splitting into smaller states, with sporadic attempts at amalgamation; in the third period, power shifted to the Phnom Penh region.

The Angkor area is known to have been inhabited from very early times. Very few traces of neolithic sites have been found, but this is not surprising after many centuries of human activity. There is considerably more evidence of Khmer occupation of the area between the 7th and 8th centuries. It seems that during that period the Angkor region formed the kingdom of Aninditapura, one of the many kingdoms and principalities into which the land of the Khmers was divided before the 9th century. We do not know how many of these kingdoms there were, and the names of only a few have come down to us—they appear in carved inscriptions, but with no indication as to their importance. However, among the various states described by Chinese travelers to this region, two can be identified and their geographical position identified: the Chinese named them Fu-nan and Chenla, but whether or not on the basis of local names is not known for certain.

Opposite
A false doorway at the temple of Preah Ko.
Very little is left of the lime mortar that covered these bricks, which formed the rough outline of the reliefs. The lintel, false doorway and *dvarapala* (guardians) in the niches, all in sandstone, are testimony to the quality of the sculpture of this period.
Preah Ko, central sanctuary in the front row, west side, about 880.
Photo: Guy Nafilyan

Following pages
A detail from a bas-relief at Angkor Wat showing the Great Battle, a scene from the Hindu epic the *Mahabharata*. The precise scene, which shows a defeated enemy being killed with lances, has not been clearly identified.
Angkor Wat, west gallery of bas-reliefs, southern half. First half of 12th century.
Photo: Luc Ionesco, Top

A bas-relief at the Bayon temple showing a military parade with elephants, cavalry, and infantry.
The parasols are an indication of rank: the greater the number, the higher the social rank.
Bayon, outer gallery of bas-reliefs, east side, southern half. End 12th century, beginning 13th century.
Photo: Luc Ionesco

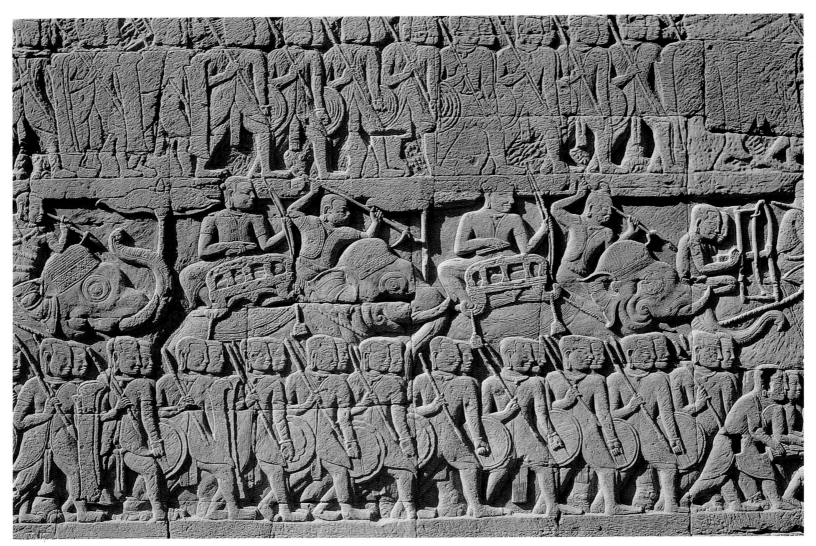

Fu-nan

A bas-relief at the Bayon temple showing a marching army.

Elephants ridden by chiefs walk between two lines of foot soldiers. The first elephant carries a kind of ballista operated by two men. The foot soldiers are carrying shields of two different types (see the unfinished section at the top of the relief).

Bayon, bas-reliefs in the south outer gallery. End 12th century, beginning 13th century.

Photo: Luc Ionesco, EFEO

The people of Funan are cunning and audacious. They take by force the inhabitants of any neighboring cities who do not pay tribute to them and make them their slaves. As merchandise they have gold, silver, and silk. Sons of rich families wear sarongs cut out of brocade; women place their heads through a length of fabric that thus forms a robe. The poor people cover themselves with a bit of cloth. The inhabitants of Funan make gold rings and bracelets and silver dishes. They cut down trees for building their dwellings. The king lives in a two-story house. They surround their enclosures with a wooden fence. Huge bamboos grow beside the sea, with leaves eight or nine feet long. These leaves are plaited to make roofs for the houses. The people also live in houses on stilts. They build boats that are eight to nine chang (ten Chinese feet) long and six or seven feet wide. The front and the back end of these boats look like the head and the tail of a fish. When the king travels, he goes by elephant. For entertainment, the people watch cock fights and pig fights.

(*Nan ts'i chou*, translated from the French of Paul Pelliot, whose own translation from the Chinese appeared in the essay "Le Fou-nan" in the *Bulletin de l'Ecole française d'Extrême-Orient*, 1904.)

This Chinese account is, I believe, the earliest surviving description of Fu-nan. The state was situated in the southern part of what is present-day

Vietnam and Cambodia. It seems to have been one of the most important states in Southeast Asia and one of the constituent parts of what was later to become the Khmer empire.

The particularly interesting feature of this Chinese text is that, as well as comments on the inhabitants' dress and crafts, it refers to several practices which continued to be characteristic of Khmer civilization for a very long time, while the image of the continual battles fought between these city states, and of the defeated peoples being taken into slavery, helps us to understand their political life. At the dawn of this civilization, settlements were encircled not with walls but with moats and with banks of earth, which were probably topped by fences of wood; it is possible that the wood was thorny. It is still possible to find traces of these enclosures in Cambodia, and also in northeast Thailand, where they have been closely studied. Some were round and some were rectangular, and occasionally they covered quite large areas. Even today the houses, in villages at least, are still built of wood and on stilts, and until recently their roofs were covered with plaited leaves of coconut palm. However, the boats, such an essential feature of the Khmer countryside, were not (and are still not) made in the shape of a fish, but in the shape of naga, which were mythical water serpents.

As far as we can tell, the kingdom that Chinese travelers called Fu-nan—we cannot be sure where its borders were, other than the one that was formed by the sea—was one of the first to absorb Indian culture, probably around the 1st century. The Indians would have crossed the Malay peninsula to reach Fu-nan in search of various goods; in particular they would have been looking for spices and other luxury commodities, such as sandalwood and perfumed resins, which they sold to the Romans, until the decline of the Roman Empire in the 5th century. As demand increased, the Indians set up small trading posts in Southeast Asia to collect merchandise between the monsoon seasons. These traders would have brought with them their culture, their religion, and their gods, all of which the indigenous people gradually adopted. The process was totally peaceful, and in spite of what has often been written, the Khmers were never "Indianized" in the real sense of the term, for they never abandoned their own culture.

In about the 6th century, which is the period of the earliest texts to have come down to us, a legend was circulating that was reported in very similar terms by both the Chinese and, a little later, by the Chams: following a dream, an Indian Brahmin named Kaundinya traveled to Fu-nan and met Soma, the daughter of the dragon-king of this country. Soon he married her and brought "civilization" to this country.

All the known Khmer kings before the 9th century claimed to be descendants of this primordial couple, though there is no point in seeking any historical fact in the legend—it turns up as an explanation of a dynasty's origins in India and even among the Scythians, as the Greek historian Herodotus relates.

In their annals, the Chinese also gave great importance to a kingdom that they called Chenla, which seems to correspond to one of the kingdoms in the interior of the Khmer territory that is referred to in greater detail in many indigenous inscriptions. The name Chenla appears to have been used only by the Chinese, who continued to use it until quite recently to refer to what we call Cambodia.

A bas-relief at the Bayon temple showing a cock fight.
This remarkable scene is very well known. The owners are holding their respective fighting cocks before the fight, and bets are being placed on the outcome.
Bayon, bas-reliefs in the south gallery, eastern half. End 12th century, beginning 13th century.
Photo: Luc Ionesco, EFEO

A naga boat.
Cambodian boats continue to be decorated with naga, mythological water serpents who safeguarded the country's prosperity. Eyes painted on the boats give them a lifelike appearance. The offering in the bow of the boat is for the particular spirit it represents. Water festival at Phnom Penh, 1964.
Photo: Luc Ionesco

The emergence of a powerful kingdom:
Bhavapura

In the second half of the 6th century, the city of Bhavapura was founded; it was named, as was the custom, after its founder, King Bhavavarman I. He was a prince from the Sambor region on the Mekong river who had not been chosen to succeed to the throne of his small home state, and so decided to carve out a kingdom for himself. Having conquered part of the central area of present-day Cambodia, he founded his capital about 30 kilometers from what is now Kompong Thom, either where Sambor Prei Kuk now stands, or not far away (the exact site has not yet been determined).

The kingdom expanded. It is clear that Bhavavarman pushed on with his conquests over a great distance, because he left an inscription to the north of the town of Battambang. His younger brother Citrasena, who had been chosen to succeed their father, was consecrated as Mahendravarman and led expeditions in the north, successfully conquering lands beyond Khon Kaen in present-day Thailand, where he left some triumphal inscriptions. For some reason Mahendravarman abandoned his conquests and, some years after 598, on the death of Bhavavarman, he settled at Bhavapura.

Mahendravarman died about 610, his son Ishanavarman I, acceding. Like all the Khmer kings, Ishanavarman felt obliged to enlarge his domain through new conquests. It is possible that he ruled almost the whole of present-day Cambodia and that he pressed on, along the route to the north of Battambang, as far as the sea, in the Chantaburi region of Thailand.

He was a great king, remembered long after his death—there is a reference to him in an inscription on the Bayon complex, dating from the 12th century. He could not have been very young when he took power and the reputation he left was of a man of great wisdom. He is important above all for the splendid state temple he built, the southern group at Sambor Prei Kuk, one of the earliest surviving examples of Khmer architecture. This group consists of brick towers within a double enclosure that measures 260 meters by 236 meters on the outside. All that remains today are seven sanctuary towers and a section of the interior enclosure wall. There are also vestiges of other towers and of some of the gopura, notably the east gopura, whose piers are covered with an inscription glorifying the king who built the monument. The central sanctuary is a magnificent, massive rectangular tower whose walls are embellished with reliefs on the outside. To the east of this sanctuary there is a tower containing a remarkable sandstone dais intended for an image of Shiva's mount, the bull Nandi, a statue that has disappeared, and that might well have been in bronze. The octagonal towers rising in quincunx arrangement (one in each corner of a square and one in the center) are very impressive, despite their ruinous condition. The interior enclosure wall was once decorated with splendid medallions in relief, but little remains of them now.

On the death of Ishanavarman I in 628, a younger son succeeded him as Bhavavarman II. However, he had nothing of his father's prestige and could neither preserve the empire's unity nor prevent the principalities regaining independence. One of these, in the north of the present-day province of Kompong Thom, whose name is not known, and which was probably not particularly important, was the birthplace of a prince who, as Jayavarman I, subsequently rebuilt the empire of Ishanavarman I.

A "flying palace."
Some temples have "flying palaces" sculpted on their outer walls. These are depictions of the dwellings of the gods who frequent the sacred area of the temple. Sambor Prei Kuk, south group, central sanctuary.
Photo: Guy Nafilyan

A temple tower enveloped by a tree.
This extraordinary sight is the central brick tower of
the south group at the temple of Sambor Prei Kuk,
before it was freed from the tree smothering it.
Photo: Guy Nafilyan

Jayavarman I
and the kingdom of Aninditapura

The earliest known date in the reign of Jayavarman is that corresponding
to Wednesday 14 June 657. On this day two sanctuaries were consecrated, one
in what is now the province of Battambang in the north, and the other in the
province of Prei Vêng in the southeast. Despite the great distance that
separated them, both their respective founders, according to the inscriptions
that they left, recognized the authority of Jayavarman I. This shows that by
that time he had almost completed his conquests.

Jayavarman I's capital was called Purandarapura. It has long been believed
that this city was in the south of present-day Cambodia, where the greatest
number of inscriptions mentioning the king's name have been discovered. If
this assumption is correct, however, it is remarkable that he himself was not

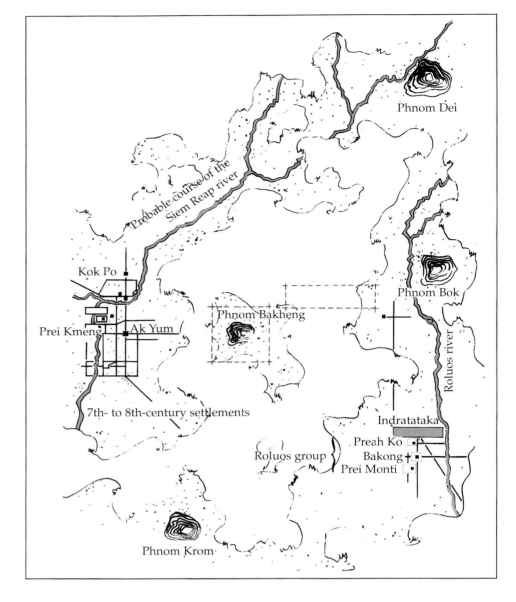

Map of the Angkor area "before Angkor."
On the left, traces of towns, including perhaps the capital of Aninditapura, which must have become Jayavarman I's capital city, Purandarapura. The course of the Siem Reap river runs well to the north of what was to become Angkor. Another group of settlements is that of Roluos, of which nothing is known until the arrival in the region of Jayavarman II. Bernard-Philippe Groslier discovered traces of a neolithic settlement at the foot of Phnom Bakheng, which was to become the center of Yashovarman I's capital. It is therefore likely that an area near to this hill was already settled in the pre-Angkor period. The square of broken red lines around Phnom Bakheng indicates the future site of the first Angkor; and the long rectangle, marks the future site of the Eastern Baray.

Map drawn by Guy Nafilyan

responsible for any of these inscriptions, not even those setting out decrees he had promulgated. It was a period when a relatively large number of sanctuaries were built, so it is impossible to attribute any temple to Jayavarman I with any certainty, even though he was remembered as a great king by many succeeding generations of Khmers. This absence of any hard facts about the monuments he built means we need to use a little imagination to form a new theory about the location of his capital.

Jayavarman I would surely not have wanted to govern his empire from his father's homeland in the outlying area of northern Cambodia, nor from the south of Cambodia, which was just as far from the center. Some traces of his presence have been found not far from Angkor, so it is not unreasonable to speculate whether he might have chosen this region, which at the time formed the kingdom of Aninditapura, as the location of his capital.

The name Aninditapura itself did not appear until later, on inscriptions dating from the Angkor period. However, it seems that the kingdom was of considerable importance; it had annexed at least the region of Roluos to the west, and it extended as far as the northern and northwestern parts of what is now the province of Battambang. Though it has never been possible to identify with certainty the site of the kingdom's capital city, either on the ground or on a map, proof of its existence is found in inscriptions. If my theory is correct, this capital city, after which the kingdom would have been named, was replaced by Jayavarman I's city Purandarapura—which was itself replaced by Hariharalaya at the beginning of the 9th century, and finally by Yashodharapura at the end of the 9th century.

The first temple-mountain: Ak Yum

One of the most remarkable pre-Angkor remains is the temple of Ak Yum. It was discovered in 1932, thanks to the fact that it had been partly buried under the southern embankment of the Western Baray when this reservoir was constructed. The temple is believed to have originally been built in the second half of the 8th century, and subsequently modified into what is the earliest known example of a real temple mountain. It is in the form of a three-tier brick pyramid, with five towers in a quincunx arrangement on the top terrace. We do not know the name of either the king who built it or of the king who later altered it. This is all the more frustrating since the later king in particular must have been of considerable importance and ambition to have undertaken such a major project, yet the historical facts we do have scarcely suggest that any such individual existed at that time. We do not know exactly what the earlier temple was like, but an inscribed pier, re-used in the main sanctuary (indicating that the text was regarded as important by the later king), contains a date corresponding to Saturday 10 June 674. In the area surrounding Prasat Ak Yum, several quite important sites have been discovered that seem to belong to the same period.

Jayavarman I, together with Ishanavarman I, undoubtedly dominates the pre-Angkor period. He died probably before 700. His immediate successor was perhaps his son-in-law Nripaditya, who reigned for only a short time, leaving the throne to his wife Jayadevi, daughter of Jayavarman I. There is evidence of her presence in the region in 713, and she is the only known queen in ancient Khmer history. Neither Nripaditya nor Jayadevi seem to have exercised their authority beyond the borders of the kingdom of Aninditapura, plus perhaps an enclave in the south of Cambodia. The rest of the country was split into small kingdoms, of which only the largest are now known by name, throughout the 8th century.

Prasat Kok Po.
Doorframe of sanctuary B, second half of 9th century.
Photo: Guy Nafilyan

Jayavarman II, "emperor of the world"

In 790 a young prince was consecrated under the name Jayavarman II. He was a member of the great family of Khmer kings, a descendant of the line of princes of Aninditapura, and came from "Java," where he is assumed to have been a "prisoner," together with his family. "Java" in this case denotes a place perhaps in the area along the border with Malaysia, the actual island of Java. Jayavarman II assumed power in the kingdom of Vyadhapura, situated more or less in the area around the modern town of Prei Ving. One of his first concerns was to hold a religious ceremony to liberate this kingdom from the control of the

43

"king of Java," from which we can deduce that the latter was the overlord of the Khmer territory. Having successfully taken over—either at the same time or subsequently—the kingdom of Shambhupura, corresponding to present-day Sambor to the north of Kratie, Jayavarman II chose as his capital Indrapura. This has been identified, possibly correctly, with the present site of Banteay Prei Nokor: an immense embankment four kilometers long lies along what is assumed to be the border separating the two kingdoms.

Pressing northwards with his conquests, he reached as far as Wat Phu (in the south of Laos), where there was a sanctuary long venerated by the Khmer kings. Then, following the south side of the Dangrek mountains, he finally conquered the kingdom of Aninditapura and established himself in the city of Hariharalaya, somewhere in the Roluos region. Probably wanting to extend his domain even further west, he founded the city of Amarendrapura, the site of which is still unknown. However, he soon abandoned this city to install himself in a city east of Angkor on the summit of Mahendraparvata, the "mountain of the great Indra," today Phnom Kulen, which overlooks the Angkor region and is the source of its water supply. Here in 802 he had himself consecrated "supreme king of kings," *chakravartin* in Sanskrit. This date was to become embedded in the mind of the Khmers as the foundation date of their empire.

The cult of Devaraja

Prasat Thma Dap.
One of the characteristics of the monuments here is that they have no inscriptions, so that there is no way of dating them, and it is impossible to know exactly who commissioned them.
Kulen style, first half of 9th century.
Photo: Luc Ionesco, EFEO

At the same time, Jayavarman II employed a Brahmin sage to create a Khmer god with a status corresponding to that which he had just conferred on himself. In each Khmer kingdom there existed, alongside the king of the people, and in parallel with him, a king of the spirits who protected the land. In establishing himself as "supreme king of kings," it was natural that Jayavarman II should have his counterpart, known as the *Kamrateng Jagat ta Raja*, the "god who is king"—translated in Sanskrit as *Devaraja*—elevated to the supreme position among the spirits of his empire. Often misunderstood, the title of *Devaraja* has given rise to a number of false suppositions. In particular, it has been applied to a god regarded as the essence of the supreme king of the Khmers, who has consequently been regarded, quite mistakenly, as a "god-king."

The king appointed a priest for the new divinity and decided that from then on this priest's family line alone should be entitled to perform the rites of this cult. Without doubt the existence of this *Devaraja* would have remained forever undiscovered, like that of many other deities, had it not been for one of the descendants of that priest, at a much later date, being given the additional post of religious tutor to king Udayadityavarman II. This appointment enabled him richly to endow his own family's temple, which until then had been relatively modest, and whose inscribed stele reveals his official function.

We do not know when Jayavarman II came down from his mountain to install himself again at Hariharalya, where he died in about 850. The end of his reign seems to have passed very peacefully. Surprisingly, it appears that after he had proclaimed himself king of the Khmer kings he did not try to conquer those kingdoms over which he claimed authority, for example in the southeast of present-day Cambodia.

Despite his great prestige as founder of the Khmer empire, modern scholars have always found it difficult to attribute to him with any certainty the building of a single temple. However, Rong Chen, a three-tier pyramid about 100 meters wide at its base, built on one of the highest points at Phnom Kulen, and today in poor condition, seems to have been built by him and might have been the setting for his consecration. This monument's almost rough-and-ready design is perhaps explained by the haste with which it was built. There are a number of sanctuaries constructed during Jayavarman II's reign, but they might equally have been built by powerful lords—in fact, this is true of most of the temples at Phnom Kulen and, with less certainty, Preah Theat Thom and Preah Theat Toch, standing within, but not at the center of, the enclosure of Banteay Prei Nokor, Jayavarman II's first capital. In the Roluos group it is more difficult to determine whether certain temples belong to his reign or to that of his son. At Sambor Prei Kuk, group C (the central group) is believed to date from his reign, but it is probable that the kingdom of Bhavapura was independent at that time.

Everything we know about this king comes from inscriptions carved in later centuries, a fact that leads some historians to believe that his legendary status grew up after his death, and that his importance was greatly exaggerated. Nevertheless it is significant that as early as the end of the 9th century he was being accorded special honors.

His son succeeded him, as Jayavarman III. This king is remembered through two narratives describing the hunt for a white elephant. In addition, he is credited with building the temple of Prei Monti, which stands in a large enclosure that might have also contained his palace. The beautiful tower of Trapeang Phong, also in the Roluos group, was probably built in this period. Jayavarman III's successor was consecrated in 877, but it is reasonable to suppose that there was a lengthy interregnum between these two monarchs, because it is hard to believe that Jayavarman III, of whom so little trace has survived, could have reigned for more than 40 years.

Indravarman I: the first great projects at Angkor

Indravarman I came to the throne of Hariharalaya in 877. His origins are very obscure, but there are inscriptions indicating his authority on the temple of Phnom Bayang in the south of Cambodia, as well as far away in the northeast of present-day Thailand. Since he was certainly no longer very young when he was consecrated king, he must have already gained control over most of his empire before receiving the title of "supreme king" of the Khmer kings.

In the space of about ten years he completed a considerable number of projects in his capital city, which does not seem to have been enclosed within walls. Construction of the Indratataka reservoir, or *baray*, started in the year of his consecration. At 3,800 meters long and 800 meters wide, it seems quite modest compared with the one built by his son at Angkor. In 877, however, it was the biggest ever constructed in Khmer territory.

In 879, Indravarman I ordered the consecration of the principal divinities of the Preah Ko temple. The function of the temple was to honor and

A typically ornate Khmer lintel, at the temple of Preah Ko.
Lintel on the south tower (first row).
Photo: Guy Nafiyan

45

The temple of Preah Ko.
Known as the "temple of the ancestors," Preah Ko
stands on the east side of a vast enclosure that
probably contained the royal palace of Indravarman
I. The temple was erected to honor the spirits of the
ancient kings who formerly ruled over the lands of
Jayavarman II, who built the temple.
Preah Ko, divinities consecrated in 879.

Photo: Luc Ionesco, EFEO

propitiate the spirits of the kings who preceded him (and not his "ancestors"
as is often stated), and especially that of Jayavarman II. This fascinating little
temple stands in the eastern part of a large area that is enclosed by a
rectangular moat 500 meters long by 400 meters wide, and that contains no
trace of any other monument. The site has never been excavated, but
Indravarman I's palace probably stood within this enclosure.

The temple of Preah Ko consists mainly of a group of six sanctuary towers
in two rows of three, all sharing the same base platform. The central tower in
the front row, standing slightly further back than the other two, was dedicated
to Parameshvara, a name given to Shiva meaning "supreme lord," and here
also a posthumous name applied to Jayavarman II. The temple to the north
honored Rudreshvara, representing Rudravarman, maternal grandfather of
Indravarman I, and the one to the south honored Prithivindreshvara,
representing Prithivindravarman, his father. We can deduce from this that
Indravarman had brought under his dominion at any rate the lands that had
belonged to these three rulers. It is also interesting to note that these three
divinities, all bearing a name that could have been applied to the god Shiva
himself, were represented not by the usual lingam but by a statue. The towers
in the row behind are smaller and were dedicated to the three monarchs'
principal queens, who are also honored under divine names.

The state temple: Bakong

Indravarman I went on to build his state temple, today known under the
name Bakong: a magnificent five-tier sandstone pyramid that rises inside two
large concentric moats. Nothing is left of the main sanctuary that originally
dominated the monument. It might have disappeared, or anyway been

severely damaged, during the turmoil that accompanied the succession to the throne after the death of Indravarman I. Was it even built of brick? We cannot be certain; perhaps it was only erected as a simple temporary shelter (built of light, non-durable materials) to house the god Indreshvara, consecrated in 881. Whatever it was, what we see today in its place is a fine sandstone tower, constructed in an archaistic style some two-and-a-half centuries later.

Everything else about the temple shows that it was planned and executed with the greatest care. Bas-reliefs were carved on the sides of the top tier; only a few fragments remain but they are enough to give an idea of the overall quality. The fourth level has 12 small sanctuaries, standing on either side of the stairways and at each corner. At the bottom of the pyramid there were small gopura at the foot of each stairway and eight massive brick sanctuaries, some of which have only their sandstone door frames still standing. One of these doorways contained a statue of Vishnu with his arms round his two wives; this statue is mistakenly known by the name of Umagangapatishvara, in other words, "the lord [Shiva], husband of Uma and Ganga."

The last certain date relating to Indravarman I is 886: it is engraved in an inscription which was discovered about 70 kilometers northwest of Ubon, in Thailand. The inscription states that the king's authority is formally recognized, even at such a great distance, by the person who has erected a statue of the Buddha. Indravarman I died in 889 at the latest, and perhaps one or two years before this. Until now historians have believed that the succession went smoothly, since the throne went to one of his sons; this, however, is a misconception.

Vishnu and his two wives.
This group was known for a long time under the name Umagangapatishvara, "the Lord [Shiva] husband of Uma and Ganga"—Shiva's consecration is recorded on the temple's stele. In fact, the four arms and the clear trace of a club show that this is Vishnu, probably accompanied by Sri and Bhu (the Earth). Originally installed in the sanctuary that stands to the east of the Bakong pyramid, north side; removed to the depository of Angkor Conservation.
Photo: Guy Nafilyan

Brick tower at the Bakong temple.
The pyramid of the Bakong temple was surrounded by eight brick towers, each one of which stands on a substantial base.
Bakong, tower to the north of the pyramid, west side.
Photo: Guy Nafilyan

Bakong

(A.D. 881)

The temple-mountain of Bakong—Indravarman's state temple—is said to be the third temple-mountain in the history of Khmer art. The first two—Prasat Ak Yum, still partly buried under the south embankment of the Western Baray, and Rong Chen, on Phnom Kulen—are not at all well known, so Bakong is regarded as the first example of a sandstone temple-mountain.

In 877 Indravarman had the immense reservoir Indratataka excavated to supply an irrigation network for his people; in 879 he built the six sanctuary towers at Preah Ko, and in 881 he erected the Shri Indreshvara lingam on a five-tier pyramid surrounded by three concentric enclosure walls and two moats, together with a large number of ancillary buildings.

The plans of this temple published by Lunet de Lajonquière in 1911 concentrated on the central part of this complex, so that the overall composition went virtually unnoticed for many years. This was partly because the summit had totally collapsed, and it was only with the restoration work carried out by Maurice Glaize between 1936 and 1943 that this building regained its former elegance and power.

The temple called Bakong, which faces due east, has four enclosures, numbered first (the central sanctuary) to fourth (the outer enclosure).

FOURTH ENCLOSURE

The fourth enclosure is a moat (today incorporated into rice fields) 30 meters wide, surrounding an area measuring 800 meters from east to west and 660 meters from north to south. This moat is intersected in the middle of each side by four entrances to the temple: those on the north and the south sides are in fact slightly to the west of center, to align with the axis of the central pyramid. Within this enclosure the remains of 22 small brick-built sanctuary towers have been found; they are arranged regularly around the third enclosure, some facing east, the others towards the pyramid.

THIRD ENCLOSURE

This consists of a wall built of laterite, 320 meters from north to south and 350 meters from east to west, enclosing a moat of 50 to 60 meters wide, with nothing else built inside it. This moat is intersected only on the east and the west by a causeway bordered with balustrades composed of naga, mythical water serpents. These naga, which are perhaps the earliest examples, are enormous, and stand directly on the ground. There are four gopura, or entrance pavilions, one on each side, in line with the two axes. The two larger ones, on the east and west, are reached via the causeways, but the smaller two, on the north and south sides, open directly on to the moat.

SECOND ENCLOSURE

The second enclosure wall, on the edge of the moat, is built of laterite and is 1.8 meters high. It has no entrance pavilions, only openings in the wall; here again, these correspond to the pyramid's two axes. The wall encloses a space empty except for a modern Buddhist monastery that now stands in the northeast corner.

FIRST ENCLOSURE

The first enclosure wall, also of laterite, surrounds all the sacred buildings in an area of about 120 meters by 160 meters. There are gopura at the axial intersections, the two larger ones on the west and east, but only the base of their walls survives. Inside this enclosure there are buildings of various types, the most important of which is the central pyramid, with a single sanctuary tower on its top terrace. In the four corners of the courtyard stand some unusual structures, in varying states of preservation. There are two in both the northeast and the southeast corners, opening towards the west, and one each in the northwest and southwest corners, opening to the east. They are built in brick, with very thick walls, and the better preserved of them show that they must have had a smaller tier above the base. They are square in plan but, because there are groups of ventilation holes in the masonry, it seems that they must have been a kind of second prototype of what later became temple libraries (the first being a single building, identical to these, at Preah Ko, the neighboring temple).

THE PYRAMID

Having passed through the east gopura of the first enclosure, the visitor walks along a paved causeway that passes first between two three-chamber edifices standing in a north-south line, then between two small laterite kiosks, which are more or less square in plan. The one to the south shelters the temple's foundation stele. Then the visitor passes between two long chambers lying on a line from east to west, parallel with the central avenue, before reaching the foot of the pyramid. This rises in a succession of five terraces, faced with sandstone, and almost square: 65 meters by 67 meters. The central platform is 14 meters above ground level.

A series of steep flights of steps climbs up each of the pyramid's sides, from one tier to the next. Each of the stairways has an

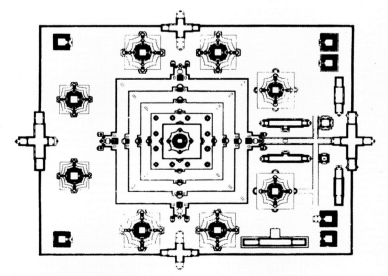

Plan drawn by René Dumont, based on an earlier plan by Maurice Glaize.

General view of the Bakong temple, from the northwest. *Photo: R. Menthonnex*

entrance pavilion at the bottom: this layout is unique in Khmer architecture, and it forms a final enclosure round the sanctuary. The five flights of stairs, rising steeply between their heavy side walls, give an impression of perspective diminution. They are guarded by lions—or what is left of them.

The tiers must represent different symbolic concepts, because the first three have monumental elephants, one at each corner, while the fourth has twelve miniature sanctuary towers. The fourth level, on which only the central tower stands, was at one time covered with bas-reliefs. Although only a few traces of these bas-reliefs survive, these fragments reveal works of outstanding quality—in fact the earliest examples of Khmer bas-reliefs of high quality—which makes it all the more regrettable that nearly all the reliefs have disappeared.

THE CENTRAL TOWER

The central tower was completely rebuilt out of its original materials (using the technique called anastylosis, something like a gigantic jigsaw puzzle) by Maurice Glaize in the early 1940s. Before that, only the base was still standing. During the restoration work it was realized, to everyone's surprise, that this tower's architectural characteristics were unlike those of the other monuments in the Roluos group and of those built in the Preah Ko

style. It became clear that its overall appearance brought to mind the mural decorations and the *devata* in the Angkor Wat style, while its base, its columns, and other elements are in the style of Preah Ko, like the rest of the Bakong monument. Therefore this tower must have been rebuilt in the 12th century, in the late Angkor Wat style, as exemplified by the latter monument's *devata*. The central tower is a sanctuary tower with a dentated square ground plan. It has one true doorway and three false, and a superstructure comprising four stepped tiers and a crowning motif at the very top.

From a vantage point on the pyramid, it can be seen that it is surrounded by eight large brick towers in the first enclosure, each standing on a base consisting of a square tier at the bottom, with the next two tiers dentated. All these eight towers face east. They were dedicated to the eight *murti*, or "forms," of Shiva. Their main body is built in brick but their doors and false doors are carved from single blocks of sandstone. The lintels are among the most beautiful in Khmer art. On the sides of the towers *dvarapala* and *devata*, sculpted in "stucco" (in reality, lime mortar) stood in niches, but very little remains of these. (Decorations dating from the 9th century made with this technique still survive at Preah Ko.)

The Bakong complex is very striking, for the sense of great power that emanates from the pyramid contrasts strongly with the elegance of the sanctuary tower. Bakong also represents the real starting point of the evolution of the temple-mountain.

CHAPTER 3
The Early Angkor Period

Angkor's wealth stemmed from the construction of the huge *baray*, or reservoirs, and extensive irrigation networks, both of which helped to counter the effects of the monsoon. The great temples and these immense reserves of managed water were created during the same period, less than a century after the foundation of the Khmer empire.

The end of Indravarman I's reign, after 886, was followed by a fierce power struggle between brothers, which was eventually won by Yashovardhana.

In connection with this conflict there is a surviving reference to a battle on Tonlé Sap, the Great Lake: "In his march towards victory, he smashed a myriad boats which appeared from all directions on the vast ocean." However, the fighting, ferocious though it must have been, was apparently confined to the area round the capital city and the royal palace of Hariharalya. The destruction of the palace was one of the main consequences of the fighting, and it was perhaps during these events that the central sanctuary in the temple of Bakong had to be destroyed, after it had been desecrated by bloodshed.

We know no more than the name of the victor, Yashovardhana, son of Indravarman I and his queen Indradevi. It seems that he was not his father's designated heir and that it was from his mother that he derived the most important of his rights over the empire.

Yashovardhana had himself consecrated supreme king of the Khmer kings in the year 811 of the shaka era—that is, between April 889 and April 890, but most probably during 889—and he took the name Yashovarman, "he whose fame is his shield."

He could not have been very young. In fact, his father must have ruled as king for a period before gaining supreme power at Hariharalaya, and so was not very young when he died. Presumably Yashovarman I was at least 30 years old at the time, and by then would have taken control of a number of territories, perhaps including the region where he would later establish his capital, though he would still have had to submit to the authority of his father. We know that he was an athlete: several inscriptions praise his

Opposite
At the Lolei temple.
In this photograph of one of the towers at the Lolei temple the bricks are clearly showing signs of the decay that affects so many Khmer monuments. In fact, this tower collapsed at the end of the 1960s and today is no more than a pile of rubble.
Lolei, south tower (first row).
Photo: Guy Nafilyan

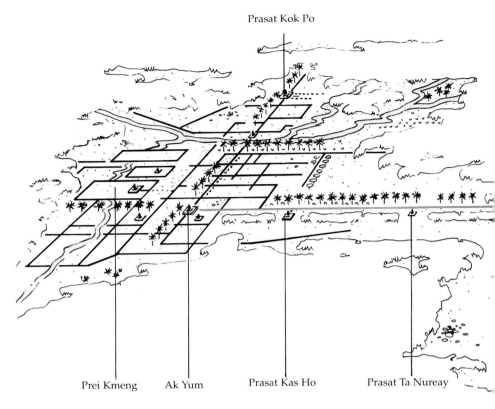

Prasat Kok Po

Prei Kmeng   Ak Yum   Prasat Kas Ho   Prasat Ta Nureay

Plan of Angkor in the reign of Yashovarman I. This plan is intended to give only an idea of what the first city of Angkor and its environs might have been like: the siting of the various buildings and other features is not to be seen as exact. Moreover, although there are still recognizable traces of the dikes and canals, the precise date when they were dug is unknown. Outside the Phnom Bakheng state temple and Yashovarman I's royal palace (the identification of whose site is still speculative, but seems probably correct), in the north of the city there is what must have been the original Phimeanakas. At the four corners of the *baray* are small shelters for stelae. To the south of the *baray* are the four *ashrama*. The causeway leading from the northwest corner of the Lolei *baray* ends in front of what is presumed to be the royal palace, and not in front of the state temple.
Drawing by Guy Nafilyan

extraordinary strength. One stated that "with a single stroke of his sword, he cut in three pieces a thick bar of hard copper." Other verses imply that he had a habit of provoking his companions into fights, which he always won.

The ashrama

Also in year 811 of the saka era, Yashovarman I found time to order the establishment of about a hundred *ashrama* all over his empire, close to existing sanctuaries. The Sanskrit name of these institutions is often translated as "hermitage" and it is the origin of the modern word "ashram," which, however, generally refers to a quite different type of institution. These *ashrama* housed communities—presumably quite small communities—of religious people who wanted to retire from the world.

The interest the new king displayed in these sanctuaries, which were spread far and wide, was in fact a way of proclaiming to all his vassal states that he was now master of all that had once been part of his father's empire. He must have carried out many other similar actions to emphasize his omnipotence, but this is the only one we know about, through references to the *ashrama* in inscriptions.

Some 20 stelae marking the site of these *ashrama* have been discovered. They all give a genealogy and a eulogy of the king, together with a set of rules for visitors. These rules provide us with some information, however scanty, about the visitors to the *ashrama* and therefore also about Khmer society. For example, to be allowed inside an *ashrama* one had to wear white clothing and no ornaments; even a parasol was forbidden. There is also a list of penalties that would be meted out to any person breaking these

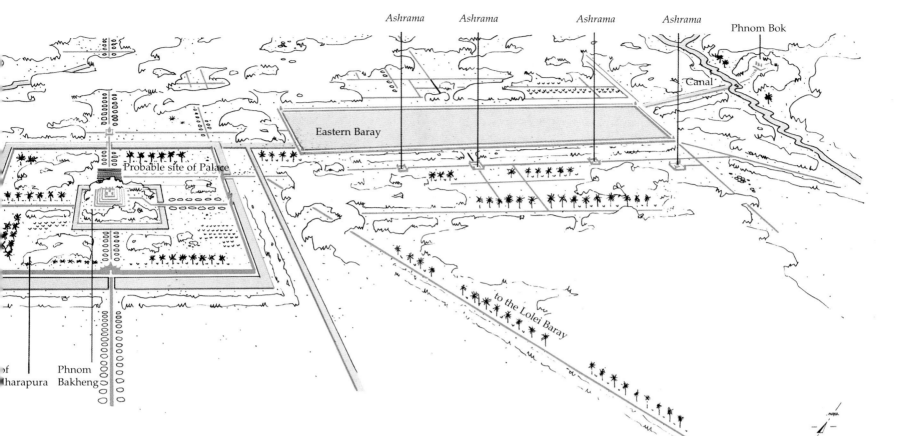

rules (they varied according to the person's rank, from "sons of kings," who had to pay 20 gold *pala*, down to ordinary people, who had to pay only three-quarters of a *pala*. If the latter could not pay, they received 100 strokes from a cane. There were also fines imposed on priests who failed to keep to their timetables, and on temple employees who neglected their duties.

These identical stelae, which have been called "stone posters," are interesting above all because they give an idea of the extent of Yashovarman I's empire. They have been found as far apart as the extreme south of Cambodia (though not in what is now Vietnam), near Wat Phu in Laos, in the region of Phnom Rung, and in the province of Chantaburi in Thailand. However, none has so far been discovered in the center of Cambodia, around Sambor Prei Kuk, which suggests that the kingdom of Bhavapura had remained independent.

The inscriptions on these stelae are the only evidence we have of the *ashrama*, which must have been built in wood and therefore rotted away. Their main characteristic is that they are "digraphic:" that is, both of their main façades have the same Sanskrit text, 50 stanzas engraved in two different scripts. One of these is traditional Khmer script; the other, which did not survive beyond the reign of Yashovarman I, and seems to have been devised by royal command, was based on a script from northern India, although with very radical alterations, since the precise Indian model has not been discovered.

The quality of the Sanskrit poetry in these inscriptions, and in others of this era, is clear evidence of a culture markedly superior to anything suggested by earlier inscriptions. Knowledge of the model for the "invented" script, and the quality of the poems, would surely have been impossible without the contribution of Indian scholars living at the Khmer court, though there is nothing else that even hints at their arrival or presence there.

Inscription in "northern" script.
This type of script, reminiscent of those from northern India, appeared during the reign of Yashovarman I. It did not survive beyond his lifetime. Fragment.
Photo: EFEO

Relocating the capital: an ambitious undertaking

Yashovarman I clearly intended to mark the extent of his empire through these inscriptions. They state, in grandiloquent terms, that he was "the supreme ruler of the Land which is bordered by the Sukshmaka and the Amrataka [these must have been peoples who lived in the Cardamom mountains and of whom nothing else is known], the ocean, China and the Champa." After setting up the stelae bearing these inscriptions, his next undertaking was to found a new capital and for this purpose he commissioned a number of works on a huge scale. Given that the war of succession had probably destroyed his father's palace and even the state temple, he would have felt free to leave the site of the old capital at Hariharalaya, which he might have regarded as unsuitable for development on the scale that he had in mind. It is reasonable to suppose that he was already familiar with the area that was to become Angkor park (I earlier suggested that he might have had some authority over this territory before he acceded to the supreme throne) and that he had perhaps long had ideas for developing it. At any rate, his project was one of the most ambitious ever realized there, and it is clear that he wanted to far outdo the already impressive works that his father had built in his own capital.

The vast Eastern Baray

The Eastern Baray.
Part of the embankment that surrounds the reservoir, not far from the temple of Pre Rup.
Photo: Matthieu Ravaux

Yashovarman needed to build a capital around a state temple and a royal palace. At the same time he wanted to introduce agricultural improvements through the construction of a *baray*. We do not know whether he started by excavating the reservoir or whether work on all these schemes was carried on simultaneously. At any rate, the *baray* he created was enormous, more than

eight times the size of the one created by Indravarman I. Nowadays it is called the Eastern Baray, but its name then was the Yashodharatataka, "Yashodhara's reservoir." It is about 7 kilometers long by 1.8 kilometers wide and had a capacity of some 17 million cubic meters of water for each meter of depth. Today, however, it is dry.

Apparently this vast *baray* was fed entirely by rainwater, which was more abundant in those days than it is now, the forest being much denser. There seems to have been a system of sluice gates at the southwest (the lowest-lying) corner, from where a network of irrigation channels may have carried water into the rice fields, or at any rate close to them. According to a recent theory, there was no method of releasing water from the basin, which was solely for purposes connected with religious rites, the supply of drinking water, and even for its aesthetic appearance. But if this was the case, why was the reservoir on such a gigantic scale and why was it sited so far from the temples and the capital?

The temple dedicated to the king's forebears: Lolei

Yashovarman I built a sanctuary, consisting mainly of four brick towers, on the artificial island that is known today as Lolei, on the Indratataka *baray* that his father had excavated near his own capital. The sanctuary was consecrated on 8 July 893, the towers being dedicated to the spirits of his parents and his maternal grandparents. Yashovarman then established another *ashrama* on the island. Two-and-a-half months before the sanctuary was consecrated, he had dedicated a large donation to two of the divinities in the temple of Preah Ko. Curiously, he chose Parameshvara (Jayavarman II) and Prithivindreshvara (Prithivindravarman), but not Rudreshvara (Rudravarman, father of his paternal grandmother), suggesting perhaps that the land Rudravarman had ruled over had regained its independence.

At the Lolei temple.
The two east towers of the temple of Lolei, before the one on the south side collapsed.
Photo: Guy Nafilyan

A sentinel lion at the Lolei temple.
Lions, portrayed in a not very naturalistic way, are among the guardians of Khmer temples.
Lolei, end 9th century.
Photo: Guy Nafilyan

Base of column at the Lolei temple.
Lolei, end 9th century.
Photo: Guy Nafilyan

The "island" of Lolei is located, unusually, at a point midway along the basin's length but quite near to the northern bank. An inscription tells us that the island could be reached through a "four-sided" gate, which has disappeared and must have been built in non-durable materials. The sanctuaries, with a square ground plan measuring about six meters each side, were built on a terrace 90 meters by 80 meters.

However, the northern towers stand exactly on the east-west axis of the terrace and there seems little doubt that this asymmetry reveals that originally six towers in two rows of three had been envisaged, as is the case at Preah Ko. The stele which records this royal foundation mentions only four divinities: it is clear from this that by the time it was engraved it had already been decided not to build the two towers that would have stood to the north.

A little later, after he had completed construction of his own huge *baray*, Yashovarman I established a series of four large *ashrama* about 450 meters south of this reservoir. They were intended to house ascetics, followers of the principal religious sects existing in his empire. All that survives of these are three stelae, reminders of the *ashrama* built for the followers of Brahma, Vishnu, and the Buddha respectively. The important absentee is Shiva: the laws of symmetry suggest that his *ashrama*, which must surely have existed, stood on the very site where the temple of Pre Rup was built about 60 years later.

The first Angkor, Yashovarman I's capital

It is worth trying to imagine the capital city of Yashovarman I, the very first Angkor, in all its splendor, arranged around the hill of Phnom Bakheng. It appears to have been enclosed within an embankment forming a square with sides four kilometers long. The city therefore covered a considerable area, the same as that of Indrapura, the first capital of Jayavarman II, and this was perhaps no coincidence. No subsequent Khmer king was to create such a huge city, except for Preah Khan in Kompong Svay. To make a comparison with France in the Middle Ages, the area enclosed by the walls of Paris built by King Philip II at the turn of the 13th century was only 273 hectares (675 acres), enlarged to 439 hectares (1090 acres) by Charles V in the 14th century, and the outer walls of Carcassonne were no more than 1,700 meters in length, or nearly ten times smaller than the enclosure surrounding Yashovarman I's capital city.

Today it is still possible to follow the embankment that enclosed the first Yashodharapura for about eight kilometers, along its south and west sides. The northern part of the west side was re-used as a dike when the Western Baray was constructed in the 11th century. The part that is still clearly visible shows that alongside the embankment there is another, smaller bank, about 300 meters away, which has led some observers to believe that originally the capital was completely surrounded by a double enclosure. In reality, however, this second, parallel embankment could hardly have been built before the middle of the 11th century, and probably later, perhaps to form a new reservoir.

The main entrance to the city was on the east, as was usually the case, near the end of a wide causeway that came from the northwest corner of the Lolei *baray*, thus linking the two capitals. Nothing is left today of a city gate on the south or west sides, but it is possible that later works closed off the embankment on these sides, concealing what might have remained of the gates. It has to be remembered that all this area has undergone numerous redevelopments over the centuries. The northern boundary of the city is not clearly identifiable: it lies somewhere in the middle of what was to be Angkor Thom, where there were many upheavals from the 11th century onwards.

The temple of Phimeanakas, built later by Suryavarman I, stood exactly at the intersection of the northern axis of the temple of Phnom Bakheng and the western axis of the Eastern Baray, a choice of location that could not have been made by chance. The temple must have been erected on the site of an old sanctuary built by a minister of Yashovarman I. This sanctuary, which was probably much less important than the one that still stands, was outside the city boundaries. The same is true of another temple, Mangalartha, dating from the end of the 13th century. This is situated in the northeastern quarter of Angkor Thom and was built over the site of a monument from the reign of Yashovarman I.

The vast square formed by the outer limits of Yashodharapura was designed so that the hill known today as Phnom Bakheng was more or less at its center. Yashovarman I decided to erect his state temple on the summit of this hill. From each of the cardinal points a causeway, bordered on either side by canals or ponds, led to the foot of the hill. Portions of causeway have been identified, especially on the east side; once again it is the north causeway that has left behind the fewest traces.

Nothing else, of course, remains of the civil works carried out at this Yashodharapura, since the buildings would have been constructed of wood. In particular, nothing is left of the royal palace. The site of this palace (assuming that it conformed with the usage that has continued right up to modern times, for example at Bangkok or Phnom Penh) must have been to the north of the state temple, and consequently somewhere in the southwest part of what was to become the city of Angkor Thom, the final capital city of Angkor.

In fact, the causeway that led from the corner of the Indratataka reservoir ended, on the left bank of the Siem Reap river, at a point on what is now the line of the south wall of Angkor Thom, and not on that of the east causeway of Phnom Bakheng. Presumably, therefore, this causeway was built during Yashovarman I's time to join up with a triumphal way that started at the royal palace and that was later completely covered over by the walls of Angkor Thom. Consequently, in this first Yashodharapura, there would have been the same arrangement of two parallel eastern avenues as in Angkor Thom, one leading to the state temple, the other to the royal palace.

In addition to this palace, there certainly would have been several houses belonging to great lords within the city, perhaps situated in parks planted with trees. And without doubt there would also have been a district, or several districts, housing people of less importance. Not all the area was built on, however: one inscription contains a reference to rice fields that had been planted within the city enclosure (or perhaps simply retained from before the building of the city).

A lion at Phnom Bakheng.
One of the two lions that guard the foot of the east stairway leading to the temple of Phnom Bakheng. Bakheng, end 9th century.
Photo: Guy Nafilyan

The state temple on Phnom Bakheng

Phnom Bakheng, the oval-shaped hill with the state temple on its summit, stood within an outer enclosure consisting of a rectangular moat 650 meters long by 436 meters wide. Running parallel with this moat was a wall that had gopura (gateways) at each of the cardinal points; the wall and the four gopura have disappeared. These gopura led immediately to the foot of the hill. Someone entering by the east gopura, guarded by two lions that are still there, would have climbed the great laterite stairway to an esplanade on the summit of Phnom Bakheng. A fine avenue then led to the gopura in an inner enclosure wall built of laterite (the gopura were sandstone, though all that is now left of them are their bases). There are sizeable remains of a similar stairway on both the north and the west sides, but not the south, though there was a gopura here, opening on to a causeway at the bottom of the hill. Perhaps the builders did not have enough time to make a stairway here, though one was definitely planned.

Once through the gopura in the inner wall, the visitor faced two buildings referred to as libraries, one on either side. There is always at least one of these buildings in the temples, always opening to the west, though here they were subsequently opened up to the east also. They must have housed divinities as well as the books that are assumed to have been there.

From this point, at the foot of the temple-mountain, the consummate artistry that produced this spectacular pyramid can be fully admired. The

A divine figure carved in bas-relief on the outer wall of the central tower of the Phnom Bakheng temple. Bakheng, end 9th century, sandstone.
Photo: Guy Nafilyan

Towers at Phnom Bakheng.
The Phnom Bakheng temple had altogether 108 sanctuary towers of varying size, in addition to the central tower.
Bakheng, end 9th century.
Photo: Guy Nafilyan

five superimposed square terraces of gradually decreasing height, which enhances the effect of perspective, are each intersected at the cardinal points by a stairway bordered by lions, also decreasing in size from one level to the next. The largest terrace measures 76 meters on each side; the top one, standing at an overall height of 13 meters, measures 47 meters on each side. On every terrace there is a small sandstone sanctuary tower at each corner and two others flanking each flight of stairs, making 12 towers in all. Finally, slightly off-center towards the west, there is a sixth terrace, measuring 31 meters on each side, and only 1.6 meters high; on this summit stand five towers, in quincunx arrangement and opening in all four directions. For the first time in Khmer art, these towers are built entirely in sandstone. The central sanctuary housed the lingam of the god Yashodhareshvara, after whom the temple is named. Altogether, counting the 44 towers that surround the pyramid, and excluding the central sanctuary, the outer enclosure contained 108 towers, the number representing the universe in Indian cosmology. The central tower symbolizes all the others, and the seven levels are also a symbol of the world.

Phnom Bakheng

(about A.D. 900)

The central tower of the temple of Phnom Bakheng. *Photo: Guy Nafilyan*

Phnom Bakheng is the state temple that Yashovarman erected on the hill of that name (which is a modern name). There are two other hills rising from the plain of Angkor, and Yashovarman also crowned these with two *prasat*, Prasat Phnom Bok and Prasat Phnom Krom, though neither of these had the appearance of a temple-mountain.

After having excavated the immense reservoir, 7,000 meters long by 1,800 meters wide, now called the Eastern Baray, and having built Prasat Lolei, the temple dedicated to his forebears, on an island on the Indratataka *baray*, Yashovarman then built his state temple on Phnom Bakheng.

This is a natural sandstone hill, which perhaps made it a logical choice as the platform to carry the pedestal of the royal lingam. In itself the hill was not enough, however: according to the rules of Khmer religious symbolism, it was necessary actually to "create" a mountain. To do this, the summit of the hill was cut into steps, and these were covered with sandstone, so that it was transformed into an image of Mount Meru, the magic mountain. This laborious process is further confirmation of the importance of imagery and cosmology in Khmer architecture. Moreover, since the mythological mountain is the center of a continent surrounded by the ocean, a moat had to be built around the perimeter.

Research carried out through detailed observation and with the aid of aerial photography, mostly by Victor Goloubew, has shown that the temple of Phnom Bakheng stands in the center of a square with sides measuring four kilometers (this square encompassed the area where Angkor Wat and half of Angkor Thom would later rise). This square was surrounded by a moat, the southwestern corner of which can still be very clearly seen, though this has now been turned into rice fields. Research carried out on the ground, with the help of a member of Cambodia's geographical department, has led to the discovery of traces of two other enclosures (the second and third), between which are numerous vestiges of small hollows that must be the site of ancient dwellings.

Here we will deal only with the first enclosure (which surrounded the sacred buildings on the summit of the hill), leaving aside the remains of entrance pavilions on the north, east, south, and west sides of the second enclosure, at the foot of the hill, which were studied by Victor Goloubew in 1932 and 1933.

THE CENTRAL TOWER

This is the earliest example of five towers in quincunx arrangement built entirely of sandstone. A central sanctuary tower is set on a base, with true doorways opening in four directions. It is surrounded by four smaller towers, all also opening towards the four cardinal points of the compass. This ensemble stands on a

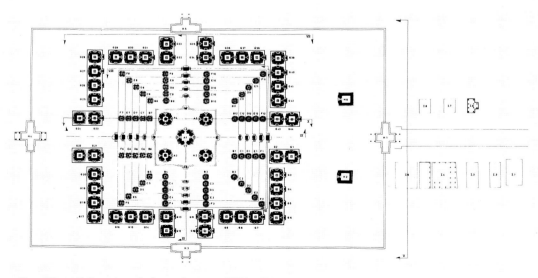

Plan of Phnom Bakheng drawn by Jacques Dumarçay, EFEO, 1971.

General view of the temple of Phnom Bakheng from the west. *Photo: Guy Nafilyan*

dentated square platform that is intersected in the middle of each side by stairways that climb between low supporting walls.

The central tower has lost its superstructure, and all we have left is the main body, which has a dentated ground plan. Its columns are octagonal, with very simple and stylized decoration. The lintels, what is left of them, are less extensively decorated with relief work than those of the previous era. The most notable decoration is that of the large *devata* on either side of the doorways, and the pilasters decorated with numerous small figures in niches. The corner towers are so ruined they have almost totally disappeared. During the recent periods of fighting this temple mountain was used as a fortress, so there was serious concern about its preservation.

THE PYRAMID

The terrace on which the five towers stand is itself on top of a pyramid with five tiers, each of which has a stairway in the center of all four sides. On each of these levels there are 12 small temples standing in a regular arrangement at the corners and on each side

of the stairways, making 60 in all. These little buildings all face east, which means that some of them open into a void while others face into the retaining wall of the terrace above (questions of accessibility were not considered!).

A series of sanctuary towers, this time in brick, surrounds the foot of the pyramid. Arranged in groups of two, three or four on the same base, there were at one time 44 of these. Some of them open towards the east, but many have openings to both east and west.

In front of this complex, that is, on the east, stand two rectangular edifices. Originally they had two doors to the west; doors opening to the east were added later. These buildings are of the type referred to as libraries. The whole complex is enclosed within a rectangular laterite wall about 190 meters long by 120 meters wide. Access was through entrance pavilions on each of the four sides, but they have disappeared.

The large number of buildings (sanctuary towers and small temples) at Phnom Bakheng is bound to stimulate a great deal of further study, particularly on the symbolism of numbers that might be revealed by this monument.

The temple of Phnom Krom from the air.
At the same time that he was building Phnom
Bakheng, Yashovarman I topped two other hills in the
area with a group of three towers. One of the hills,
Phnom Krom, overlooks Tonlé Sap, the Great Lake.
Phnom Krom, end 9th century, sandstone.
Photo: Guy Nafilyan

The construction of the temple-mountain of Phnom Bakheng was an undertaking of gigantic proportions. The summit of the hill had to be leveled off, leaving behind only as much as was needed to form the body of the pyramid, which stands directly on the hill's sandstone.

The monument's sculpture (to be seen particularly on the central sanctuary, which has reliefs carved on the outside of its walls) is of superb quality. The artists continued the earlier work done at Preah Ko and at Bakong; this time they were working not in stucco but in sandstone, which was harder to sculpt and so forced them to modify the designs slightly, making them less exuberant. The lintels show less imagination. There are no pendants and fewer small figures.

About 907, the principal god of the Phnom Bakheng monument, whose name Yashodhareshvara ("the lord who brings glory") was linked to that of the king, must have been consecrated together with the most important statues. However, the towers still had to be built and the sculptures carved, so it is not certain that the king, who probably died in 910, ever saw his state temple completed.

It is generally believed that at the same time as building the Phnom Bakheng monument, Yashovarman I also built temples in the Angkor region, on the summits of Phnom Krom, a hill overlooking the Great Lake, and Phnom Bok, not far from Phnom Kulen. Perhaps these were the work of some of his high officials. Nevertheless, these two temples are designed according to exactly the same plan, with three sandstone towers in a row, the one in the center dedicated to Shiva, that on the north to Vishnu, and that on the south to Brahma. The dates when they were consecrated do not appear in any surviving inscription.

After Yashovarman I

Yashovarman I was succeeded by one of his sons, Harshavarman I, whose reign lasted more than ten years. He cannot have had the energy or the influence of his father and he wielded much less real power. Nonetheless, he was responsible for the pyramid of Baksei Chamkrong, a structure of fine proportions and construction. Built in laterite, it stands at the northeast foot of Phnom Bakheng. Harshavarman had statues of Shiva and of Shiva's wife Devi consecrated on Phnom Bakheng, in memory of his parents. The temple therefore played a similar role to that of Preah Ko and of Lolei. Although he built the tower on the top of the pyramid, he did not manage to decorated it: this task was undertaken by Rajendravarman, less than half a century later.

Harshavarman I was succeeded in about 923 by his brother, Ishanavarman II, whose authority over the empire seems to have been weak, despite his title of *chakravartin* ("emperor of the world"). He died in 928 or just before. There is no temple known to have been built by this king. It was not even during his reign that the temple of Prasat Kravan at Angkor was built, or its twin, Prasat Neang Khmau, "the temple of the black lady," far away near the modern town of Ta Kev, south of Phnom Penh. The splendid brick bas-reliefs, inspired by the cult of Vishnu, inside the two sanctuaries at Prasat Kravan, deal with the same subject as the only mural paintings surviving from this era: these are painted on the inside walls of Prasat Neang Khmau, but are now in a very poor state.

At the temple of Baksei Chamkrong.
The fine pyramid of Baksei Chamkrong was built by Hasharvarman I, son of Yashovarman I. He also erected the sanctuary tower, but did not complete its decoration.
Baksei Chamkrong, beginning 10th century, laterite, brick and sandstone.
Photo: Guy Nafilyan

There are other bas-reliefs in brick, but of much cruder quality, in a monument of similar date at Phnom Trop, situated not far from the outlet of Tonlé Sap, the Great Lake, in the province of Kompong Cham.

The manpower required for the projects

Prasat Kravan: Vishnu's Three Steps. This bas-relief illustrates the legend of Vishnu's avatar (incarnation) as the Dwarf. Prasat Kravan, interior of central tower, south side, bas-relief in brick. About 925.
Photo: Luc Ionesco, EFEO

Prasat Kravan: Vishnu astride Garuda. Prasat Kravan, interior of the central tower, north side, bas-relief in brick. About 925.
Photo: Luc Ionesco, EFEO

Up to now, we have looked at the temples and other remarkable projects, but hardly at all at the people who carried out these works; yet an enormous amount of manpower must have been needed for these almost superhuman achievements.

Take the Eastern Baray, for example. As we have seen, it is 7 kilometers long and 1.8 kilometers wide. The cross-section of the dike surrounding it formed a trapezoid approximately 120 meters wide at its base, 15–20 meters at the top and 10 meters high. This meant that roughly 700 cubic meters of earth, probably taken from the excavated basin, had to be moved per linear meter: a total of over 12 million cubic meters of earth. To make a contemporary comparison: on average, 100,000–150,000 cubic meters of earth have to be moved for each kilometer of motorway built (about five times less than for the *baray*. Moreover, it is estimated that in motorway construction, an average of 5,000 cubic meters of earth a day are shifted over a period of several months.

The French archaeologist George Groslier, in attempting to calculate the time taken to build the great Banteay Chmar temple in the 12th century, estimated, on the basis of practical experiments, that a workman could transport about two cubic meters of earth a day over a distance of some 30 meters. Using this figure as our starting point, we can calculate that it must have taken roughly six million working days just to build the embankment surrounding the Eastern Baray. With 6,000 workers (a reasonable enough figure, given the other large-scale projects under way at the same time) the construction would have taken 1,000 days, or about three years, assuming that all these laborers worked with no rest days, and without taking into account periods of bad weather.

This shows that the Eastern Baray, which was started in 889, could not have been completed before 892 at the earliest, and that very likely it took somewhat longer than this.

To get an idea of the size of population required to provide all these workers and also to feed them, the hypothetical figure of 6,000 (plus all the skilled technicians who would have been needed as well) will have to be multiplied by five or six, and perhaps even by seven or more. It is unlikely that the region of Angkor alone could have supplied so many workers. This therefore leads to the supposition that large numbers of people were forcibly transported, doubtless from vanquished kingdoms, a practice described in an earlier time by Chinese observers and, unhappily, frequently adopted in Southeast Asia in subsequent times, as recorded in the royal chronicles.

The Eastern Baray was of course far from being the only construction project during the reign of Yashovarman I. Taking only the biggest of these

schemes, there was also the building of his capital city with its 16-kilometer walls and, at its center, the state temple (which involved leveling off the hill first), as well as the construction of the causeway embankment that linked this complex to the Lolei *baray*, more than ten kilometers away.

Taking into consideration all these facts and figures, and using just a little imagination, we can begin to have some idea of what an astonishing undertaking the building of Yashovarman I's great capital city was.

A bas-relief at Prasat Kravan: the goddess Lakshmi and two figures praying.
Ptarat Kravan, interior of the north tower, west side, bas-relief in brick. About 925.
Photo: Luc Ionesco, EFEO

CHAPTER 4

Relocating the Capital

Pre Rup and Ta Keo

In the middle of the 10th century, after having been abandoned for about 20 years, Angkor was brought back to life when King Rajendravarman relocated his capital to Pre Rup, south of the Eastern Baray, to facilitate the systematic development of the area to the north of this reservoir. The century ended with a long and peaceful reign, during which the temples of Banteay Srei and Ta Keo were built.

O n the death of Ishanavarman II in about 928, the supreme throne passed to a king who until then must have been his vassal, Jayavarman IV. The latter had reigned since at least 921 at Koh Ker, the capital of a small kingdom about a hundred kilometers northeast of Angkor. He was the uncle of Ishanavarman II and of his brother, Harshavarman I; his principal wife was Jayadevi, one of the younger sisters of Yashovarman I. He was probably not all that young in 921; at any rate, he was sufficiently powerful and rich to have already built the fine brick complex of Prasat Thom at Koh Ker, and he had doubtless already started the development of his capital at that date, and perhaps a few years earlier.

Jayavarman IV and his provincial capital Koh Ker

This is why in 928 Jayavarman IV decided to reject Angkor as a capital and instead to remain in his own, where he proceeded with his ambitious projects, erecting in particular an imposing state temple. During a period of 20 years or so from 921, a large number of less important temples were also built in this district, which covered about 35 square kilometers. These projects illustrate the great wealth of Jayavarman's capital, which was located in what is today one of the poorest regions in Cambodia.

Just as previous kings had constructed *baray* at Angkor, so Jayavarman IV had a *baray* built at Koh Ker, the Rahal. Compared with Yashodharatataka (the Eastern Baray) at Angkor, it was of modest dimensions, 1,200 meters by 560 meters. However, its construction must have presented greater difficulties: because of the topography, the *baray* had in part to be cut out of the rock, while its alignment had to be almost north-south, which was unusual. The remains of a laterite sluice gate for allowing water to flow out and irrigate the surrounding lands are still visible. Yet this reservoir alone can hardly have been responsible for the obvious sudden prosperity of Pre Rup. What must have occurred—and there is evidence of this—is that the rich and powerful families of the kingdom who had been living at Angkor moved to Koh Ker in order to serve their new supreme king, bringing with them their possessions, their servants, and perhaps even their own slaves.

For his state temple, Jayavarman IV erected a seven-tiered sandstone pyramid, 35 meters high and today in a ruinous condition. In cross-section it almost forms an equilateral triangle, with its base covering a square with 62-meter sides and its top terrace forming a square with sides measuring about 12 meters. The unusual thing about it is that it has only one stairway, on the east side. This temple is the eastward continuation of another temple already dedicated to the gods of the kingdom. Jayavarman IV presumably did not have the time to complete his new temple, not even to build the central sanctuary, which would have been of similar proportions and was to have topped the pyramid. At the summit of this pyramid there is only an enormous pedestal, intended to support a lingam so unusually large that it is celebrated in several inscriptions.

Prasat Thom at Koh Ker.
West entrance pavilion of the third enclosure (east side), giving access to the Prang enclosure, which can be seen in the background. In front of the sanctuary (left) a figure with the head of a bird stands guard (see illustration opposite).
Photo: Guy Nafilyan

The Prang at Koh Ker.
It is not really known why this name, Prang, which seems to be of Sanskrit origin, was given to this pyramid, Jayavarman IV's state temple, which was probably never completed. The word is little used in Cambodia but common in Thailand. The king erected his temple alongside Prasat Thom, in an unusual manner: the western part of the third enclosure of Prasat Thom formed a common wall with the new temple. It is likely that the Prang, being sited here, was not exactly in the center of the king's capital city.
Photo: Guy Nafilyan

A statue of Ganesha at Koh Ker.
This magnificent statue of Ganesha, the Hindu god
with the head of an elephant, and son of Shiva,
sits enthroned in the center of Prasat Bak, about
2.5 kilometers from Prasat Thom.
Sandstone, 1.45 meters high.
Photo: Guy Nafilyan

A statue at Prasat Thom, Koh Ker.
Figure with the head of a bird standing guard
at the east side of the west entrance pavilion of the
third enclosure.
Photo: Guy Nafilyan

The most striking feature of the art of Koh Ker is the huge size of the blocks of stone used for both the building work and the sculpture. There was plenty of sandstone available nearby, so there was obviously not the same problem of transportation as at Angkor. Also, it is possible that Jayavarman IV wanted to show that a "provincial" king was capable of accomplishing projects that were as impressive as, if not more so, those of Angkor. There are also several sizeable sanctuaries in brick, notably Prasat Kraham, "the red sanctuary." Possibly rebuilt after Jayavarman ascended to the supreme throne, this sanctuary formed the east gopura, housing an immense statue of a dancing Shiva with five heads and eight arms. Unfortunately, this statue was discovered in pieces, though the high quality of the sculpture still shines out.

Jayavarman IV probably died in 941, which seems to have been the year when his son Harshavarman II ascended the supreme throne (though this might have taken place slightly earlier). The accession of the new king probably did not take place peacefully, because an inscription tells us that he "achieved kingship thanks to a friend and to his two strong arms." One of his generals had to wage war against the city of Indrapura, Jayavarman II's first capital, and he himself apparently had to keep fighting throughout his short reign. After only three years, Harshavarman II disappeared in unknown, but probably violent, circumstances.

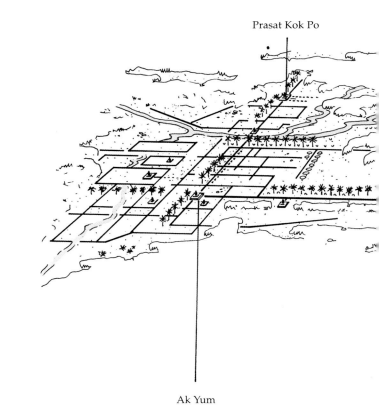

Prasat Kok Po

Ak Yum

Plan of Angkor as it was in the reign of Rajendravarman. Rajendravarman abandoned Yashovarman I's capital, perhaps because it was in too ruinous a state after having been deserted for 20 years. He installed himself further east, not far from the middle of the southern bank of the Great Baray. His palace was subsequently given the name Eastern Mebon and his state temple, Pre Rup. He transformed the whole area north of the *baray* through irrigation, by creating a diversion canal from the Siem Reap river, which flowed about eight kilometers to the north. Important dignitaries were responsible for some of the temples, such as Bat Chum, as well as other large-scale projects, including in particular the creation of Sras Srang, the "royal bathing pool."
Drawing by Guy Nafilyan

Rajendravarman: the return to Angkor

The small kingdom of Bhavapura, founded by King Bhavavarman around Sambor Prei Kuk in the center of Cambodia during the 6th century, seems to have remained largely independent of the "supreme kings" up till this point.

About 940 the king of Bhavapura, Rajendravarman, a ruler who was clearly full of energy and who had succeeded his father Mahendravarman some years earlier, decided he was going to ascend the supreme throne. In 944, only three years after the consecration of Harshavarman II, Rajendravarman duly ousted him. The court poets declared the new king to be "greater" than his predecessor "in age and in his list of virtues." This was not the kind of observation that normally would have been made, and it might have been a way of justifying a somewhat violent assumption of power. Rajendravarman was the cousin of Harshavarman II, since his mother Mahendradevi was sister of the great Yashovarman I and of Jayadevi, though this relationship clearly did not give him any particular right to the throne.

A great admirer of Yashovarman I, Rajendravarman planned to rebuild from scratch the capital of the Khmer empire on the site of Angkor. Initially he doubtless installed himself in the old royal palace. His first major pious work was the restoration of the nearby temple of Baksei Chamkrong, which had perhaps been abandoned during the Koh Ker interlude. Harshavarman I had not had enough time to complete the decoration of his sanctuary tower: Rajendravarman is said to have "added the splendor of a decoration in stucco," which has since been lost. The principal divinity of this sanctuary was consecrated on Wednesday 23 February 948, and it is even possible to specify that the ceremony took place at about 9:40 A.M. This was a "gold" statue of Parameshvara, and not a lingam as might be expected in the case of Shiva. It seems that Rajendravarman chose this title in order to evoke the

70

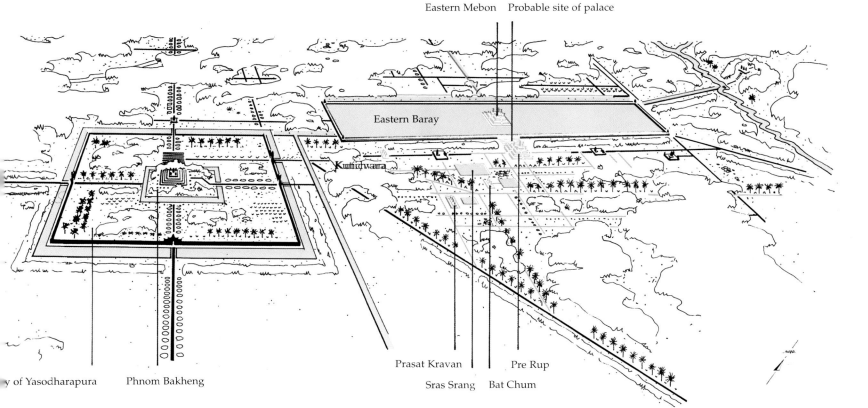

Eastern Mebon   Probable site of palace

Eastern Baray

Kutishvara

Prasat Kravan   Pre Rup

y of Yasodharapura   Phnom Bakheng   Sras Srang   Bat Chum

posthumous name of Jayavarman II, Parameshvara, particularly since this temple also housed the "shades" of all the previous kings of Cambodia. They are cited in the very fine inscription that covers the piers of the tower's doorway. It is thanks to this text that we know that the Khmers' account of their own history started with a number of totally mythical kings.

The kingdoms become provinces

Rajendravarman certainly needed the protection of all these legendary past kings. He was evidently very badly received right from the start and he had to deal with rebellions throughout his reign. First he had to gain control of those kingdoms that had separated from the empire during previous reigns. Presumably it was because this proved very difficult that he adopted the drastic measure of simply turning all the Khmer kingdoms into *vishaya*, provinces. Doubtless this radical reform was not welcomed by the rulers of these territories, who were formerly his equals.

He also waged war beyond the frontiers of his empire. At some point he sent out an expedition during which "the city of the king of Champ, which is bordered by the deep moat of the sea, was reduced to ashes by warriors obeying his orders." The description is very vague, because most Cham cities were not far from the sea, but at any rate the city in question was a long way from Rajendravarman's own base.

There are several traces of Rajendravarman in areas along the border with Thailand; he certainly seems to have managed, without much difficulty, to regain control of all the territory Yashovarman I had ruled.

71

A new capital
south of the baray

Rajendravarman chose the middle of the south bank of the Eastern Baray for the site of his capital, of which nothing is now visible except his state temple, Pre Rup. This location would have made it easy to reach surrounding areas, in all directions, across this immense reservoir.

According to the normal practice, Rajendravarman would have built his royal palace somewhere between the temple of Pre Rup and the *baray*, that is, to the north of the state temple. No trace of this palace has ever been discovered, however, perhaps because no one has ever really searched for it. To direct this project, the king brought in Kavindrarimathana, whose name (or title) means "destroyer of enemies, king of poets." This man was not only an army chief and on occasions the king's personal envoy, but also an architect. His name has come down to us only because he left a monument, which we will consider shortly.

Rajendravarman's plan was to build a temple on an artificial island in the middle of the Eastern Baray, which was called Yashodharatataka ("the reservoir of Yashodhara"), as if to put the finishing touches to the great *baray* of the former king whom he so much admired. This is the temple nowadays called the Eastern Mebon, whose principal divinity, called Rajendreshvara, "the Lord of Rajendra[varman]," was consecrated on Friday 28 January 953, at about 11 A.M. The king again brought in Kavindrarimathana for the building of this temple, "at the invitation of everybody," according to an inscription.

The Eastern Mebon temple.
On the island at the central point of the Eastern Baray, which might have been created at the time when this great reservoir was excavated, Rajendravarman built the Eastern Mebon temple, some time after 950. The water would have actually lapped round the walls of the temple.
Photo: Guy Nafilyan

This Buddhist architect also built for himself, or rather for the good of his karma, the small temple of Bat Chum with its three brick towers and pond. What is unusual here is that each of the towers bears an inscribed eulogy of the founder, each written by a different author, as if there had been a kind of competition and that the three best examples had been "published." The temple was consecrated in 953 and Kavindrarimathana most likely died soon afterwards.

The Eastern Mebon temple.
The central terrace with its towers in quincunx (five-point) arrangement.
Photo: Guy Nafilyan

Near to this temple there was a pagoda housing Buddhist priests, with dwellings and other buildings all around. These have all completely disappeared, of course, but to the north of this we can still admire another of Kavindrarimathana's personal projects, the "small" *baray* known as Sras Srang, the "royal bathing pool." This reservoir, still filled with water, was originally 400 yukta ("arm's length") by 200 (approximately 700 meters by 350 meters), and was surrounded in the usual way by earth dikes. Inscriptions at the temple of Bat Chum stipulate how the reservoir was to be cared for: "...in this *baray*, which has been filled with water for the good of all creatures [...], above all, no one must allow a herd of trained elephants to climb on the dikes, as this would destroy them." And then: "...in this *baray*, whose waters are fresh thanks to the trees growing on the banks, no one must allow elephants to bathe; if any are seen trying to do so, conscientious people should stop them." Sras Srang was radically altered two centuries later by

Sras Srang.
Probably the architect who created this reservoir (literally "royal pool") had envisaged a wooden landing stage on more or less the same spot as this terrace, which was not built until the reign of Jayavarman VII, over 200 years later.
Photo: Luc Ionesco, EFEO

74

The Eastern Mebon temple.
Each of the four corners of the Eastern Mebon temple is guarded by an elephant, guardian of the midway points of the universe.
Photo: Guy Nafilyan

The Eastern Mebon temple.
A detail from a lintel of the south false door of the northwest sanctuary. An elephant (Ganesha?) astride what looks like a horse.
Photo: Luc Ionesco, EFEO

Jayavarman VII, who shortened the reservoir, embellished it with a charming landing stage, and had all of its banks encased in sandstone.

The whole of this district was quite densely inhabited: Kavindrarimathana had erected another Buddhist sanctuary nearby, while to the northwest of Sras Srang a high official built the temple known as Kutishvara. Since the reign of Yashovarman I there had been a Hindu temple to the west of the same *baray*, on what was to be the site of Bantea Kdei temple two centuries later.

Also during this period, some ten kilometers north of the Eastern Baray, a sluice was constructed on the Siem Reap river, feeding a canal that subsequently became this river's main course; a few laterite blocks and a small temple can still be seen at the place where this diversion canal was built. The canal enabled a considerable area of land to be developed for agriculture.

Pre Rup:
a classic temple-mountain

All that is known today of Rajendravarman's capital city, which must never have had a moat, is the state temple, Pre Rup. This temple stands exactly to the south of the Eastern Mebon temple and perhaps, as I suggested earlier, on the site of the *ashrama* built there by Yashovarman I for worshippers of Shiva. At any rate, there is a shelter there similar to those housing the stelae of the other three *ashrama*, and the temple is situated almost at the point where the missing *ashrama* must have been.

The principal divinities of Pre Rup temple were consecrated in 961 or the beginning of 962, about eight years after those of the Eastern Mebon, and

Pre Rup

(A.D. 961)

Prasat Pre Rup is a classic example of a temple-mountain, and the last without continuous galleries. Its name, which means "turning the body," relates to a ritual recounted in Khmer legend.

The upward thrust of its composition is much more marked than at the Eastern Mebon temple: there is a first level with the second or outer enclosure; a second level with the first or inner enclosure; then a pyramid with three tiers of unequal sizes on which, between the four corner towers, the central tower stands upon two further steps and a pedestal.

THE ENCLOSURES

The temple is first of all surrounded by the inevitable moat: the Ocean that surrounds the Universe.

The second enclosure wall, built in laterite, has four imposing entrance pavilions, one on each side. These pavilions have five chambers with entrance and exit porches. Within this enclosure there are two very different groups of buildings: on the north, west, and south sides, standing on a slightly raised terrace, there is a series of

The name of the monument, Pre Rup, which means "turning the body," refers to a rite that took place during a cremation, and is linked to the cremation of a legendary king. However, the "cistern" that inspired the use of the name here was really only the pedestal of a statue of the bull Nandi, Shiva's mount.
Photo: Luc Ionesco, EFEO

Left: Pre Rup: a view of a long hall from the north. *Photo: Guy Nafilyan*

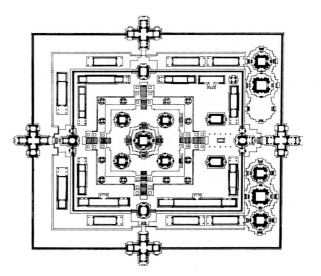

Plan drawn by Henri Marchal, from L'Architecture comparée dans l'Inde et l'Extrême-Orient, *1944.*

An aerial view of the Pre Rup temple from the northeast.
At the northeast corner of the first enclosure, between two halls, there is a small building of the same type as those that house the stelae bearing

inscriptions of the rules of the other *ashrama*. This suggests that Pre Rup was built on the site of the *ashrama*, which has never been discovered.
Photo: Menthonnex

long chambers. On the east side there is no terrace and in the corresponding space there are instead five brick sanctuary towers. A sixth had been planned at the south end of the northern row but it was never built; in fact, the other towers were never fully built. This unfinished state allows us to see on the lintels the various stages of decoration, from the first outline to the finished work.

On the next level, the first enclosure's laterite wall is intersected by four small gopura consisting of single square chambers, built in brick, with those on the east and west having entrance porches. In addition to the central pyramid, this enclosure contains buildings of several types:

• two libraries, on the north and south sides, with a real door opening to the west and a false door to the east

• nine assorted long chambers, aligned with the wall of this first enclosure and foreshadowing the galleries that run round the perimeter of later temples

• in the northeast corner, a small kiosk of the type created for containing a stele, built in laterite and with a corbeled vault in the "cloister arch" or "priest's hat" form.

THE PYRAMID

In the center rises the pyramid, with three superimposed terraces of decreasing height. The first has a series of 12 small brick temples. The second is bare, but on its east side there are two additional stairways leading to the top tier, one on either side of the main stairway, and aligned with the axes of the secondary north-east and southeast towers on the top tier, but hardly useable, since they start right at the outer edge of the terrace!

The final level forms the plateau on which the five sanctuary towers stand in the usual quincunx pattern. The four towers at the corners have a dentated square ground plan. In the middle, standing on two steps on top of a pedestal, is the larger central tower, with a ground plan of the same shape. All these towers are in brick with the usual sandstone decoration around the doorways. On their sides, flanking the main doors, divinities are roughly carved in the brick; at one time they were covered with the coating of lime mortar that is referred to as "stucco" with which the Khmer sculptors and decorators put the finishing touches to bas-reliefs.

even longer after the completion of Rajendravarman's new royal palace. This is quite a long delay, particularly since this temple is smaller than those his predecessors built.

Towards the end of his reign the name of one of the king's most loyal advisers appears: Yajnavaraha, the scholarly guru of the future king Jayavarman V and grandson of Harshavarman I. The king granted him land along the banks of the Siem Reap about 30 kilometers to the northeast, not far from the foot of Phnom Kulen. Here he built a settlement and together with his brother erected the famous temple of Banteay Srei: famous not only for its beauty but also for the somewhat exaggerated interest that the French writer André Malraux took in its sculptures.

Rajendravarman was able to see the central divinity of this charming monument consecrated, on 22 April 967. Nevertheless he cannot have seen the temple completed: he disappeared at the beginning of the following year, very probably following a palace revolution. It is possible that during this revolt the fine palace built for him by Kavindrarimathana was destroyed.

Jayendranagari:
"Capital of the conquering king"

The son of Rajendravarman ascended the throne as Jayavarman V. Although still a youth, he got down to work immediately: already on 3 July 968 he signed a decree granting certain privileges to the temple of Banteay Srei and to other temples founded by Yajnavaraha, his guru. Another decree signed in the same year concerns the old temple of Phnom Bakheng, which suggests that he had returned to the palace of Yashovarman I.

All this activity on the administrative front does not mean, however, that he did not have to fight hard in order to impose his authority: "At the time of the great battle for possession of the land, when they suddenly discovered the devastation caused by the flying arrows of this powerful king [...], even the bravest of the enemy were terrified and everysingle one of them fled, abandoning their insane audacity."

Opposite
The temple of Pre Rup.
This view of the east stairway of the pyramid at Pre Rup shows how steep the approaches to the sanctuary often were. The stone pillars probably supported a kind of canopy that sheltered the bull Nandi, Shiva's mount. *Photo: Luc Ionesco, EFEO*

The temple of Pre Rup.
Southeast corner of the central sanctuary (as it was in July 1989). Abandoned for almost 20 years, most of the temples have been reclaimed by nature.
Photo: Claude Jacques

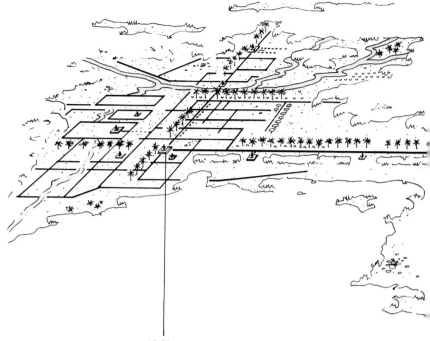

Ak Yum

Plan of Angkor at the time of Jayavarman V.
Jayavarman V had to abandon his father's capital and he first
returned to a place near Phnom Bakheng, probably in what
remained of the former palace of Yashovarman I. His new
capital would certainly have been easier to defend. He built it
to the west of the Eastern Baray, with Ta Keo as his state
temple. But it was probably his successor, Jayaviravarman,
who completed the city's defences with a wall to the north
and perhaps also to the west. These defenses, however, were
to prove ineffectual against the assaults mounted by
Suryavarman I.
Drawing by Guy Nafilyan

The temple of Ta Keo.
The monument seen from the east, in the 1960s.
Photo: Guy Nafilyan

The temple of Ta Keo.
The temple seen from the southeast, surrounded by
undergrowth (photographed in July 1989).
Photo: Claude Jacques

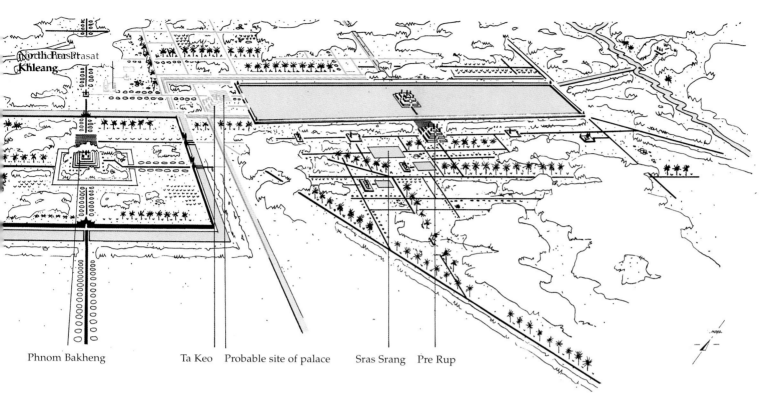

Phnom Bakheng   Ta Keo   Probable site of palace   Sras Srang   Pre Rup

A few years after coming to power, Jayavarman V decided to establish a new capital; his father's palace had doubtless been destroyed. He wished probably to choose a site that would be easier to defend than those chosen by his father and Yashovarman I. He set up his capital on the western bank of the Eastern Baray and called it Jayendranagari, "capital of the conquering king," instead of Yashodharapura, the name used by all the previous kings who had based their capital cities in the Angkor region.

About 975 work began on the temple of Ta Keo, referred to in inscriptions as Hemashringagiri, the "golden-tipped Mountain." At the same time, work also started on the royal palace, of which nothing now remains apart from the sandstone landing stage built exactly in the middle of the western embankment of the *baray*. However, signs of some major terracing work in this area are still noticeable, some of which might have been re-used by Jayavarman VII for the great enclosure wall round his capital city.

The temple of Ta Keo is in a less finished state than the other temple-mountains. The sculpting of the stones was only just started, but this in itself gives the monument an air of great strength. It was an ambitious project: the pyramid, almost entirely encased in sandstone, consists of three levels, the uppermost level being subdivided into three tiers; the overall height of the pyramid is 21.35 meters. At ground level the pyramid is a rectangle measuring 122 meters by 106 meters, and the top terrace measures 46 meters by 44 meters. On this top tier there are five sanctuaries in quincunx arrangement, with the largest one in the middle, raised above the others, as was the custom. The long chambers that surrounded the pyramid at Pre Rup have here become continuous galleries, built on the second level. The causeway on the east was flanked by two pools, and the whole complex was surrounded by a moat, 225 meters on the longer sides, 195 meters on the shorter sides. The sculpture that does exist at Ta Keo is of the highest quality.

The monument that we see today was not entirely completed during the reign of Jayavarman V. Its construction seems to have been continued during

Ta Keo

Ta Keo is the finest and most classical example of a Khmer temple-mountain. It possesses all the individual elements, assembled in a simple and logical composition:
- sanctuary towers in quincunx arrangement and with successive stories of decreasing size
  - a three-tiered pyramid, on which the sanctuaries stand
  - superimposed and concentric platforms that form the base of the enclosures (of which here there are two)
  - concentric enclosures: here one is formed by a gallery, the other by a plain wall
  - entrance pavilions to these two enclosures, placed on the axes of the temple
  - corner pavilions (or constructions representing these), at the corners of the gallery-enclosure
  - two libraries on the second platform, at the foot of the pyramid, one either side of the principal entrance axis
  - four long chambers, of various shapes, two on each platform
  - stairways, on the principal axes of the temple, climbing up between their own stepped walls, from one level to the next.

Ta Keo is therefore a typical Khmer temple-mountain, except for its simple, unfinished state, which is almost bare of ornamental details. This rough-hewn quality produces an impression of power and mass but, at the same time, the few examples of decoration that were started, and in some cases completed, do make it a cause for regret that the monument was never finished.

SYMBOLIC IMAGE

Ta Keo is also a striking example of the temple as an image, with elements that apparently serve no practical purpose. The most obvious demonstration of this symbolic character is the fact that the gallery on the second level (the earliest example of a sandstone gallery standing on a platform) is totally inaccessible: there is no doorway allowing entry, either from the courtyard or from the entrance pavilions. The only way to get into the gallery would be to climb in through one of the windows, which would be far from easy. Moreover, the windows overlooking the courtyard would have been lined with stone balusters. As for the windows on the outside of the gallery, they are blind (and even so they have balusters on the outside).

The corner pavilions, in the shape of small sanctuary towers, look like turrets, with false openings looking outwards. The entrance pavilions on the temple's axes are accessible only through their central doorway: the side doors on the outside open on to a void. The central stairways have steps measuring 36 centimeters high and their steepness varies from 44° to 57° (Jacques Dumarçay, *Ta Keo*).

The Ta Keo complex consists of the following components:
- a moat representing the ocean upon which floats a continent, itself represented by the temple's platform
- a terraced platform carrying the temple, which is reached on the east side via a paved causeway, flanked by two pools (there is another access on the north side, via a simple terraced causeway).

THE TEMPLE

The temple itself has three components:
- a platform surrounded by a wall
- a platform surrounded by a gallery
- a stepped pyramid, with five sanctuaries on the upper level.

The first platform, or first level, is 1.73 meters high and has an enclosure wall—the second enclosure—broken by four axial entrance pavilions (those on the north and south sides are shifted slightly westward, so that they are aligned with the axis of the pyramid's stairways; they are also smaller than the gopura on the east and west). In the courtyard there are two long halls, aligned with the east wall.

The second platform, or second level (or first enclosure), stands 5.73 meters above the first and has the earliest example of a gallery that stretches all around a temple, broken only at the axial intersections by entrance pavilions. The corners of the gallery are shaped like pavilions on their two external sides. This gallery was probably vaulted in brick. The courtyard that the gallery surrounds is wider on the east side than the others, to make space for some ancillary buildings. There are two libraries, opening to the west and square in plan, and a small entrance vestibule with a door and two

Cross-section showing false triple nave form (from a north library on the second level at Ta Keo). This form appeared at Koh Ker at the beginning of the 10th century, whereas the true triple nave form did not appear until the 12th century, at Angkor Wat.

Plan and drawing by Jacques Dumarçay, EFEO 1971

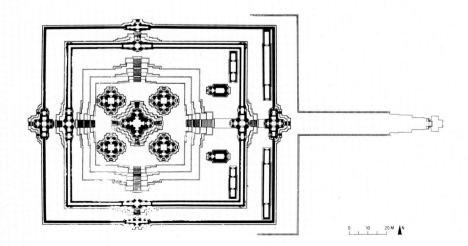

An aerial view of the Ta Keo temple, from the east. The overall layout and the unfinished state of the temple are particularly noticeable. *Photo: Henri Stierlin*

windows. The cross-section of the main chamber of the libraries has the shape of a "false triple nave," lit by two windows in the upper part of the chamber, the "attic." The "false triple nave" is another demonstration of the idea of image that is at the heart of Khmer architecture. It is astonishing to note how early this form appears, given that the true triple nave form does not appear until the start of the Angkor Wat style in the 12th century. The outside looks like a raised nave, flanked by two side aisles, whereas in fact the interior consists of a single-space nave, which in cross-section follows the shape of a triple nave.

THE PYRAMID

The courtyard of the first enclosure contains another two small "long halls"—they are much shorter than those in the second enclosure because of the placing of the libraries. Finally, on this first enclosure platform, slightly to the west of center, stands a pyramid, whose base is more or less square (its sides measuring about 47 meters). The pyramid, 13.89 meters high, has three superimposed terraces, respectively 5.69, 4.60 and 3.60 meters high. Access to the terraces is by stairways hemmed between their stepped side walls. These flat-topped walls rise beside the steps, two levels for each

terrace, but the stairs form a continuous flight, though their width gradually reduces as they climb. All the examples of progressive diminution give an effect of perspective, but really they are a product of the layout conventions of this architecture: the rules of perspective were completely unknown to the Khmers.

THE SANCTUARY

Five sanctuary towers stand on the upper plateau of the pyramid, in quincunx arrangement, which is the most usual layout in Khmer architecture, especially for temple-mountains. The four corner towers are also typical: each stands on its cruciform base, square in plan, with four doors reached through four vestibules, which themselves have an entrance bay and two side windows.

One of these towers, on the northeast, was the subject of an in-depth study by Jacques Dumarçay that is a mine of information on the building and the rules of proportionality it displays.

In the middle, the central tower stands on its base, which in turn stands on a double cruciform platform. It is the first example of a sanctuary with double vestibules on each side: this model reappears in later periods, the finest example being that at Angkor Wat.

Opposite
A guardian divinity at the temple of Banteay Srei.
Banteay Srei, north sanctuary, southeast corner,
east side.
Photo: Claude Jacques

The temple of Banteay Srei.
General view of the temple from the northeast.
Photo: Guy Nafilyan

that of Jayaviravarman, his successor at Angkor. A different type of sandstone was used for the towers on the upper terrace; there is no explanation for this other than that, perhaps, political changes along with the change in ruler might have meant the quarries used earlier were no longer accessible.

Several temples, including one near Siem Reap, within the enclosure of Wat Preah Einkosei, were built by Divakarabhatta, a Brahmin scholar who was born in India near Mathura on the banks of the Yamuna river. It is not known how he arrived in Cambodia, but he married Indralakshmi, one of the younger sisters of Jayavarman V, during the lifetime of Rajendravarman. He had been in the service of Jayavarman V for some time already, and he might have been the author of the exceptionally fine poems that are engraved on the stelae at the Eastern Mebon and at Pre Rup.

The temple of Banteay Srei, started and consecrated in the previous reign and the work of that king's guru, Yajnavaraha, was also completed during Jayavarman V's reign. Often called "the jewel in the crown of Khmer art," it is small—the overall height of its central sanctuary is only 9.8 meters—but its composition, its perfect proportions, the quality of its sculpture and the richly imaginative scenes decorating the tympanums, together with the red tint of the sandstone, all combine to make it entrancing.

Despite its stormy beginnings, the reign of Jayavarman V seems to have been subsequently one of the most peaceful in a history that saw few such periods. After his consecration, calm seems to have prevailed. Nevertheless, it is possible that he did engage in battle in order to extend his father's territory into what is now Thailand, where a good number of Khmer

Banteay Srei

(A.D. 967)

For some people, captivated by the special charm of Banteay Srei, its remarkable state of preservation and the near-perfection of its ornamentation, this is without any doubt the finest of all the monuments at Angkor. (Maurice Glaize, *Les Monuments du groupe d'Angkor*)

Banteay Srei is by far the prettiest of the Khmer temples, and it certainly merits the description of "jewel" or "gem." In addition, it is also one of the most impressive in terms of layout, and its proportions are as perfect as its decoration. Its history alone would merit a whole chapter—the history of its creation and that of its discovery, misadventures, and admirable reconstruction.

OVERALL PLAN

The smallness of Banteay Srei is a surprise, but it does make it easy to gain an idea of the whole monument. The distance from the end of the east entrance pavilion on the fourth enclosure to the end of the west entrance pavilion on the third enclosure is actually quite long (200 meters). Nevertheless, it is a small temple, almost as if it had been built to half-scale. The door of the cella of the central sanctuary is no more than 1.08 meters high, so visitors have to bend down in order to enter this "holy of holies." The east entrance pavilion of the first enclosure is so small inside (each of its wings is only about 30 centimeters wide) that squeezing into it is difficult.

It was long believed (and I was once of the same opinion) that what is always referred to as the "east pavilion of the fourth enclosure" actually did stand on the east side of a fourth enclosure concentric with the three others. There was thought to have been some form of fence, made of planks or posts. No one has ever looked for traces of posts in the soil (wood is sometimes preserved in soil in certain conditions), but in any case, an earth bank is what one would expect, being the more usual solution. Not even a trace of one remains now. Therefore we have to accept that this temple was designed as it now stands, while the buildings situated outside the third enclosure will continue to be referred to as belonging to the "fourth enclosure," even if one never existed. Aerial photographs show a large pool to the northeast of this pavilion, with no visible trace of a link between the temple and the pool.

Drawing by Jacques Dumarçay, EFEO 1988

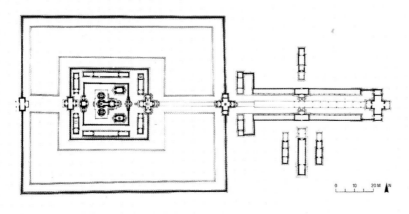

Guardian divinities surrounded by filigree carving in stone. Central sanctuary of Banteay Srei, southwest corner. *Photo: Guy Nafilyan*

Therefore, the overall plan of Banteay Srei is in the shape of a square racket or paddle, the handle represented by the group of buildings (galleries, various long halls, and entrance pavilions) outside the temple on its east side. All these buildings were once covered with tiles attached to timber frames.

ACCESS TO THE TEMPLE

Access to the temple is by the entrance pavilion, or gopura, on the fourth enclosure. This comprises a central cruciform chamber, whose north and south wings are lit by windows that have stone bars. These wings extend into two small passages, which have doors with very high thresholds. The main passage is reached through a porch on square pillars. Above this porch was once, probably, a triangular pediment on a sandstone architrave. The doorway of the gopura consists of the usual grouping of ornamental columns, lintels, pilasters, and pediment. The latter is triangular and has signs of where roof timbers were once sited; its decoration on the other hand is wavy in form, typical of the classical Khmer pediment. The exit to the west of the gopura is through an identical porch.

From here there is a paved causeway about 75 meters long, bordered by stone posts, across a long courtyard flanked on the north and the south by two galleries. These galleries comprise a solid wall on the outside and a row of square pillars on the inside. At the mid-point of this long courtyard, there are two pavilions, one on either side, and both preceded by a porch and lit by windows fitted with balusters. These pavilions give access to the outside: to the north, to a long, three-chambered building and to the south, to a group of three long buildings, a large one in the middle (with three chambers) and two smaller ones, each with four chambers. At its western end, the long courtyard widens and here joins on to two small, three-chambered halls.

We are now at the temple proper, with its three concentric enclosures, moat, entrance pavilions, halls, libraries, and sanctuaries. In short, it is the archetypal Khmer temple. The description that follows starts from the center and works outwards.

THE SANCTUARY

The central sanctuary consists of a sanctuary tower, with a dentated square ground plan, one real door and three false doors. Linked to it by a round chamber with false windows (which nevertheless have the usual stone balusters), is an antechamber with side doors and real windows, also with balusters. On the east side of this antechamber is an entrance vestibule, which has side windows without balusters. A sanctuary tower stands on either side of the central tower. The north-south axes of these side towers are just a few centimeters westward of that of the central tower, and the towers are also slightly smaller than the central one. They are classic examples of the isolated sanctuary with one true and three false doors, and are referred to as such by Maurice Glaize, Jean Boisselier, and many others.

These three buildings are decorated all over their external surfaces, but their interiors are bare. On the sides of the central tower there are *dvarapala* in niches, while on the north and south towers there are *devata*. The antechamber is covered with a simple "tapestry" decoration forming a check-pattern with two alternating motifs.

This group of sanctuaries stands on a molded terrace whose T-shaped ground plan has projections corresponding to the shape of the various buildings on it. Stairways flanked by stepped walls lead to the three entrances of the antechamber and to the doors of the side sanctuaries. Behind the group, opposite the false door of the central sanctuary, is another staircase leading up to the terrace.

THE FIRST ENCLOSURE

Two libraries, north and south, with true doorways opening to the west and false doorways to the east, stand on either side of the antechamber in the northeast and southeast corners of the first enclosure. They are built of sandstone, with some infilling in laterite, but they are vaulted in brick and their cross-section is in the shape of a false triple nave, a form that is seen in many of the libraries (perhaps starting from Banteay Srei?). They are lit by long, low windows in the false attic story.

The Hindu god Indra on the elephant Airavata.
At this time it was common for the lintels or pediments to show the ruler of the corresponding cardinal point: Indra rules the east.
Photo: Guy Nafilyan

The first enclosure forms a square with sides measuring 24 meters. It is built of brick, as is its west entrance pavilion. There are two rather odd things about this pavilion. First, it occupies a square-shaped site measuring 3.2 meters on each side, the same size as that of the central sanctuary and the antechamber. Second, it has no door on the west side, which suggests that it should perhaps be regarded as a sanctuary in itself, rather than as a passageway. We know nothing about what its superstructure was like. The east entrance pavilion of this enclosure has been entirely rebuilt and is totally of sandstone. It has five components: an axial passage with a cross-vault and, on either side, two small chambers with lengthwise vaults that diminish in size like a telescope. These chambers have blind windows with stone balusters on the east side. They are so narrow that it is almost impossible to enter them—this exaggerated smallness is partly a consequence of the idea of the temple as image rather than functional building, and partly just a consequence of the overall small scale of this particular monument.

THE SECOND ENCLOSURE

The second enclosure is 42 meters long and 38 meters wide and is built of laterite. It contains six buildings that foreshadow the gallery-enclosures of the classical age (they first appear at Ta Keo, in about 1000). These laterite buildings, with three rooms each, were once covered with tiles attached to a timber framework. The east entrance pavilion in this enclosure, with three passages, comprises a cruciform chamber in the middle, preceded and followed by porches on pairs of square pillars, and two square side rooms forming lateral passages. The east façade of the central chamber is lit by real windows with real balusters. This gopura boasts magnificent triangular pediments finished with spiral motifs of great elegance. On the west side, at the exit, there is a small figure of a bull (Nandi, Shiva's mount) looking towards the temple. Of the west entrance pavilion, in brick, nothing remains but its doors with their round ornamental columns and their lintels.

THE THIRD ENCLOSURE

The third enclosure, constructed of laterite, measures 94 meters by 109 meters. It contains only a very wide moat, which represents the ocean upon which the temple-mountain "floats"—in the rainy season, in fact, it is possible to see both the temple and its reflection in the water. The east entrance pavilion of this enclosure is cruciform, with a central chamber and four other chambers that are extensions of the arms of the cross. There is a porch on plain square pillars on both the east and the west sides. The building was once covered with a timber frame. At the east end of the central chamber there are real windows barred with stone balusters. The side chambers have open bays that perhaps mimic doorways, though they have no access stairs.

To go back to the overall composition, the temple can be described as a square with a triple enclosure and, at the front, an access structure—a kind of entrance channel. In this same position at Angkor Wat there is a vast cruciform terrace, at the Bayon a long terrace, and at numerous other temples an approach avenue. So this idea of a structure in front of the enclosures is quite typical, though here it is developed in a much more elaborate way.

It would be possible to discuss at length the decorative work at Banteay Srei, which resembles exquisite stone jewelry and is of a quality unequaled in the Khmer monuments, and also the complex organization of its layout, and the beauty of its libraries' elaborately carved pediments. But this would require a book in itself.

A guardian divinity at the temple of Banteay Srei, detail.
Photo: Guy Nafilyan

A scene from Hindu mythology at the temple of Banteay Srei.
Sita, wife of Rama, is being abducted by the demon Viradha, an episode in the Hindu epic *Ramayana*. Banteay Srei, central sanctuary, lintel of the south false door.
Photo: Henri Stierlin

inscriptions have been found that refer to him—in the northeast and as far away as Nadun, about 100 kilometers north of Buriram.

Many inscriptions dating from Jayavarman V's reign are decrees concerning the temples of his empire, and some of them provide information about disputes over land. For example, there is an account, taken from a Sanskrit poem, of a lawsuit brought by Sahadeva, great-grandson of a certain Gavya and apparently heir to land he left, against people who had tried to take possession of this land, claiming they were the owners:

Upon the death of Gavya, three men, Hi, Pu and Ke, wishing to take possession of this land by force, declared: "This land is ours."

Hem instructed Pu himself to remove the boundary stones that were placed on these lands by order of the king.

Gavya's descendant, Sahadeva, informed in writing king Jayavarman [V] about all the offences committed by these people.

This action on the part of Pu and the others was the object of a thorough investigation by ministers and court advisers and was declared by the king to be manifestly criminal.

"Hem's lips shall be cut off and Pu's hands shall be cut off, in accordance with each man's misdeed": this was the order of the king.

And Sahadeva asked the king to give him Ke, son of his maternal grandfather, together with his family and his land.

The temple of Banteay Srei.
Internal courtyard, southeast corner of the central sanctuary and south sanctuary. Instead of lions, the guardians of the temple are monkeys, soldiers of Hanuman, Rama's helper.
Photo: Henri Stierlin

Later, four men called Pan, Ap, Gadakesha and Ishanasiva, together with a woman called Ayak, again laid claim to Gavya's land.

Even though they had seen and heard tell of the misfortune that had befallen those who earlier had tried to seize this land, they were foolish enough to want to take possession of it.

Sahadeva again complained to king Jayaviravarman, who ordered an investigation.

By order of the king, Ap had his feet crushed and this caused him suffering; Pan had his head crushed and he died as a result.

As for the woman, Ayak, she had her head crushed, and her relations, very frightened, fled hurriedly in all directions to hide themselves.

(From an inscription on a stele at Tuol Prasat, stanzas XXI to XXVIII and XXXI to XXXII. From the French of George Cœdès.)

The poem provides an indication of the punishments inflicted on wrongdoers. We learn of many more types of punishment from other inscriptions: placing in a "cage," slapping the face, strokes of a rod, the cutting-off of the ears or the nose, or, for people of the highest castes, large fines. Capital punishment certainly existed as well, but no precise example of it has come down to us through inscriptions.

Jayavarman V died in about 1000: a new period of violent unrest began for the Khmer empire.

90

CHAPTER 5
Angkor in the 11th Century

During the 11th century the fierce struggle for power meant that for the first time a royal palace had to be surrounded by walls. In the middle of Angkor, the Phimeanakas temple, erected by Suryavarman I, was regarded as too modest by his successor, who created the grandiose temple of Baphuon, south of the Phimeanakas, as well as the temple of Western Mebon on a platform in the middle of the Eastern Baray.

O n the death of Jayavarman V in about 1000 (at which point his immediate family disappears from history), the Khmer empire found itself once again in a state of disarray.

We know from inscriptions that first of all there was a king called Udayadityavarman I, consecrated in 1001. His mother was the sister of one of Jayavarman V's wives, which in itself would definitely not have given her son any right to the supreme throne, despite what has been written to the contrary in the inscriptions. She was said to have belonged to the "line of the kings of Shreshthapura," but in fact this single reference to an ancient legend clearly shows that the new king had no direct link with his immediate predecessors.

His maternal uncle had been a general under Jayavarman V; it is possible that this was the very uncle who was behind his accession to the throne. There is no doubt at all that the throne was won only after a hard-fought struggle. However, we have no clues as to who his main adversaries might have been—they were presumably close relatives or direct descendants of Jayavarman V.

Opposite, top
Two bas-relief scenes at the Baphuon temple.
Top: Rama consoling Sugriva after the death of her brother Valin (second level, north axial pavilion, south façade).
Photo: Guy Nafilyan

Opposite, bottom
Horses fighting (second level, west axial pavilion, east façade).
Photo: Guy Nafilyan

Jayaviravarman defends himself at Angkor

Since there is no evidence of Udayadityavarman I ever having been at Angkor, it is not certain that he went there as sovereign. An inscription at Koh Ker reproduces an edict of this king bearing the date of Friday 13 February 1002: perhaps he tried to install himself in this former capital in order to assert his power, which was being challenged. Whatever the truth, he was to die soon after that date, but we know nothing of the circumstances.

In this same year, 1002, two rival princes claimed to have been consecrated "supreme kings" of the Khmers: Suryavarman I and Jayaviravarman. The latter had established himself at Angkor, apparently in the palace of Jayavarman V, and he continued with the construction of the temple of Ta Keo. He supposedly belonged to the (legendary) "line of Kaundinya and Soma"—as vague a reason for taking the throne as that put forward for Udayadityavarman I, which suggests that once again the crown was won through violent means.

Jayaviravarman certainly ruled over the regions of Angkor, Battambang to the west and Kompong Thom to the east, where there are some traces of his jurisdiction. His domain probably did not extend much beyond these regions, though it is possible that stones in other areas, inscribed with his edicts, were destroyed by his successor.

In the province of Kompong Thom he receives a particular mention not far from Koh Ker: so perhaps he was responsible for the disappearance of Udayadityavarman I. The last known inscription from Jayaviravarman's reign reproduces an edict promulgated on Saturday 25 May 1006, though everything points to his having continued to rule up to 1010.

At Angkor, he might have been responsible for a construction which to date has received little attention, even though it has been known about since the beginning of the 1930s. This is an imposing wall, some ten meters high, running more or less from the northeast corner of Angkor Thom to the northwest corner of the Eastern Baray. It is clearly defensive, and is the first example of its type in this region. In fact, Jayaviravarman was soon under threat from Suryavarman I—a very real threat, for Jayaviravarman soon disappeared from view, so it is easy to understand why he needed to defend himself effectively in his capital city.

An incidental point worth noting is that the presence of this wall means that in those days the river did not follow the same course that it does today, contrary to the commonly held belief. In fact, it flowed much further north along a course which, despite some breaks, is identifiable for the whole of its length. The water course we see now was in that era only a part of the irrigation network.

An examination of the plan of Angkor shows that Jayaviravarman's defense wall forms an almost perfect square with the east embankment of the Eastern Baray, the present west wall of Angkor Thom, and the causeway embankment that leads from the Eastern Baray to the east gate of Angkor Thom. The latter, called "the Gateway of the Dead," obviously had not yet been built, but this does not mean that the causeway did not already exist. It seems likely that this square was actually the enclosure of the capital city built by Jayaviravarman.

At a later date, the north wall was breached to allow the Siem Reap river to flow through, and to follow what is its present-day course, but there is nothing to indicate that this gap was made before the 16th century.

If this hypothesis regarding the layout of Jayaviravarman's capital is correct, then the state temple would have been far off the center point of the city, which is most unusual. However, this anomaly could be explained by the fact that the temple and the enclosure were built by two different people, and that the second probably had to adapt very quickly to what he found already there. Under growing threat from his rival Suryavarman I, Jayaviravarman might well have been forced to ignore the traditional rules of layout based on symbolism, according to which the state temple, representing Mount Meru, center of the world, had to be sited at the center of the capital, itself representing the world.

The Prasat Khleangs

Opposite the royal palace of Angkor Thom there are today two buildings that at one time would have been covered with tiles, and that stand symmetrically on either side of the avenue leading to the palace. They are not normal temples in that they are without an actual sanctuary tower, and the name given to them by the Khmers in modern times is Prasat Khleang— "temple-stores" or "temples of the royal treasure." Both their location and their function are puzzling. Two points worth noting are that the North Prasat Khleang is the older of the two, and the symmetry we see today was not necessarily planned at the outset. The siting of the earlier monument therefore is not to be interpreted on the basis of how it appears now. Originally it would have been relatively isolated, though close beside it to the east there is a small sanctuary in the slightly earlier Banteay Srei style, so the area had already been built on.

The North Prasat Khleang contains several inscriptions ordered by Jayaviravarman. It consists mainly of a building more than 40 meters long and 4.7 meters wide, and open at both ends; its finely decorated sandstone walls are 1.5 meters thick. Later, its single, immense interior space was

North Prasat Khleang.
The exact function of this building with its unusual layout is not known, but it was clearly a religious monument, originally standing outside the capital.
Photo: Guy Nafilyan

divided into two by a central tower; at its east end, galleries enclosed a courtyard. This building must have served a religious function, though this function is difficult to determine from the building's layout.

When Suryavarman I was establishing his palace, his architect doubtless decided to improve the vista of the royal square by creating a symmetrical feature, using the existing Prasat Khleang. Therefore the South Prasat Khleang was built, but with less finesse than the first, and it was left unfinished. The appearance of the two buildings has been considered sufficiently distinctive to give rise to a named style, a style also seen at the temple of Ta Keo, the gopura of the royal palace, and the temple of Phimeanakas.

Although he reigned for some ten years, Jayaviravarman is excluded from the list of great Khmer kings. This is most unusual, since Khmer kings generally harbored no rancor towards those whom they had ousted. However, in this case, the victor Suryavarman I, consecrated in the same year as Jayaviravarman, 1002, would have found it impossible to admit that two "supreme kings" existed at the same time.

The long reign of Suryavarman I

Suryavarman I is said to have descended from the maternal line of Indravarman I, a line that had remained in the background until then. Initially, he could have been "supreme king" only of the ancient kingdom of Shambhupura, where he must have been consecrated.

During the first decade of the 11th century, Suryavarman I made gradual encroachments on the domain formerly ruled by Jayavarman V and by his predecessors, now under the jurisdiction, with the exception of one or two territories in the hands of some minor prince, of Jayaviravarman. The king progressed slowly towards the temple of Bhadreshvara at Wat Phu, as though he were on his way to that ancient sanctuary to seek the protection of the country's past rulers. Then he marched towards the west of the empire, passing to the north of Angkor and following the line of the southern slopes of the Dangrek mountains.

In the region of Aranyaprathet, which was held by princes loyal to Jayaviravarman, there is evidence in several places that he encountered fierce resistance. He then with difficulty made his way down to Angkor, where he finally succeeded in defeating Jayaviravarman, at a date which must have been shortly after 1010.

Total victory took some time to achieve, however; according to an inscription, Suryavarman I's war lasted nine years. Although there is some evidence of his administration in the area around the modern town of Battambang from 1007 onwards, the first trace we have of him in the Angkor region dates from about five months before the day in 1011 when he had all his "officials" swear an oath of allegiance to him. The words of this oath were subsequently engraved on the walls of the east gopura of his royal palace, together with the names of the people who had taken the oath—nearly 500 names are still legible. On Sunday 9 September 1011, all these men solemnly promised:

East gopura of the royal palace.
The main entrance of Surayavarman I's royal palace was buried under the terraces that were built during the reign of Jayavarman VII. The words of the "officials' oath" and the thousands of names of those who took the oath were engraved inside this gopura. This photograph of the monument with encroaching undergrowth was taken in July 1989.
Photo: Claude Jacques

All of us offer our life and our unfailing grateful devotion, to our Lord Shri Suryavarman... We will not revere any other sovereign but him; we will not be hostile to him and we will not collude with his enemies...
It concludes:

If any one of us should break this oath, we ask that future sovereigns inflict on them all manner of royal torture. If there should be any traitors amongst us who do not abide fully by this oath, may they be reborn in the 32 hells, for as long as the Sun and the Moon shall last. If we keep this oath without fail, let the sovereign give orders for the maintenance of religious foundations in our own homelands and for the subsistence of our families.
(Translated from the French of George Cœdès.)

It is impossible to say whether this practice of oath-taking had existed earlier, but the solemnity that was obviously accorded to the ceremony was without doubt a new feature. The king clearly intended to ensure the loyalty of the people in his service, having learned the lesson of earlier events. An oath to the king, strangely similar to this one, was taken every year until quite recent times by assembled officials at Phnom Penh.

Having taken control of Angkor, which must have brought him great prestige, the king still had several obstacles to overcome. First, there is clear evidence of a "purge" in the capital. Then he had yet to conquer the rest of the empire, particularly the south. This does not seem to have caused too many difficulties for Suryavarman I, now that he had for some time been able to maintain order in his country.

Defining the empire's frontiers: four lingam

In 1018, as if to mark out the boundaries of his domain, the king ordered the consecration of three lingam called Siryavarmeshvara—"Suryavarman's Lord." One was installed in the north at Shikhareshvara, "Lord of the Peak," which today is Preah Vihear, a magnificent temple built on a ridge in the Dangrek mountains. The second was installed at Ishanatirtha, a site which

Plan of Angkor at the time of king Suryavarman I.
Suryavarman I was to alter radically the Angkor landscape by
moving away from the Eastern Baray area. Returning towards the
west, he surrounded his royal palace with walls, and completed the
royal square by building the South Prasat Khleang symmetrically
opposite the Khleang to the north. He was also responsible for the
construction of the immense Western Baray. It has often been said
that this new *baray* had to be made because the one to the east had
dried up. This was not the case at all: there is evidence that the
Eastern Baray still existed long after the 11th century; besides, it is a
fact that no temple was built there apart from the Eastern Mebon,
while temples continued to be built all around the *baray*.
Photo: Guy Nafilyan

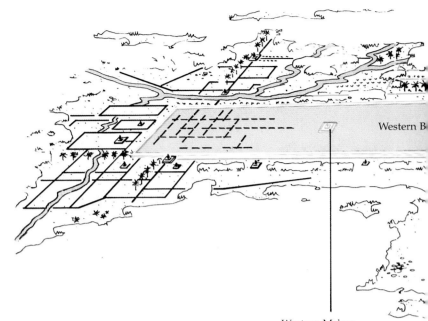

Western Mebon

At the temple of Preah Vihear: a pavilion on the
monumental stairway that led to the temple.
Photo: Guy Nafilyan

At the temple of Preah Vihear: a view of the
monumental stairway leading to the temple.
Thailand lies in the background.
Photo: Guy Nafilyan

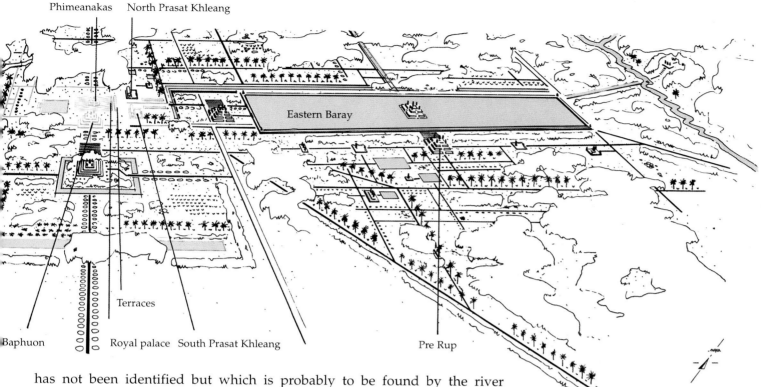

Phimeanakas   North Prasat Khleang

Eastern Baray

Terraces

Baphuon   Royal palace South Prasat Khleang   Pre Rup

has not been identified but which is probably to be found by the river Mekong, in the east. The third was set on the hill of Suryadri, the present-day Phnom Chisor, 60 kilometers south of Phnom Penh. While he was still making his conquests, Suryavarman had already erected a lingam in the west, at Jaykshetra, "field of victory," now Wat Baset, near Battambang.

He has also been attributed with important conquests in territory that today is in Thailand, and he is believed by some to have reached as far as present-day Lopburi, where a stele has been discovered bearing one of his edicts, dated 1022. This stele, however, might have been transported there from somewhere else. It is very doubtful whether he made any conquests in the Malay peninsula. The truth is that there is nothing concrete to show that he went much further into Thailand than the territory that had been controlled by Jayavarman V, except, perhaps, in the Lopburi region.

A fortified palace

At Angkor, Suryavarman I rejected the palace and state temple of Jayavarman V, probably because they had been the property of his enemy and therefore would have been the scene of the final battle. He made a gift of this complex to one of his ministers, who was also his son-in-law, Yogishvarapandita, a descendant of Jayavarman II, who had been in the service of his predecessor and who therefore might be suspected of treason.

The king moved to a spot close to the earlier Angkor and built for himself a palace that for the first time was surrounded by walls. This is the present royal palace of Angkor Thom, whose enclosure was to be utilized by many other kings in later ages. There are good reasons for thinking that this palace was established on a property long owned by the family of Suryavarman I and that the king was all the more ready to establish himself there because he knew he would have the protection of his ancestors.

Within the enclosure he erected the small temple-mountain today known as the Phimeanakas. With its relatively modest dimensions it resembles a palace

97

Aerial view of the Phimeanakas temple.
Photo: Guy Nafilyan

A divinity at the Phimeanakas temple.
Around the Phimeanakas, which was first a state
temple and then a royal chapel, carved stones of
various dates have been gathered. This one is from
the time of Jayavarman VII.
Photo: Guy Nafilyan

chapel rather than a real state temple. It is smaller than the temple of Pre Rup
(whose sides measure 50 meters): it measures only 35 meters by 28 meters at its
base, compared with the 120 meters by 100 meters of his immediate
predecessors' temple of Ta Keo. Moreover, unlike the previous state temples, the
pyramid of the Phimeanakas, which is built of laterite, was topped with a single
sanctuary tower. To frame the doorway of this sanctuary, which has
disappeared, he re-used old stone piers bearing an inscription in Sanskrit and
Khmer recalling the merits of a minister of Yashovarman I. This is what leads
me to suppose that there was some link between this minister and Suryavarman
I, because the use of the piers in this important position could not have been
merely by chance. In front of his palace, he had the second Prasat Khleang built.

A variety of buildings

Outside Angkor, Suryavarman I established a considerable number of
religious foundations. In particular, in the south, there is the temple of
Suryadri or Siryaparvata, "the mountain of Sirya," today called Phnom Chisor;
in the north is the splendid temple of Preah Vihear, where he made alterations
to an old religious center apparently founded by a son of Jayavarman II. Also
attributed to him are some buildings in the large city of Preah Khan. Nearer
Angkor, the temple of Chau Srei Vibol, recently renamed Prasat Wat Trach,
also dates from his reign, which lasted over 40 years. This king, of whom so
little is really known, was probably one of the greatest builders among all the
Khmer kings and may well have carried out many more projects during his

The temple of Phimeanakas.
This pyramid must have been constructed on the site of the old sanctuary erected during the reign of Yashovarman I, at the intersection of the axes of the temple of Phnom Bakheng and the Eastern Baray.
Photo: Guy Nafilyan

long reign. It was he rather than his successor who built the second great *baray* of Angkor, the Western Baray, even more impressive than the earlier one. It is 8 kilometers long, 2.2 kilometers wide. It has often been stated that it was created because the Eastern Baray by that time had completely dried up. I find this difficult to believe: first of all, the terrace that Jayavarman V had constructed to the east of his palace only a short time earlier would have been pointless unless it was next to water; moreover, a 13th-century inscription still mentions this *baray*. Several inscriptions celebrate Suryavarman I for the important civil projects, such as roads, bridges, shelters for travelers, and numerous reservoirs, that he built all over his empire.

Suryavarman I, one of the great names in Angkor civilization, disappeared from the scene in unknown circumstances in 1049, after a reign that, counting from the date of his consecration, lasted 47 years.

A troubled reign, and the construction of the Baphuon

Suryavarman I's successor, Udayadityavarman II, was consecrated in February or March 1050. They had no blood ties, but the new ruler of the Khmer empire seems to have been related to Viralakshmi, his predecessor's principal queen, who belonged to the line of Yashovarman I's wife, mother of Harshavarman I and of Ishanavarman II. The reign of Udayadityavarman II seemed subject to many upheavals, recounted in epic terms—very unusually—in an inscription celebrating his loyal general Sangrama. Early in

99

A bas-relief at the Bayon temple complex:
a battle scene.
Photo: Claude Jacques

A bas-relief at the Bayon temple showing a battle
scene.
In the midst of the battle, a dancer is apparently
trying to draw divine assistance to his side.
Photo: Claude Jacques

the reign, in 1051, this general crushed a rebellion by a certain Aravindahrada, who up to then had successfully held out against several generals sent by the king. Later, in 1065, Sangrama was sent to an area just to the northwest of Angkor, to subdue Kamvau, a general who, despite having been showered with honors by Udayadityavarman II, "blinded by the glare of his own grandeur and plotting in his heart the downfall of him to whose mighty favor he owed this grandeur," had turned against his king. A short time later, there were new disturbances in the east, fomented by individuals about whom we know nothing. Once again Sangrama was given the task of bringing them to heel and, if we are to believe the general's panegyrists, he quickly defeated them, took them prisoner, and despatched them to his king.

I cannot resist quoting the very lively account of the battle between the loyal Sangrama and the traitor Kamvau:

The sky was suddenly lit up, reflecting the flashes of scimitars, sabres, lances, spears, weapons of all kinds that were being brandished to and fro on either side.

Many brave enemy captains covered in wounds slept the sleep of death, their limbs stained with streams of thick blood, rows of them like mountain ranges.

On seeing the enemy chief who was advancing on him, bow in hand, Sangrama, a practiced speaker, shouted at him in a proud, deep voice:

"You insane, depraved individual, I have been seeking you for a long time! How can anyone who attacks Indra be without fear, however foolish he is?"

"Stop, stop, great hero! Show me your valor. As soon as I have tested your valor, I'll send you to the dwelling-place of Yama [god of the underworld]."

Thus addressed, the proud hero replied in a haughty tone:

"Stop trying to scare me, O hero! In a little while you will see my heroism! This sharp and virile arrow that I am about to aim at you will send you swiftly to the dwelling-place of Yama. So, with your fine words, do your best to evade it!"

Thus they exchanged fearsome declarations to frighten each other: they took up their bows, made especially taut for the combat, and made them reverberate, the one more strongly than the other.

Kamvau adjusted his arrows, images of his thoughts, on his shining, tightly bent bow and, having aimed at the general's jaw, pierced him.

And the general, struck by these sharp arrows as though by a shower of flowers, was no more disturbed than is the king of the mountains by a shower of rain.

Swiftly, with three well-feathered arrows, resonant like the humming of Agni's dart, he pierced his enemy in the head, the neck and the chest at one and the same time.

Torn by these sharp arrows, the enemy, falling to the ground, gave a terrible cry, as if announcing the sad news to his followers.

(From the stele at Preah Ngok, side C, stanzas 38–49. Translated from the French of Auguste Barth.)

A bas-relief at the Baphuon temple: animals next to windows in the entrance pavilions of the second level.
These animals might be some of the rulers of the 12 cyclical years, of Chinese origin, which start to appear during this era.
Photo: Guy Nafilyan

The temple of the Baphuon

These disturbances, however, did not prevent Udayadityavarman II from being very involved in the establishment of his capital. "Seeing that the Golden Mountain, dwelling-place of the gods, rose in the middle of Jambudvipa, he had a golden mountain built at the center of his own city, as if in imitation."

This golden mountain was in fact the great temple of the Baphuon, the magnificent pyramid that stands to the south of the royal palace and that, more than two centuries later, was to impress the Chinese envoy Zhou Daguan. During the 1960s, its enormous ruined mass was the subject of Angkor Conservation's most important restoration project, using the anastylosis method. Unfortunately, the civil war interrupted this work.

Access to the temple was through a magnificent gopura with three cruciform entrances, situated on the edge of the royal square. The temple was then approached by way of a fine causeway 200 meters long and interrupted at mid-point by another cruciform pavilion. The base of the pyramid measures 120 meters from east to west and 100 meters from north to south. Its three tiers are of almost equal height and are surrounded by continuous galleries, broken only by gopura. The two upper tiers are both placed on bases so high they act as additional tiers. At the summit, there was only one sanctuary tower, standing on a base with a cruciform ground plan, later transformed into a square. The gopura of the second level are extensively decorated with charming bas-relief panels, arranged one above the other; viewed from the bottom upwards, they illustrate episodes from Indian mythology and legends.

Udayadityavarman II probably had some kind of enclosure built around his city, covering approximately the same area as that of the city of Angkor Thom. This enclosure must have disappeared during later construction work.

101

The Baphuon

The Baphuon, state temple of king Udayadityavarman II, was founded about 1060. In the 13th century the Chinese envoy Zhou Daguan wrote with enthusiasm about this temple-mountain. It was certainly a very beautiful temple, from what we can see today, despite its current ruinous state. An inscription tells us:

> Seeing that the Golden Mountain [Meru], dwelling-place of the gods, rose in the middle of Jambudv(pa, he had a golden mountain built at the center of his own city, as if in imitation. On the summit of this golden mountain, in a golden temple, shining with celestial radiance, he erected a golden Shivalingam. (Translated from the French of George Cœdès.)

Today, except for those parts of the monument that are being reconstructed, it is basically a shapeless mound with a few precarious remains on the west face that give just a hint of what the Baphuon once was. Its ruinous state is due mainly to the ancient Khmers' lack of knowledge about building techniques, especially those concerning retaining walls. Nevertheless, its layout is one of the finest, for its sense of order, for its simplicity, and also for a number of innovative features, such as the walkway raised on round pillars, a dome, and a gallery with finial decoration.

The following description makes use of the plan published by Maurice Glaize in his guide, with the addition of some observations we have made on site and through a study of photographs.

LOCATION

The Baphuon stands within what today is the enclosure of Angkor Thom. It was erected on a north-south line running from the Phimeanakas to Phnom Bakheng, a kind of "sacred meridian," and in an astonishingly restricted space, between an earth bank on which stands its south enclosure wall, and the south wall of the royal palace. Between these parallel lines, the temple's enclosure forms an elongated rectangle, about 425 meters by 125 meters, surrounded by a high wall made, most unusually, of sandstone. In fact, the bank to the south is the ancient dike marking the northern boundary of Yashovarman's capital, which had Phnom Bakheng at its center.

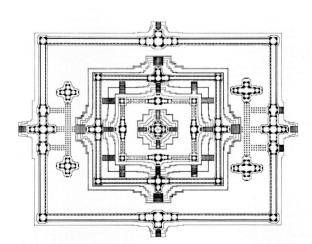

Plan of the Baphuon temple drawn by René Dumont, based on one by Maurice Glaize.

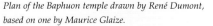

At the far eastern side of this space there is an entrance pavilion comprising three cruciform sections joined by galleries. These galleries align with the entrance to the royal palace. The entrance pavilion was linked at a later date, perhaps not very successfully, with the Terrace of Elephants. The sparse remains of this triple gopura, which stands on the fourth enclosure, were restored by Bernard-Philippe Groslier, using the anastylosis method.

After the triple gopura, the approach to the temple on its pyramid is along an astonishing causeway made of "long paving stones placed on stilts formed by three rows of columns" (Maurice Glaize). This avenue raised on sandstone piles had been transformed into a dike by the addition of infilling and two side walls. Glaize removed the walls and the hypostyle causeway was restored to all its elegant simplicity and grandeur (it is 200 meters long). "At about two-thirds of the way towards the temple, the causeway is barred by a cruciform pavilion." This pavilion, which in Glaize's day was in ruins, likewise underwent anastylosis restoration, as complete as was possible with what fallen stone was found on the spot. To the south of this pavilion there is an ornamental basin whose sides consist of sandstone steps, and this too has been restored.

The temple-mountain of the Baphuon has five tiers altogether; the first level of the pyramid has just one tier, but the second and third levels both consist of two tiers. Each level has a gallery running round its perimeter.

THE FIRST LEVEL

The first level consists of an enormous retaining wall more than six meters high, with massive moldings. Its gopura are reached by climbing four stairways of the usual type, between side walls. However, on the east side, on either side of the central stairway, there are two "images" of stairways, leading to the secondary entrances to the east gopura of the third enclosure. I use the term "images" because these stairways are virtually unusable: the steps are 10 centimeters deep but 48 centimeters high! They are there only because their presence at this point is a requirement of the temple's overall plan (*yantra*). On the platform of this level there is a gallery, raised up on a base and running round the perimeter, with four corner pavilions and four entrance pavilions at the axial intersections.

The sandstone gallery (or what is left of it) consists of an outer wall with blind windows, which once would have had stone balusters, and an inner wall that, before it collapsed, had real windows, which doubtless would also have had similar stone balusters. It is likely that this wide gallery was not vaulted and that it had a tiled roof supported by a timber frame.

The east entrance pavilion on this level is large and complex and underwent complete anastylosis restoration under the direction of Bernard-Philippe Groslier. It consists of a central space, square in plan, between two wings, each of which has two chambers, the one leading out of the other. The outer chambers had doors and were on a line with the illusory stairways referred to earlier. A double vestibule on the outside gave access to the main space of the pavilion, and the exit was through another, single-space vestibule. The side chambers have their fine original vaults again, thanks to the reconstruction. The central chamber, which also has been rebuilt, is of an extremely unusual shape. Above the main level there is another story, smaller in size, which is quite usual, but on top of that there is a dome-shaped vault, square in plan and in what is known as "priest's hat" or "cloister arch" shape. This form is new in Khmer

The Baphuon temple in 1989. The east entrance pavilion was reconstructed during the 1960s. *Photo: Claude Jacques*

art, and to my knowledge it is found only in the little "chapels" spread around the interior courtyards of Preah Khan at Angkor. The gopura is crowned with a beautiful lotus-petal motif. The west entrance pavilion, now destroyed, is erroneously depicted as identical to its counterpart on the east side, whereas Maurice Glaize speaks of "three other gopura with a single passage." Only the gopura on the south still has some of its walls standing.

In the eastern part of the courtyard of the third enclosure, there are the remains of two buildings that, according to Lunet de Lajonquière and Maurice Glaize, were cruciform in plan and were used as libraries. These are thought to have been linked by small footbridges raised on stone pillars. However, what is visible today is insufficient to confirm the existence of these footbridges. As to the libraries, the one on the north side has the remains of a molded base and all that is left of the one on the south is a small shapeless mound. On the west side of this enclosure there are the vestiges of a similar group of structures.

THE SECOND LEVEL

The second level occupies a platform on two tiers, both about 4.8 meters high. Access to this level is by stairways at each axial intersection, climbing extremely steeply between side walls. From this point, the monument is more or less completely ruined, and those components that had not collapsed were knocked down during later construction work. The description that follows is based on earlier accounts. The only surviving part today is the southern portion of the west side.

The second level was surrounded by a very narrow, vaulted gallery, built in sandstone; a part of this remains. There were square pavilions at the corners, today all in ruins. Only one gopura, on the west side, is still visible. The gallery had true windows on both sides. The outer walls of the gopura were covered in delightful bas-reliefs. According to various sources, the four gopura of this enclosure were in the form of sanctuary-towers (a design that was not used again at Angkor Wat but that reappeared in the style of the Bayon, and above all at the Bayon itself). They had two side aisles and a projecting vault on their exterior side.

THE THIRD LEVEL

The third level of the pyramid occupied almost all the area ringed by the second enclosure. Today it is reduced to a shapeless mass. Formerly, it rose on two successive tiers, both about 5.4 meters high, and stairways, even more steep, led to entrance pavilions on the axial intersections.

An anomaly needs pointing out here: the plans published by Lunet de Lajonquière and by Maurice Glaize show stairways opposite the axes of the corner towers. However, these do not look like the usual Khmer stairways, which are *always* set between heavy side walls. Old photographs show something like buttresses on the outer sides of these corner towers. This raises a question that cannot be answered until the monument is rebuilt: were these really stairways, or were they buttresses designed to reinforce the corner towers? Either theory could be correct, even though stairways without supporting side walls are not the Khmer style. But in either case, it must be a very ancient feature, because at Angkor Wat there are stairways leading to the corner towers, well built and designed as an integral part of the overall composition.

The platform of this third level was once surrounded by a vaulted gallery built of sandstone. Unusually, this was divided lengthways by a wall running parallel to (and between) two walls that were partly open to the outside with either a series of windows and piers, or else a row of pillars; the gallery is in too ruinous a state to tell which.

The corner towers and the gopura have disappeared and the only surviving section of retaining wall, in the southern wing of the west side, has dangerous cracks in it; it could fall down any day. All that is left in the middle of this third level is a shapeless mound, with some traces of molded base: it seems that there was a square base framing another, cruciform base.

The shape of the central *prasat* can only be guessed at. Maurice Glaize goes as far as to state that it must have been built of non-durable materials. Although this is possible, it is more likely that the central sanctuary was a sandstone tower. It will be a long time (not until restoration work is completed) before we know what it looked like, when once again it rises on top of this pyramid, which soars more steeply than any other Khmer monument.

A bas-relief at the Baphuon temple.
Detail of an unidentified scene.
Baphuon, north entrance pavilion on the second
level, western portion of south side.
Photo: Guy Nafilyan

It is during his reign that the first reference is made to the *Devaraja*, created two-and-a-half centuries earlier by order of Jayavarman II on his consecration as "supreme king" in 802. A member of the family that had been put in charge of the cult of this divinity had been appointed to a very important position at court. He was already married to a younger sister of Viralakshmi, the principal queen of Suryavarman I, and he became guru to Udayadityavarman II who, in gratitude, granted him the royal title of Jayendravarman and offered him lavish gifts, a list of which survives.

The Western Mebon in the middle of the baray

Just as Rajendravarman had built a temple, the Eastern Mebon, on an artificial island in the middle of Yashovarman I's *baray*, Udayadityavarman II had the Western Mebon erected in the middle of the Western Baray, which was constructed during the reign of Suryavarman I. It is an unusual monument, comprising an earth embankment enclosing a large square terrace edged with sandstone steps, about 100 meters long on each side. The bank was topped by a wall with windows and also pavilions, three on each side, dividing it into equal lengths.

In the middle of the terrace there was a sandstone platform whose sides measured about ten meters. This was linked to the east bank of the *baray* by a laterite causeway. Sunk in this platform was a well 2.7 meters deep, neatly faced. At the bottom of this well a large fragment of a splendid reclining Vishnu in bronze has been found; originally the figure must have been more than four meters long. Today the fragment is displayed in the National Museum in Phnom Penh. It is particularly interesting that the few large Khmer statues in bronze that have come down to us all date from this era.

During the reign of Udayadityavarman II, people of very high rank used to withdraw to the hermitages of Phnom Kulen and Phnom Kbal Spean; in the river bed or on nearby rocks they carved lingam and images, many of them inspired by the cult of Vishnu.

Udayadityavarman II died in 1066 or just before; he was one of the very few Angkor Khmer kings not to have been given a posthumous name. Uncertainty about the date when his successor was consecrated might indicate that there was a troubled interregnum, and that as a result his cremation did not take place in normal conditions.

A lotus-flower crowning motif on top of a tower. It is most unusual for such tower crowns to have been preserved; nearly all have fallen off.
Photo: Guy Nafilyan

Harshavarman III: a lackluster reign

In about 1066 or 1067, Harshavarman III succeeded his brother Udayadityavarman II. He was to rule for some 14 years. Later inscriptions do not tell us much about his reign, perhaps because he was replaced by a king who descended from a different line. Like his brother, he probably had to deal with serious internal troubles, but all we know of him—and this from foreign sources—concerns his expeditions into neighboring countries.

Through Chinese sources we know that in 1076 the emperor ordered the Khmers and the Chams, whom he regarded as his subjects, to help his troops in attacking his former Vietnamese vassals on their southern frontier. According to the Chinese sources, the campaign he launched against the Vietnamese was unsuccessful—the Chams seem to have remained somewhat cautious and it is not known how far the Khmers themselves committed themselves to the battle. There is no information about this in any inscriptions.

In any case, this particular alliance between Khmers and Chams lasted only a very short time. Harivarman IV, a Cham prince who ruled from 1074 to 1081, claimed to have won a victory at Someshvara (the name of a temple that must also have been the center of a city, whose location is now lost to us) over Khmer troops commanded by a royal prince named Nandanavarman, of whom no mention has been found in any Khmer inscriptions. The prince was taken prisoner and, as was the custom, the temple was emptied of its treasures. In 1080 these were offered to a god of the Chams, Ishanabhadreshvara, at the "national" temple of Mi Son.

Harshavarman III disappeared from the scene also in 1080: given the serious unrest that characterized his reign, he perhaps died a violent death.

CHAPTER 6

Suryavarman II and Angkor Wat

Khmer art reached the height of its glory in the 12th century. Angkor Wat, the most balanced, the most harmonious, the most perfect Khmer temple, was built by Suryavarman II, the warrior king who led his troops well beyond the frontiers of his empire. He and his great lords also built (or started) other temples of exceptional quality not far from the capital: Thommanon, Chau Say, Tevoda, Banteay Samre and, farther away, Beng Mealea.

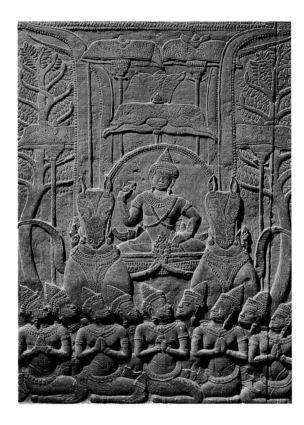

A bas-relief at Angkor Wat.
Northwest corner pavilion, decorated inside with scenes from the Hindu *Ramayana*. Here we see Surya ("The Sun") on his chariot.
Photo: Luc Ionesco, EFEO

T he end of the reign of Harshavarman III marks a change at the head of the Khmer empire. At this point, a king appears who, most unusually, does not claim descent from any previous Khmer king. Jayavarman VI, consecrated in 1080, was the son of a certain Hiranyavarman, possibly a minor ruler and a vassal of Angkor. He declared himself to be descended from a "royal" family that had been established for several generations at Mahidharapura, a kingdom or city whose precise location is unknown to us, though, according to one plausible theory, it was in the northeast of present-day Thailand. Modern historians have used this name of Mahidharapura to designate the new "dynasty." At any rate, the radical change of royal family line suggests that, once again, succession to the supreme Khmer throne was probably accompanied by violence.

Jayavarman VI: a long reign without monuments

Jayavarman VI was consecrated at Yashodharapura in 1080 by Divakarapandita, a Brahmin sage who was his guru and who had been in the service of Udayadityavarman II and of Harshavarman III. Only one piece of written evidence of his 27-year-long reign has been discovered at Angkor. On

Opposite
Angkor Wat after cleaning.
The west gallery, southern portion.
Photo: Claude Jacques

The temple of Phimai.
The shape of the tower, new in Khmer architecture, was to be the model for the towers at Angkor Wat. This temple has recently been entirely rebuilt, with French aid.

Photo: Claude Jacques

the other hand, very few inscriptions relating to this king have been found in the rest of the empire. An inscription carved at Pre Rup states that the reign was "extremely peaceful," so perhaps it is not too fanciful to apply to Jayavarman VI the adage that happy people have no history.

He is credited with the alterations carried out to the third level of the Baphuon, at the base of the central sanctuary tower. These works involved the splendid cruciform base being buried under a new, square one, which also is very fine. It was also probably he who had the approach causeway to the temple modified, raising its height along its length from the first east gopura up to the sanctuary, transforming it into a kind of sandstone bridge resting on three rows of elegant columns, which are still there.

This shows that he retained his predecessor's state temple, and was happy just to introduce a few minor alterations. It is probably not the first time that a king representing a new royal line decided not to build a new state temple for himself. Jayaviravarman before him had utilized Jayavarman V's Ta Keo, so it is clear that a king did not feel obliged to build a new state temple if there was an existing one that was considered suitable. Jayavarman VI also retained the royal palace of his predecessors, which suggests that if violence did accompany his accession to the throne, then it could not have occurred at Angkor.

Jayavarman VI is mentioned after his death in a few inscriptions as having created various religious foundations at existing prestigious sites, such as the temples of Wat Phu and Preah Vihear, and also that of Phnom Sandak—all situated near the northern frontiers of present-day Cambodia. However, no new monument is attributable to Jayavarman VI himself, which is extraordinary, given the length of his reign.

The temple of Phimai, far from Angkor

However, it was shortly before the death of Jayavarman VI that a magnificent temple was built in the center of the city of Phimai, today in Thailand. If it is true that the Mahidharapura dynasty had its origins in this region, then it is hard to imagine that Jayavarman VI played no part in the construction of such an important monument, given that the city was obviously under the control of the king of Angkor at that time. There is an important fact that weighs against this supposition, however: the foundations established by Jayavarman VI everywhere else were in Hindu temples, whereas this one appears clearly to be a Buddhist temple. On the other hand, many other kings contributed to the foundation of temples dedicated to divinities other than those of their own religion. Moreover, perhaps the temple of Phimai was not originally built for housing the Buddha. Although the decoration of its lintels is inspired by Buddhism, its great pediments are not, in particular the most important of them, which is on the south side and displays a magnificent dancing Shiva.

A very unusual feature of this temple is that it opens to the south. This has sometimes been explained as being due to topographical constraints; or, more often, by the fact that the temple is thereby turned towards Angkor. However, the more plausible explanation is that, given that a temple's south side was regarded as that of the ancestors, this temple housed the spirits of Jayavarman VI's family line.

On the other hand, it is clear that an important part of the sanctuary housed the local god, who must have been powerful, since he even had in his service his own "general," named Trailokyavijaya, "conqueror of the triple world." Despite his Sanskrit name, the general too must have been strictly local to the Phimai area.

The temple of Phimai contains certain innovations that seem to have inspired architects of a later date: in particular, the unusual shape of its principal tower was the model for the towers at Angkor Wat.

On the death of Jayavarman VI, in 1107 or shortly before, he was succeeded by his elder brother, since the designated crown prince, his younger brother, had died prematurely:

> Dharanindravarman [I], without having desired royalty, when his younger brother was restored to heaven, out of simple compassion and acquiescing to the prayers of the multitudes who were now without a protector, governed the land with prudence.

With prudence, perhaps, but with insufficient firmness to unify the kingdom: it is known that round about that time there were two Khmer empires in existence and doubtless many other principalities as well.

Dharanindravarman I did not have time to build any monuments. Five years later, in his capital that was "without defenses," he was overthrown "in a one-day battle" by one of his nephews, who was to reign under the name of Suryavarman II.

The new king was the maternal grandson of a sister of the two previous kings: a "normal" royal lineage in a country where lines of descent were matrilineal. It was also the rule that those in line to the throne had to wait their turn, something that Suryavarman II clearly was not prepared to do.

Once again, the accession was preceded by what was in effect the conquest of the Khmer empire, or rather, the two empires: one of them was ruled by Dharanindravarman I, but the name of the rival emperor is not known.

Having conquered Yashodharapura, Suryavarman II had himself consecrated as king in 1113 by the same Brahmin, Divakarpandita, who by this time must have been very old, and who had already consecrated his two great-uncles, who were his predecessors.

For us, Suryavarman II is above all the builder of Angkor Wat. For his contemporaries, he was above all a great conqueror, and this is how he was depicted, together with his generals and his armies, on a bas-relief at the great temple.

The lions of Angkor Wat.
Two meters high, these elegant lions guard the entrance.
Photo: Guy Nafilyan

Angkor Wat,
the supreme harmony

Suryavarman II's crowning glory is the creation of Angkor Wat, to the south of the capital that preceding kings had occupied. Possibly Dharanindravarman I's palace suffered great damage during the "one-day battle" in which the king was killed, but the reason why the new ruler decided to built a new state temple is that he belonged to the Vishnuite sect. Although there is no clear trace of a city, or of a palace, inside the boundaries of the great temple, there is little doubt that the enclosure (a square with sides measuring 1.5 kilometers) did also surround the capital and that the palace

A naga at Angkor Wat.
These raised naga heads are at the ends of the
balustrades that are formed by their bodies.
Commonly used as decoration in Khmer art over a
very long period, naga reach a peak of artistic
perfection in the age of Angkor Wat.
Photo: Guy Nafilyan

A view of the Angkor Wat temple across the
west moat.
Photo: Luc Ionesco, EFEO

Angkor Wat.
It can easily be imagined how this scene looked when the houses of the city stood on either side of the causeway and the royal palace probably stood to the north of the temple.
Photo: Guy Nafilyan

must have been to the north of the temple, very likely opposite the north "carriage" gate. At any rate, the site of the palace of Angkor Thom would not have been suitable, since it was too far away.

It is difficult to describe Angkor Wat and at the same time do justice to its great beauty. The approach from the west is along a raised causeway that stretches across a moat 200 meters wide. Visitors then go through a gopura with five passages, and finally are rewarded with a magnificent view of the whole temple, more than 400 meters ahead. From this point, a sandstone-paved causeway about 1.5 meters above the surrounding ground level leads up to the temple. In the early morning the temple seems lost in the mist; at midday it shimmers in the dazzling light; but in the evening, gilded by the setting sun, it is a scene from a fairytale, gradually fading until all that is visible is its silhouette in the darkness of night.

This causeway takes visitors to a stairway that in turn leads to the elegant cruciform terrace. Here there are bas-reliefs carved on the outside wall of the third enclosure: 200 meters of sculptures, two meters high, and covering all four sides of the temple. There is a high degree of order in the overall

composition: on the southern portion of the west gallery a single panel measuring 200 square meters depicts the terrible final battle scene from the Mahabharata, the great Hindu epic; at the end of the gallery, the interior of the southwest corner pavilion is completely carved with bas-reliefs representing various episodes from the legend.

If instead, on arriving at the temple, visitors turn left and walk northwards, they see the battle of Langka, which is narrated in that other great Hindu epic, the *Ramayana*, still familiar to everyone throughout Southeast Asia. The story is told here in sculptures carved in tableaux decorating the northwest corner pavilion. Some of the images can no longer be interpreted, and possibly they depict episodes added by the Khmers.

On the western section of the south side of the temple, the famous Historical Gallery shows Suryavarman II on his throne, surrounded by his advisers, ministers and Brahmins. Farther on there is the depiction of a great military parade, an opportunity here for a series of portraits of the king's military leaders; minuscule inscriptions provide their names but nothing more.

On the eastern section of this same gallery, the Gallery of Heaven and Hell,

Apsaras at Angkor Wat.
No one has ever counted these celestial dancing maidens at Angkor Wat, with their wide variety of costumes and facial expressions.
Photos: Guy Nafilyan

113

Angkor Wat.
Inhabitants of the Ocean of Milk. The Khmer
sculptors could allow their imagination free rein in
depicting these fantastical scenes. The feet of the
gods pull the serpent that turns Mount Mandara,
using it as a churn.
The Churning of the Ocean of Milk, east gallery of
bas-reliefs, southern portion.
Photo: Claude Jacques

sculptures depict the judgment of Yama, the god of the afterlife, and also celestial beatitude in the company of *apsaras*, while sinners undergo abominable torments that are depicted in minute detail.

Arriving at the temple from the East, visitors find on the left another scene from Indian legend, the famous bas-relief the Churning of the Ocean of Milk, which produced ambrosia, the nectar that conferred immortality. The nectar was created by Mount Mandara, which was transformed into a churning rod. This rod is turned with the aid of the serpent Vasuki acting as a cord, pulled one way by the gods, and the other by demons—the gods and demons for once in alliance. Vishnu appears twice, first in his incarnation as a tortoise, which functions here as the pivot of the mountain, and then in his usual form, at the summit of the mountain. The scene does not correspond exactly to the Hindu epic: in particular, there is an anomalous appearance of Hanuman, the general who leads Rama's loyal monkeys. The tableau as a whole displays perfect symmetry, and the observer is torn between admiring this and the astonishing imagination shown by the Khmer artists in their portrayal of the sea teeming with fish and other aquatic creatures, which get caught up in the eddying waves near the churning rod.

To the right of the east gopura, the bas-reliefs are of a different quality: this part, like the east half of the north gallery, was not decorated during the reign of Suryavarman II, doubtless because there was not enough time. These bas-reliefs were not carved until the 16th century, when the king Ang Chan was restoring the temple. Probably the northeast and southeast corner pavilions would have been given the same bas-reliefs, had the king been able to complete his temple.

Finally, on the west section of the north gallery there is an immense battle scene. In among the mêlée of warriors, all the great gods of the Brahmanic pantheon can be identified—21 in total—each engaged in single combat with a demon.

Arriving at the temple from the west, visitors enters the Gallery of a Thousand Buddhas, so-named because of the large number of statues that were amassed in this hall by devout Khmers in recent centuries. Today it is almost empty: the conservator of the Angkor monuments had the finest of the statues removed at the start of the civil war in order to protect them, and the Khmers Rouges took away and destroyed almost all those that remained.

Bas-reliefs at Angkor Wat.
Torments inflicted on the damned.
South gallery of bas-reliefs, eastern portion.
Photo: Claude Jacques

Bas-reliefs at Angkor Wat.
The great battle scene from the Hindu *Ramayana*: monkeys attack an army of demons.
West gallery of bas-reliefs, northern portion.
Photo: Luc Ionesco

Angkor Wat

Angkor Wat was built in the first half of the 12th century by Suryavarman II. Of all the Khmer monuments, this is the most ordered, the most beautifully balanced, the most harmonious. It is also the biggest, because the Bayon and the eastern Preah Khan, in Kompong Svay, are smaller, lost within their disproportionately large enclosures three or four kilometers long on each side.

THE COMPLEX AND ITS POOLS

Angkor Wat occupies a rectangle 1,300 meters from north to south by 1,500 meters from east to west; and, most unusually, it faces towards the west. This area is surrounded first by a moat about 200 meters wide and entirely faced with stone steps. On the west side, this moat is crossed by a raised causeway built of laterite and sandstone, paved and bordered with naga balustrades. Stone lions guard the entrance. On the east side, access is by way of a plain earth causeway.

The area of the fourth enclosure, surrounded by a laterite wall, measures 840 meters from north to south and 1,030 meters from east to west. Four gopura allow access to this enclosure. Those of the north, east and south are relatively small (59 meters long) and consist of a single axial passage running across a cruciform chamber with side-aisles and extended laterally by additional chambers at either end. However, the west entrance pavilion, formerly known as the Western Gateways, is nearly 230 meters long. In its central part it has three passages, each with a sanctuary tower above, and at its north and south ends, entrances for vehicles—since there are no stairs here, carts and elephants could pass through this gopura. Within this fourth enclosure, the temple's platform is approached by a paved causeway bordered by naga balustrades and with six pairs of stairways leading down to the lower ground level on either side. At the midway point the causeway is flanked by two libraries and, further on, by two pools.

The actual temple stands on a platform about one meter high, with a sandstone wall supporting a naga balustrade, and before the platform is a large cruciform terrace. The platform can be reached by 12 stairways, three to each side. The temple consists of three levels: the first is on a molded base about 3.3 meters high, the second on a molded base about 5.8 meters high, and the third is on top of a two-tier pyramid with a total height of about 11 meters. The summit of the central tower is 65 meters above ground level.

THE FIRST LEVEL, OR THIRD ENCLOSURE

A gallery runs right round the perimeter of the first level. Its vault is supported on the inner side by a solid wall, which has false windows on its exterior face, overlooking the courtyard. Inside the gallery, this wall is decorated with the great bas-reliefs of Angkor Wat, covering an area almost 700 meters long and two meters high, not counting those on the corner pavilions. On the outer side of the gallery the vault rests on square pillars and on a semi-vaulted side aisle supported by smaller pillars. Access to this level is by stairways: three on the north and south sides and five on the west and east. However, the axial stairway on the east side was not actually constructed, and since the molding of this platform is continuous, the omission was evidently intentional.

The gallery-enclosure is punctuated by four entrance pavilions, those on the east and west being cruciform in plan and having a triple passage, while those on the north and south comprise a single passage. The one on the west joins up with the west entrance pavilion to the second enclosure, which is of the same composition, through a series of covered passages forming a kind of cruciform cloister made up of triple-nave galleries with sides formed by rows of pillars.

There are porches at the axial intersection of both the north and the south sides of this cloister. They open towards the two libraries of the third enclosure, which are rather smaller than those of the fourth enclosure, but standing on a high base, are visible from outside, rising above the gallery of the third enclosure. This gallery also has corner pavilions.

THE SECOND LEVEL, OR SECOND ENCLOSURE

The second level also has its gallery-enclosure, but this one has a single nave and its vault rests on two walls. The outer wall is completely solid, while the inner one has some windows opening on to the courtyard of the second enclosure.

Opposite
Top: Angkor Wat at sunset. *Photo: Guy Nafilyan*
Bottom: The cruciform gallery: an aerial view from the northeast. In the south arm of the cross, called the Gallery of a Thousand Buddhas (Preah Poan), there was a group of statues that were not taken to the Angkor Conservation depository during the civil war and they were destroyed by the Khmers Rouges. *Photo: Henri Stierlin*

An *apsaras* sculpted on a pillar in the third enclosure of Angkor Wat. *Photo: Guy Nafilyan*

Angkor Wat (continued)

The west entrance pavilion is linked to the "cruciform cloister" by a series of covered flights of stairs, forming an astonishingly subtle composition. The north and south gopura are cruciform and dissymmetrical, while the gopura on the east side is larger. The corner pavilions are of an unusual type, the only other known example before this date being at the Baphuon. They are really sanctuary towers, square in plan, with four vestibules on the outside, which make the overall plan into what is sometimes referred to as "false cruciforms." Their superstructures

An interior courtyard at Angkor Wat. The pattern formed by the broken line of roofs and bases is particularly striking. *Photo: Guy Nafilyan*

consist of a series of ever-decreasing tiers crowned with a lotus-flower motif.

In the courtyard of this second enclosure there are two small libraries, linked to each other as well as to the west entrance pavilion of the second enclosure and thus to the stairway that climbs the pyramid by means of a bridge paved with sandstone and supported on small piles, also made of sandstone. These libraries are also linked to the overall composition: their north-south transverse axis crosses two secondary doorways in the gallery-enclosure. Two other secondary doors, in the eastern portion of the courtyard, create another north-south axis, but this is purely by chance, or so it seems.

The Third Level, or First Enclosure

Leaving the bridge that links the libraries of the second enclosure, visitors climb the central massif formed by the temple-mountain. This pyramid, 11 meters high, has only two tiers. The stairways climb in a single, vertiginous flight: their side walls rise in four stages, two to each tier.

The gallery of the first enclosure runs round the plateau at the top of the pyramid. It has a principal nave with outer wall lit by true windows that have stone balusters. On the inner side, the vault rests on square pillars; then there is a side aisle, semi-vaulted, supported by smaller square pillars. In the corners there are sanctuary towers, slightly bigger than those of the second enclosure. At the axial intersections, cruciform entrance pavilions give access to the central sanctuary by way of triple-nave galleries on pillars. These linking galleries, the first example of their kind, have two small stairways, one on either side, leading down into the corner courtyards of the first enclosure.

Plans drawn by Guy Nafilyan, EFEO 1969

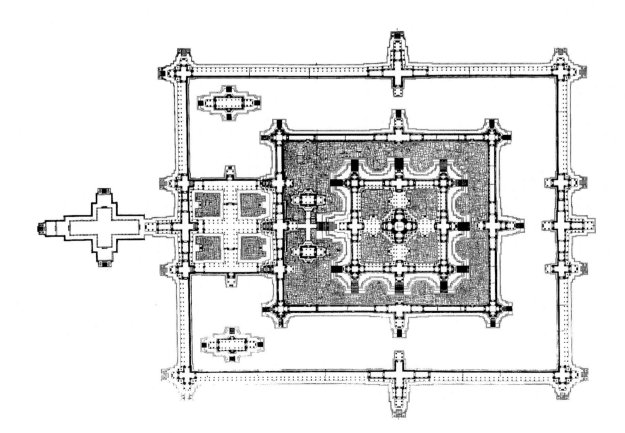

Aerial view of Angkor Wat from the northeast. *Photo: Menthonnex*

THE CENTRAL SANCTUARY

The central sanctuary rises in the geometric center of the third level, standing on a base that lifts it above the level of the four corner sanctuary towers. It consists of the following elements:

• the main body of the sanctuary, enclosing the cella, which is slightly dentated, with four true doors (at present walled up); it rises to a considerable height and its surfaces have a variety of projecting features

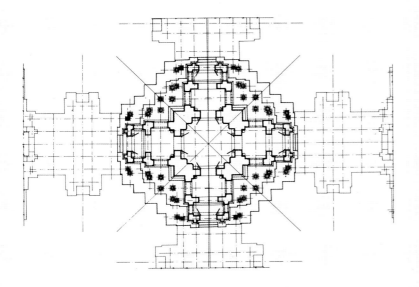

• a series of four two-tier structures projecting from the main body of the sanctuary

• a series of four single-tier structures projecting from these two-tier structures

• a system of vaulted side aisles, supported by pillars and projecting from the body of the sanctuary and from the projecting structures referred to above.

The towers, when viewed in elevation, give the impression of having numerous tiers, but in fact they have very few:

• the central tower, above its main cornice, has only four tiers, decreasing in size towards the top and crowned with a motif consisting of three layers of lotus petals, the top of a lotus bud

• the towers of the first enclosure also have four tiers in decreasing size, with the same crowning motif as the central tower

• the towers of the second enclosure are smaller than the others, but follow the same model.

Altogether, then, there are nine sanctuary towers on the temple itself, and three at the Western Gateways, making a total of twelve. This figure also applies to the number of stairways on the pyramid, those on the platform, and those on the approach causeway. There are other recurring numbers, relating to the steps in the stairways, the bays, the windows, both true and false, and so on. However, no texts have been found that could elucidate the numerology underlying the design of this temple, or of any of the other temples, and it is highly unlikely we shall ever find any.

At Angkor Wat: window barred with carved balusters.
The long galleries of the upper levels are lit by these windows. Soft light is diffused through the beautifully turned balusters that look as though they were made of wood.
Photo: Henri Stierlin

Opposite
A bas-relief at Angkor Wat: detail of an *apsaras*.
Photo: Guy Nafilyan

Following pages
Angkor Wat at dawn, viewed from the west.
Angkor Wat emerges romantically from the morning mist.
Photos: Luc Ionesco, Top

Higher still, having climbed up one of the steep stairways, visitors finally arrive on the plateau with its five towers, the walls decorated with *apsaras*. The four doorways of the principal tower, which were once open, have been walled up, possibly in the 16th century, and these wall surfaces have been carved with figures of the Buddha. The tower probably originally housed a statue of Vishnu, but it has never been discovered.

Here the visitor comes face to face with the breathtaking beauty of Angkor Wat's famous bas-reliefs, finely chiseled on walls, piers, and plinths, a thousand pediments displaying the glory of the gods or recounting their exploits, often repeating the same stories—the Churning of the Ocean of Milk, the Battle of the Monkeys, and episodes from the life of Krishna. Here, soft light penetrates the galleries through the window balusters; here the modern visitor is tempted to imagine the temple as it was, with its various idols served by hundreds of priests and enclosed within the sanctuaries (which today appear more like passages because their doors have disappeared), and the spectacle of great feasts celebrated amid the grandeur of these decorations.

120

The ambition
of a great conqueror

Under the reign of Suryavarman II, diplomatic relations with China, which had not been mentioned for a very long period, were resumed. Through Chinese annals we learn that the Khmer king sent "embassies" there in 1116 and 1120. It seems that the purpose of these missions was more economic than political or strategic.

The Khmers had always been in conflict with the neighboring Chams. The independence of Vietnam, at the start of the 11th century, had changed the political equilibrium of the region. Starting with the reign of Suryavarman II, relations between the Khmer empire and Champa were to change utterly and there were no more of the local raids that seem to have been common previously. The Khmer king had no hesitation in exerting his authority in the Cham territory, which suggests that he had friends in one or several of the Champa kingdoms.

Suryavarman II's plans were particularly ambitious here; it is not certain that he wanted to annex the Cham territory right at the beginning of his reign, but it was from here that he launched his war against Vietnam, involving the Cham kings in this rash venture whether they liked it or not. Furthermore, towards the end of his reign, in 1145, Suryavarman II installed prince Harideva on the throne of the Cham kingdom of Vijaya (in the present-day

The temple of Thommanon.
The central sanctuary and east entrance pavilion.
Photo: Guy Nafilyan

region of Qui-nhon), having killed the previous incumbent, the younger brother of one of his own wives, a Cham herself. In so doing, he aroused the fury of another Cham king, Jaya-Harivarman I, who killed Harideva in 1149 and proclaimed himself "supreme king of the Cham kings," a title adopted doubtless as a defiant gesture against the Khmer king. This was the starting point for the unrelenting wars between the Chams and the Khmers.

Suryavarman II was not content with waging war in this region alone; he had no difficulty in taming the provinces situated on the other side of the Dangrek mountains, right up to the Lopburi region, and retaining them within the Khmer empire. And he led his armies much further into the north of present-day Thailand and well down the Malay peninsula. The Chinese annals give an approximate description of the extent of his empire in the middle of the 12th century: "Cambodia borders Champa to the north, the sea to the east, the kingdom of Pagan to the west and Grahi to the south." Grahi corresponds to the present-day region of Chaiya and Nakhon Si Thammarat.

The last years of Suryavarman II are obscure and the date of his death is unknown. The latest inscription naming him during his lifetime bears the date 1145, but it is just possible that he led one more campaign, a disastrous failure, against Vietnam in 1150.

Other temples
in the style of Angkor Wat

The building of the temples of Thommanon and Chau Say Tevoda is believed to have been mostly carried out at the end of the reign of Suryavarman II. These small "symmetrical" temples stand one on either side of the causeway that led to the royal palace of Angkor Thom and that of Jayavarman V. However, at the time when the temples were built, there was nothing special about this causeway, because the center of the empire would have been around the site of Angkor Wat. Also, it cannot have been planned at the outset that they should be symmetrical, because they are not exactly alike and Chau Say Tevoda seems to be of a slightly later date.

Detail of a pediment at the temple of Chau Say Tevoda.
Photo: Guy Nafilyan

The temple of Chau Say Tevoda: an access causeway raised on small columns, seen from the north.
Photo: Guy Nafilyan

Far away, near the east bank of the Eastern Baray, the very beautiful monument of Banteay Samre must have been constructed during the same period by some grand dignitary, but there is no written document relating to this temple.

On the way from Angkor to Phimai, about 60 kilometers before arriving at the latter, the route crosses a long hill called Phnom Rung; from at least as far back as the days of Rajendravarman, ascetics had retreated to this hill and built sanctuaries there. However, in the 12th century, a first cousin of Suryavarman II, Narendraditya, retired there after an illustrious military career. He was responsible for building most of a temple that has been restored by Thailand's archaeological department. This sanctuary is not very big in itself, but its location on top of the hill and the long causeway leading up to it, as well as the quality of the construction, make it one of the most important Khmer sites. Moreover, the large *baray* that lie at the foot of the hill and the temple of Muang Tham, built in the previous century, are clear evidence of the great wealth of this region.

The temple of Chau Say Tevoda.
The east entrance pavilion seen from the west.
Photo: Guy Nafilyan

The temple of Banteay Samre, between the first and second enclosures.
Photo: Guy Nafilyan

A pediment at the temple of Banteay Samre.
Photo: Guy Nafilyan

An aerial view of the temple of Banteay Samre from the southeast.
Photo: Guy Nafilyan

It was also probably during the reign of Suryavarman II that construction work was at any rate started on the great temple of Beng Mealea, situated at the foot of Phnom Kulen, some 40 kilometers east of Angkor. This is a most impressive construction, in an area where there are scarcely any traces of earlier monuments. It does in fact lie on the route to the "Great Preah Khan," about 60 kilometers farther on, a temple whose history is equally little known.

Beng Mealea, a magnificent temple, has a large *baray* in front of it to the east. It can be compared to the greatest Angkor monuments, in terms of both size and the skill with which it was executed. Its layout is very close to that of Angkor Wat, but the temple, slightly smaller, stands at ground level. As at Phimai, this is a Buddhist sanctuary and must have been built by a very powerful lord, but we know nothing about him, since no inscription relating to him has ever been found.

Great architectural and restoration works: Yashovarman II

On the death of Suryavarman II, about 1150, the supreme crown passed to Yashovarman II, whose origins are totally unknown. For a long time it was believed that between Suryavarman II and Yashovarman II there was another king, Dharanindravarman II, father of the future ruler Jayavarman VII. But there is really no trace of any such reign and it is more likely that this royal personage never ascended the supreme Khmer throne, even though he might have ruled over a part of the empire, which was again in a state of disunity.

With regard to Yashovarman II, it is worth noting that his name does not appear in the "genealogy" of Jayavarman VII, which shows that he did not belong to the Mahidharapura family. The troubles discernible at the end of Suryavarman II's reign suggest that the new king's accession was not quite straightforward. As it happens, not one contemporary inscription ordered by Yashovarman II, or even one mentioning him, has been found—it could be that his successor, who brutally eliminated him, had something to do with this.

Although nothing is known about Yashovarman II other than the approximate date of his accession, 1150, and the probable date of his disappearance, 1165, nevertheless some major architectural works were begun or continued during his reign, which lasted for about 16 years. It is unlikely, in fact, that the temple of Beng Mealea or even the smaller ones such as Thommanon and Chau Say Tevoda, or Banteay Samre, had all been completed by the time of Suryavarman II's death.

Furthermore, there is a case for ascribing to Yashovarman II the restoration of the ancient temples of the Roluos group. A long time ago it was noticed that the central sanctuary of Bakong belonged to the "Angkor Wat style," as did at least one statue found at the Lolei site. The particular interest shown in these temples might indicate that a descendant of the lines who built them had reappeared. This descendant was not Suryavarman II, as we know; but Yashovarman II seems to be the perfect candidate. Clearly, he would have been aiming to obtain the favor of his great ancestors, whose achievements were still celebrated.

It is thought that Yashovarman II abandoned the Angkor Wat area to establish his royal palace on the site of what is now the temple of Preah Khan.

The temple of Beng Mealea.
Situated 40 kilometers from Angkor, the superb temple of Beng Mealea poses numerous questions: in particular, who was responsible for building such an important complex, and for what purpose was this city built?

Photo: Guy Nafilyan

The temple of Beng Mealea.
Largely dilapidated, this temple has still not received the attention it deserves, given its great beauty.
Photo: Guy Nafilyan

Doubtless it was here that on returning from an expedition to Lavodaya (the present-day Lopburi in Thailand) he was overpowered by a rebellion mounted by one of his "mandarins." The latter soon had himself crowned with the name of Tribhuvanadityavarman, in about 1165. As soon as the future Jayavarman VII learned of these dramatic events, an inscription tells us, he hastened to the Cham kingdom of Vijaya, situated in the region of Quinhon (in modern Vietnam), to give his support to the legitimate king—he is perhaps to be suspected of having coveted the supreme throne already at that time, though without success.

The Cham invasion

Tribhuvanadityavarman the usurper—the only supreme king acknowledged as such in Khmer inscriptions—was to reign at Angkor for about a dozen years and was in his turn eliminated by a king of Champa, Jaya-Indravarman IV.

Nothing is known of the monuments constructed duringthe reign of Tribhuvanadityavarman and no mention of his name survives, except for one at Angkor itself denouncing him, an inscription that was engraved during the following reign, and another on a copper tray found far away, south of Phnom Bayang in the south of present-day Vietnam.

However, in 1177, the Cham king Jaya-Indravarman IV decided to launch a raid on Angkor, doubtless having been provoked by a number of serious Khmer incursions into his own territory. In fact, it was by no means a simple undertaking: the Chinese annals claim that the Chams traveled to Angkor by water, along a tributary of the Mekong to Tonlé Sap, the Great Lake, itself, all with the help of a Chinese pilot. But we know also that another army, "transported on chariots," had no hesitation in making the long march across the mountains that separated the two countries. Furthermore, there must have been Khmer kings who were supporters of Jaya-Indravarman IV and enemies of both Tribhuvanadityavarman and of the future Jayavarman VII , and who tend to be forgotten. In the face of these combined forces, Angkor fell and its usurper king met his death. Another chapter in Khmer history was about to open.

CHAPTER 7

Angkor Thom

Capital city of the great Jayavarman VII

The late 12th century was the period of greatest expansion for the Khmer empire. Despite the fact that it took him several years of fighting to gain the supreme throne, Jayavarman VII, the dynamic builder of Angkor Thom and the Bayon, of Ta Prohm, Preah Khan and other monuments, will remain the greatest Khmer king of all.

W hen the usurper Tribhuvanadityavarman took power from Yashovarman II in about 1165, a Khmer prince—the future Jayavarman VII—hurried to the Cham kingdom of Vijaya to help defend its king. He arrived too late: the coup was over and he had to abandon any idea of mounting a challenge to the new ruler in the immediate future. Although his principal wife, Princess Jayarajadevi, strongly urged him to seize the supreme throne, he patiently waited more than 12 years for the right moment; we do not know where he was during this period. Then, once he had learned the news of what was happening in his country, with the downfall of the usurper at the hands of the Cham king Jaya-Indravarman IV, Jayavarman VII quickly returned to Angkor at the head of his army.

In the Bayon temple, much of the bas-relief decoration in the south gallery shows a huge naval battle between Khmers and Chams. This scene is identified by all scholars as the battle on Tonlé Sap, the Great Lake, that must have preceded the recapture of the capital, and that here is given due importance. But other fierce encounters were to follow, right up to the last battle and final victory. It seems likely that this took place at the royal palace, whose site eventually became that of Preah Khan. At any rate, an inscription by Jayavarman VII describes a "lake of blood" in connection with the royal palace, and Jaya-Indravarman IV is known to have met his end at this palace.

Although this victory gave Jayavarman VII the city of Yashodharapura, it did not give him the Khmer empire. The expedition that brought the empire under his control is too often referred to today as a "liberation." This is both unrealistic and anachronistic: the inscriptions themselves state that Jayavarman VII had to reunify an empire "sheltered by numerous parasols," each parasol presumably representing a king; and the task of pacifying the country—and ensuring that all these kings accepted the new supreme ruler—

Presumed head of King Jayavarman VII, found at the temple of Preah Khan, Kompong Svay. National Museum, Phnom Penh. Height 41 cm.
Photo: Luc Ionesco, EFEO

A bas-relief at the Bayon temple: battle scene. Chams against Khmers, with elephants and foot soldiers.
Bayon, southern portion of east side, outer gallery of bas-reliefs.
Photo: Luc Ionesco, EFEO

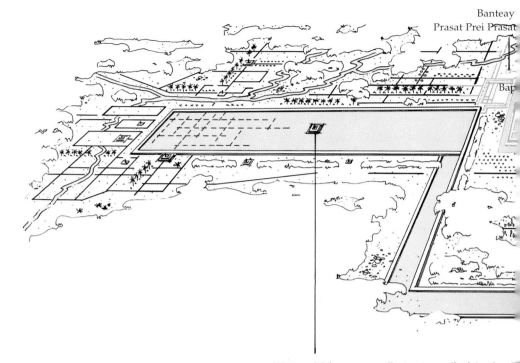

Banteay
Prasat Prei Prasat

Bap

Plan of Angkor at the time of King Jayavarman VII.
It was during the reign of Jayavarman VII that the Angkor
site acquired its definitive appearance, first through the
creation and interior arrangement of the fortified city of
Angkor Thom (with the Bayon temple at its center, the
palace with its royal terraces and so on), then through the
establishment of the cities of Ta Prohm, Preah Khan,
Banteay Kdei, and probably others as well, and finally
through the alterations made to the old Sras Srang and to
the *baray* at Preah Khan (with the temple of Neak Pean in
its center). In fact, the landscape had already undergone
great alterations since the time of Suryavaraman I. First,
alongside the royal palace, the powerful mass of the
Baphuon was built (and the Mebon temple in the middle
of the Eastern Baray). Then the city of Angkor Wat was
developed, and various temples, not necessarily of royal
foundation, appeared: Thommanon, Chau Say Tevoda,
Banteay Samre. Finally, Yashovarman II seems to have
established himself in a palace that stood on the site of
Preah Khan.

Plan drawn by Guy Nafilyan

Western Mebon   Perimeter wall of Angkor 1

was perhaps not such an easy one. In fact, it was not until 1181, four years
after the battle with the Chams, that Jayavarman VII was consecrated as
supreme king, and it is certain that rebellions were still breaking out in areas
not far from Angkor for several years afterwards.

We know the names of the new king's direct antecedents: his father was
Dharanindravarman II, and for a long time historians considered him to be one
of the greatest Khmer kings of his age. This is in fact very unlikely, but since
the empire had been considerably fragmented since the end of the reign of
Suryavarman II, or at any rate that of Yashovarman II, he might very well have
been the ruler of one of the small "independent" kingdoms of that period. This
Dharanindravarman was son of the younger brother of Suryavarman II's
mother, in other words, first cousin of Suryavarman II, but this relationship
clearly gave him no particular right to the supreme throne, and gave his son
even less right. The mother of Jayavarman VII, Jayarajacudamani, was the
daughter of a king called Harshavarman, who must also have been a minor
Khmer king. There are certain grounds for thinking that the center of his
domain must have been the site of Banteay Chmar, northwest of Angkor.

It often seems as though we know Jayavarman VII much better than the other
Khmer kings, perhaps because of the "statue portraits," as George Cœdès called
them, which show him meditating. Also, the abundance of pious works that he
instituted, particularly the hospitals, which are described in two great Sanskrit
poems, serves to enhance his image as a king who appears to be totally occupied
with the care of his subjects. However, the bellicose aspect of his career should
not be forgotten: he spent the first part of his life fighting in the Cham kingdom
of Vijaya and he had to lead many expeditions in order to reunify his own fragmented empire before having himself consecrated as supreme king in 1181.

Even after his enthronement, Jayavarman VII still needed to struggle in
order to maintain stability in his empire. For example, we learn from a Cham
inscription that the city of Malyang, believed to have been situated in the
region of today's Battambang, rose up in rebellion several times. In the end,
the king sent a young Cham prince to subdue the city; he had taken an

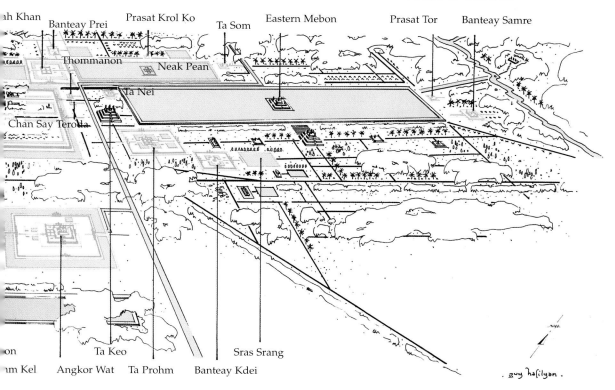

ah Khan
Banteay Prei   Prasat Krol Ko   Ta Som   Eastern Mebon   Prasat Tor   Banteay Samre
Thommanon   Neak Pean
Ta Nei
Chan Say Teroda
on
m Kel   Ta Keo   Sras Srang
Angkor Wat   Ta Prohm   Banteay Kdei

. guy hafilyan .

interest in this prince, Vidyanandana, "since his earliest youth," and he himself had trained the young man in the martial arts.

The fact that Jayavarman VII put a Cham prince in command of such an expedition implies that he did not have much confidence in his Khmer generals. Moreover, following this campaign, he conferred on Vidyanandana the important title of *yuvaraja*, "crown prince."

Ta Prohm,
the romantic temple

Leaving aside the various wars, it would still be possible to gain some idea of the reign of Jayavarman VII just from the list of monuments he built. The first of these at Angkor was the great temple-monastery of Ta Prohm, which at the time was called Rajavihara, the "king's monastery." It was surrounded by a city, which today is no more than forest and thicket, and whose enclosure covers an area of 60 hectares (148 acres), while the temple itself covers only just over one hectare (2.5 acres). The inscription tells us that altogether 12,640 people were occupied at the monastery, most of whom, if not all, must have lived within the city enclosure. To feed all these people, no fewer than 79,365 people worked in the villages attached to this temple.

The principal divinity of Ta Prohm, Prajnaparamita, "perfection of wisdom," was consecrated in 1186. The sculpture, modeled on Jayavarman VII's mother, was surrounded by 260 other divinities, distributed among the various sanctuaries of this complex temple. The monastery also housed the administration center for the royal supplies distributed to the 102 hospitals throughout the empire, to which we will return later.

The temple has been deliberately left as it was discovered, amid the encroaching jungle, so that the visitor today experiences something of the sense of wonder that the first European explorers must have felt.

Following pages
At the temple of Ta Prohm.
Kapok trees clasp the sanctuaries in their mighty roots. Courtyard of the central sanctuary.
Photo: Guy Nafilyan

A half-hidden bas-relief of a divinity at the temple of Ta Prohm.
Photo: Guy Nafilyan

Pages 136-137
The temple of Ta Prohm, west gopura, with guardian of the gate, and the terrace in front of the temple.
Photo: Guy Nafilyan

The university of Preah Khan and its ancillary temples

Another large temple was then built on the site of the palace of Jayavarman VII's immediate predecessors—also the site of the battle that ended in Angkor's downfall at the hand of the Chams. The enclosure contained a city covering an area slightly smaller than that of Ta Prohm, at 56 hectares (138 acres), but the actual temple is appreciably larger, occupying a rectangle 200 meters by 175 meters. More than a monastery, it was really a kind of university, housing a number of masters and students. Unfortunately, most of the lines of the inscription that relate to them are lost, but it seems there were over one thousand teachers here. As at Ta Prohm, a large crowd of people worked in the temple, serving the needs of even more numerous gods. This required support on a huge scale: 97,840 people who supplied, among other things, about ten tons of white rice a day. On the basis of an estimated daily ration of 650 grams (23 ounces), this would have fed some 15,000 people.

The temple of Preah Khan is particularly complex, containing even more sanctuaries than Ta Prohm. In this case, however, the inscriptions give us precise information about which god was housed in each cella, enabling us to form a clear idea of the temple's structure. Preah Khan is a veritable pantheon, sheltering Buddhist, Shivaite, and Vishnuite divinities, not to mention local spirits.

In the middle there was the Buddhist temple, the most important. The statue of the principal occupant, the bodhisattva Lokeshvara, sculpted in the image of Jayavarman VII's father, was consecrated 1191. Around him there are 282 secondary divinities that included, alongside deities of the Buddhist pantheon, a number of recently deceased dignitaries who had become protectors of their family lines, and also Khmer heroes such as Arjuna and Shridhara of Devapura, who died while defending the palace of Yashovarman II when it was attacked by Tribhuvanadityavarman.

The temple of Preah Khan.
Frieze of dancers on a lintel of the Hall of Dancers.
Photo: Guy Nafilyan

The temple of Preah Khan.
The elephant god Ganesha installed in the central tower of the Shivaite temple (in the north). This idol is definitely not in its original place, and must once have occupied a sanctuary further away.
Photo: Guy Nafilyan

The temple of Preah Khan.
Boundary stones lining the approach causeway to the city of Preah Khan from the east. Lion-atlantes and niches from which figures of the Buddha have been carved out.
Photo: Guy Nafilyan

Nevertheless, in front of this temple there was the sanctuary of the god Tribhuvanavarmeshvara. This name is too much like that of the "usurper" king Tribhuvanadityavarman to be a mere coincidence, especially given that the temple lies on the site of his former palace. It is important to remember that a Khmer king, once consecrated, was a protector of his country, whatever he might have done in his past life.

To the south of the central group stood the temple of the former kings, in the middle of which dwelled the spirits of king Yashovarman II, surrounded by 32 divinities, heroes, and important personages. Later, after the death of Jayavarman VII, Yashovarman II had to make way for the great king and he was moved to a secondary sanctuary nearby.

To the west, and opening to the west like Angkor Wat, was a temple dedicated to Vishnu, with 30 images of his principal avatars and of the usual divinities who surround him. Enthroned in the center of the temple was the god Campeshvara, whose name does evoke that of the people whose country the king was aiming to annex, but in fact it relates to an incarnation of Vishnu, known through older inscriptions in India as well as in Cambodia.

Following page
The temple of Preah Khan.
Terrace and east entrance pavilion of the temple's enclosure.
Photo: Guy Nafilyan

The temple of Ta Som.
Giant faces on the tower of the west entrance
pavilion imprisoned in tree roots.
Photo: Gerster, Rapho

Finally, north of the central group there was a temple dedicated to Shiva, housing a total of 40 divinities. In the prime position in this temple was a representation—exceptional in Hinduism—of Shiva's footprints. The temple's enclosure also contained 42 other lesser divinities, those whose task it was to protect the ambulatories and the entrances, and those guarding the hospital, the travelers' accommodation, and the rice store.

To complement this ensemble, Jayavarman VII built to the east of it a *baray* of considerable size, called the Jayatataka, 3.5 kilometers long and 900 meters wide. In the middle, on an "island" 350 meters square, was the astonishing ensemble known today as Neak Pean, "intertwined serpents," named after the two serpents that twine around the base of the principal sanctuary.

The island also has a total of 13 pools. The best-known today are the five stone-faced cross-shaped pools that have been restored. Outside the central pool, which is 70 meters square, there are at the cardinal points of the compass four smaller square pools. Water can flow into these, in theory at any rate, from the central pool by means of spouts sheltering under a sandstone canopy: the spout to the east is in the shape of the head of a man, to the south that of a lion, to the west that of a horse, and to the north that of an elephant. In the middle of the central pool, on a circular base, stands the ensemble's single sanctuary tower, quite small and built of sandstone. Eight other ponds, not faced in stone, fill the remaining area of the island; four of them were of a complicated shape that is now difficult to make out.

The ensemble, surrounded by a wall, housed "fourteen divinities, including a group of one thousand lingam," according to the stele at Preah Khan. In the basin itself, on the west side, an image of Vishnu reclining has been discovered and, on the north side, some Shivaite lingam. The image on the

south side is no longer recognizable but, in accordance with the layout of Preah Khan, it might have related to former kings. Finally, on the east, is the famous statue of the horse Balaha.

The Neak Pean ensemble has been seen as a representation of Anavatapta, a miraculous lake in the Himalayas that cures all illnesses—a very Buddhist image. However, there are many objections to this theory: the stele at Preah Khan that describes the island makes no allusion to Anavatapta, and Neak Pean's old name, Rajyashri, "the kingdom's fortune," bears no relation to it, not to speak of the presence of Hindu gods and other details. However, it seems clear that such an elaborate layout was intended to represent a definite place, even taking into account alterations made to the site at the start of the 13th century. Perhaps the key to the puzzle will be found by chance, by someone studying Indian writings—unless Neak Pean was of purely Khmer inspiration.

East of the Jayatataka is the temple of Ta Som, famous for the tower of faces at its west gopura, which until recently was clasped by the branches of a banyan tree. This could be the temple named Gaurashrigajaratna, the "jewel of the auspicious white elephant," which housed 22 divinities. The stele also mentions a monument named Yogindravihara, "monastery of the King of the *yogin*," as being in the Preah Khan group. The inscription says it housed 16 divinities, the same number as each of the two small pools adjoining it. Since the monastery is mentioned in the same stanza as Neak Pean, it possibly stood nearby, but to date it has not been identified.

The date 1191, when the principal divinity of Preah Khan was consecrated, cannot be regarded as that of the whole ensemble of sanctuaries described on the stele. They were probably built a little later, though still during the reign of Jayavarman VII.

The temple of Neak Pean.
The central sanctuary, from the northeast. To the east are the raised heads of the naga before them is the well-known group of the horse Balaha.
Photo: Guy Nafilyan

Detail of Balaha group, Neak Pean.
Lokeshvara became a horse to help some merchants escape from an island of ogresses. This view shows them hanging on to his tail.
Photo: Guy Nafilyan

The temple of Banteay Kdei and the Sras Srang

It was long believed that Banteay Kdei was the sanctuary called the Eastern Buddha in inscriptions. However, this Eastern Buddha was without doubt much farther away, to the east of Angkor, and probably should be sought in one of the large-scale complexes such as Preah Khan at Kompong Svay or Beng Mealea.

Unfortunately, no stele bearing invaluable information, such as those at Ta Prohm and Preah Khan, has ever been discovered at this temple. Given its size, it would seem reasonable to attribute its creation to the king. It was established over the ruins of an old Buddhist temple that must have been built by Kavindrarimathana, the architect of Rajendravarman. Some elements of the old monument were reused in the new one. Initially small it was soon considerably enlarged and provided with an outer enclosure comparable to that of Ta Prohm, and became the center of another walled city.

Probably it was when work began on expanding the monument that it was decided to restore the old Sras Srang *baray* that lay to the east and which had also been created by the architect Kavindrarimathana. Jayavarman VII had this small reservoir magnificently refurbished: the surface area was slightly decreased and sandstone steps were built right round its sides. Also, the graceful terrace, referred to earlier, was added, aligned with the axis of Banteay Kdei (and not with that of the *baray*). This reservoir well deserves its modern name Sras Srang, "royal bathing pool."

Pages 146-147
The royal palace, Angkor Thom.
Terrace of Elephants, after the monsoon. In the foreground is a typical naga.
Photo: © Guy Nafilyan

The royal palace, Angkor Thom.
Dwarf spirits standing on lotus leaves (at the feet of an unidentified five-headed horse).
Terrace of Elephants, north side, inner bas-relief. End 12th to beginning 13th century.
Photo: Claude Jacques

Ta Nei, the solitary temple

Ta Nei is a small temple standing not far from the west bank of the Eastern Baray, midway between Ta Prohm and Preah Khan. It could be approached only from the south, however, since the wall built by Jayaviravarman formed a barrier on the north side; this means that it was off the beaten track, as it still is today.

It dates from the early years of the reign and differs from the large temples of the same period in that it was very little altered after it was first constructed. Other distinguishing features are its two long moats that border it on the north and south sides. There is nothing to suggest that this temple was commissioned by the king himself.

Prasat Tor, temple of Shiva

Prasat Tor, which was constructed during the reign of Jayavarman VII, is a fairly small temple built in laterite and standing at the northeast corner of the Eastern Baray, thus complementing Banteay Samre.

It is one of the rare known examples of a temple dedicated to Shiva from this era, apart from those that were an integral part of the great royal temples. Jayavarman VII, right at the beginning of his reign, had a statue installed there that was "incomparable, in gold" (it would in fact have been gilded

The temple of Banteay Kdei.
Third enclosure, west entrance pavilion viewed from the east.
Photo: Guy Nafilyan

bronze), modeled on his maternal grandfather, Harshavarman. We do not know, unfortunately, which divinity this statue represented or why it was there, but it seems quite likely that there was a special link between that king, and therefore also Jayavarman VII, and the family that owned Prasat Tor.

The great capital, Angkor Thom

At what point did Jayavarman VII decide to create his own capital city? Presumably he had it in mind right from the start of his reign, even if the temple of Preah Khan does seem like a state temple, given the gods it houses. The city's enclosure wall forms an immense square with sides three kilometers long, marking the boundaries of what is today called Angkor

The Gate of Victories, Angkor Thom.
The Gate of Victories is one of the two east gates that correspond to the entrance to the royal palace.
Photo: H. Serraillier

Thom, the "great city," with its five monumental gates, four of them corresponding to the Bayon's entrances, the fifth opening via a triumphal way directly to the royal palace, as in the old capital of Yashovarman I. The city walls were originally intended to be defensive: an inscription seems to state this explicitly. They are eight meters high and on the inside there is an earth bank, forming a route running all the way round. On the outside of the walls is a moat 100 meters wide. The monumental gateways did not originally have their famous towers bearing gigantic faces; these were applied at a later date to older structures.

Access to the gateways was along causeways across the moat that were edged with carved serpents held by divine beings. Paul Mus suggested that these figures illustrate the famous story the Churning of the Ocean of Milk, which is so frequently represented in Cambodian art. Certainly this is the legend that first springs to mind, but in fact it is not really so clearly represented. Instead, the regal nature of these gateways, underlined by the fine images of the god Indra on his three-headed elephant, seems to support Jean Boisselier's notion that these were serpents guarding the capital's riches. At each corner of the city there is a sanctuary tower. These are called the Prasat Chrung ("corner sanctuaries") and each houses a stele engraved with poems celebrating the king, composed by various authors, as were those carved on the four stelae of the Eastern Baray in the time of Yashovarman I.

Above: Angkor Thom, south gate.
The giants, guardians of the city's riches.
Photo: Guy Nafilyan

Right: Angkor Thom, south gate.
The Avenue of Giants, seen from the north in the late afternoon. The giants form the parapet of the causeway that crosses the city's moat.
Photo: Guy Nafilyan

Below: Angkor Thom, east gate.
Head of a demon fallen to the ground. The round eyes are a demonic sign. *Photo: Guy Nafilyan*

A forest of heads: the Bayon temple

The temple-mountain of the Bayon, rising in the center of the city, has been the subject of much conjecture. It has been identified in turn as a temple dedicated to Shiva, to Brahma, and to the Buddha. We know now that it is all these, and much more—like Preah Khan, whose ground plan its own resembles, though it is in a way a "compressed" version. It is a veritable pantheon that housed, or was intended to house, all of the divinities worshiped in Jayavarman VII's empire, which then encompassed not only the actual Khmer kingdom, but also those of the Chams and other vassal states. It is easy to see why the Bayon should be devised as a pantheon, more so than in the case of Preah Khan, since the Bayon is the state temple.

The Buddha sat on the throne of the central sanctuary, of course. In the following century, when there was a change of divinity, his statue was broken up and thrown down the well that represented the earth's axis. The statue has been retrieved and restored and can now be viewed on a nearby terrace. It is likely that a replica of the famous statue of Jayavarman VII meditating was placed in a sanctuary that served as a kind of antechamber to the central sanctuary. Clearly this had nothing to do with the idea of a *Buddharaja*, the

The Bayon temple viewed from the east.
Photo: Luc Ionesco, EFEO

The Bayon

The Bayon has aroused more enthusiasm and attracted greater attention than any other Khmer monument, and research into this temple is far from completed. It has enormous defects—it is badly built and clumsily sculpted, and its plan is disorganized, or so it seems. But it also has indisputable qualities, particularly the extraordinary display of gigantic faces on its sanctuary towers and, above all, the air of mystery it radiates.

The apparent disorder of this great pile of badly cut stones resolves itself, when analyzed, into a plan as well ordered as that of Angkor Wat... well, almost as well ordered, because its complexity makes it difficult to comprehend fully.

A visit to this temple can be an intoxicating experience: after having wandered around dark and uneven corridors and clambered up almost vertical stairways, visitors emerge onto the upper platform to find themselves in another world. It is a sight to be experienced by the light of the moon or of flaming torches.

The Bayon is the center of Jayavaraman VII's city and dates from the end of the 12th century. It is a Buddhist temple; in fact a kind of hybrid, something between a stupa, the typical Buddhist monument, and a *prasada* or *prasat*, the normal type of Khmer monument of that era.

CHARACTERISTICS

The temple has three principal characteristics:
- its complexity, displayed most markedly in what is called the gallery of the first enclosure, in the form of a dentated cross, surrounding the central massif, which opens in eight directions and comprises superimposed tiers
- the shape of the main body of the "mountain," also that of a dentated cross, and giving the impression of expanding outwards until it almost touches the galleries of the second enclosure
- above all, the unusual way in which the temple's orientation is marked: while in all the earlier *prasat* stairways and entrance

pavilions marked the four cardinal points of the compass, here it is the sanctuary towers with huge faces carved on their sides which powerfully define these points, their significance reinforced by the towers that mirror them on what is the second enclosure, where this merges with the first.

The fact that certain chambers between the second and third enclosures, called "passageway chambers," have been completely razed to the ground, and that there are a number of clearly visible signs of alterations (such as pillars integrated into stone walls) suggests that the layout underwent some modifications.

The Bayon is situated at the geometrical center (within 20 centimeters or so) of the three-kilometer-sided square that forms the city of Angkor Thom and that must be regarded as its fourth enclosure. The temple itself is an ensemble of galleries and sanctuary towers that is almost square, 160 meters long and 140 meters wide. In front of it is an access terrace, giving the whole complex the shape of a racket, which is seen so frequently in the layout of Khmer monuments as to be almost the norm.

THE THIRD ENCLOSURE

The third enclosure, which is the first that the visitor encounters, forms a kind of quadrangle of galleries, which were once vaulted, and which consist of a great central nave with a solid wall on one side and a row of pillars on the other, and a side aisle supported by pillars. The walls of these galleries display a series of bas-reliefs on historical themes showing the battles fought by Jayavarman VII, together with scenes of everyday life. This peripheral gallery is broken on the axes of the cardinal points and at the corners by entrance pavilions and corner pavilions, which all have the same layout: a central cruciform chamber on pillars, flanked by semi-vaulted side aisles. The latter extend into adjoining chambers and these too are designed on a triple-nave plan. In front of the entrance pavilions are pillared porches, with either one or two bays. All the pavilions were vaulted, with the usual corbeled construction, the central part having the form of a groin vault. However, the entire vaulting of the third enclosure has collapsed because of defects in the way it was built. The temple

General plan and plan of central plateau of the Bayon temple drawn by Jacques Dumarçay, EFEO 1967

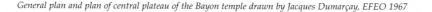

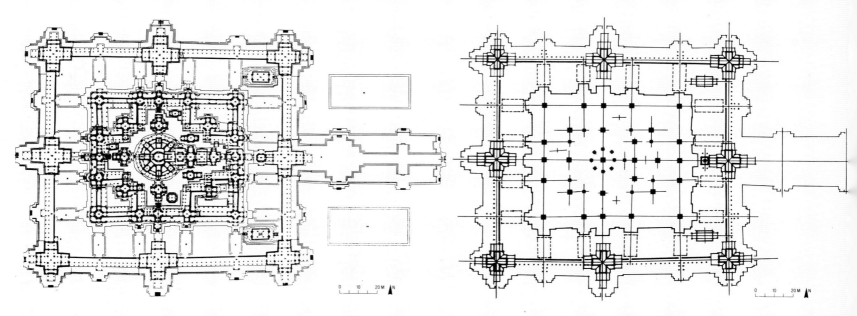

Above: In the foreground, the outer gallery of bas-reliefs, east side of the Bayon temple. *Photo: R. Menthonnex*
Below: Terrace of the third level of the Bayon temple. *Photo: Luc Ionesco, EFEO*

could be entered principally through the entrance pavilions at the axial intersections, but not at all through the corner pavilions. There were also other entrances, of lesser importance, marked by porches projecting from the exterior side aisle, at the base of the corner towers of the second enclosure gallery. Other entrances, simple doors in the gallery wall, give access to the "passageway chambers."

All that remains of these passageway chambers are the stone platforms on which they stood. There were four passageways on each side, dividing the space between the third and second enclosure galleries into 16 small rectangular courtyards. To judge by traces left on the gallery walls and in the ground, these passageway chambers were well built and it seems that they must have been deliberately demolished at some point. This is one of the Bayon's many mysteries.

The courtyard of the third enclosure contains, in its northeast and southeast corners, two libraries, each with an entrance on both its east and its west side. The libraries are perched on high bases, similar to those in the third enclosure at Angkor Wat.

THE SECOND ENCLOSURE

The rest of the temple is a far cry from the simplicity and clarity of the earlier temple-mountains (Pre Rup, Ta Keo, Baphuon, and even Angkor Wat), and distinguishing between the second and first enclosures requires an effort of understanding. Several authors, notably the French scholar Henri Parmentier and, more recently,

151

The Bayon (continued)

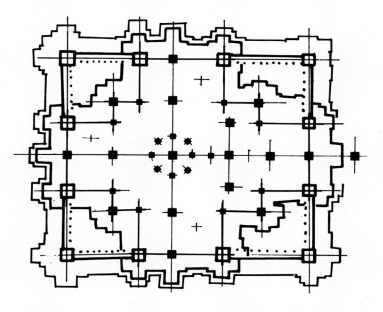

Jacques Dumarçay, have tried to explain the complexity of the Bayon's layout as being a result of modifications introduced during construction. Perhaps the actual construction work was faulty, as a consequence of the plan being so innovative, with its circular central sanctuary, chapels radiating outwards in eight directions, with its cruciform and dentated "mountain," and with the first and second enclosure galleries merging into each other along certain stretches. These, also, are among Bayon's mysteries.

The second enclosure, standing on average 1.3 meters higher than the courtyard of the third enclosure, forms a rectangle that has the four corner towers and the lower galleries that link these towers to the dentated cross of the first enclosure. These are triple-nave galleries: a central nave between two side aisles. Some sections of the first enclosure could equally be regarded as belonging to the second.

The First Enclosure

The first enclosure, raised on average three meters above the second, is in the form of a dentated cross. This shape can also be seen as the superimposition of a square (or rectangle) on a cross,

and this gallery enclosure has at each of its corners, either projecting or inset, a sanctuary tower with faces carved on its sides. These towers are linked by triple-nave galleries.

The first enclosure surrounds the central "mountain." The horizontal part of this mountain forms the "central plateau" and is about 4.6 meters above the average level of this enclosure. The sanctuaries and libraries stand on this plateau.

The central mountain occupies all the space between the galleries of the first enclosure, rather as a cake or a soufflé fills a baking tin. This part can also be likened to the main body of a stupa.

The ground plan of the central plateau is in the shape of a multidentated cross, with every angle in place, including those made by two small chapels in the lower level. However, there is a third chapel, placed in an entirely irregular position, and its presence in this position has not been acknowledged by a corresponding extension of the terrace on which it stands.

Apart from the central massif itself, the most striking features are the cruciform sanctuary towers on the north, west and south arms of the cross, and on the east arm, a series of three towers, also cruciform, and with an intermediate pavilion. After the temples of Ta Prohm and Preah Khan, this is an entirely new development, even more distinct than the sanctuary towers on the cardinal axes.

The Central Sanctuary

The central sanctuary (or central massif) is yet more remarkable. Examined separately from the sanctuary towers on the east arm of the cross, the central part displays a circular ground plan. The cella looks oval in shape but is in fact a badly made circle; the ambulatory that surrounds it is much closer to a circular shape. The rest of the building has a ground plan radiating out in eight directions. This plan is translated in the superstructure into the eight towers or turrets, each with three carved faces (the fourth existing only in imagination, facing inwards). This is truly a representation of the compassionate bodhisattva Lokeshvara, the radiant "universal Buddha" who faces in all directions.

Moreover, this central group of towers carved with faces is surrounded by others, those of the double enclosure. Altogether there are 49 towers and almost 200 faces of Lokeshvara, "Lord of the World."

This temple, together with the Buddhist temple complex of Borobudur in Indonesia, is without doubt the most imposing realization of cosmic and religious symbolism anywhere in the world.

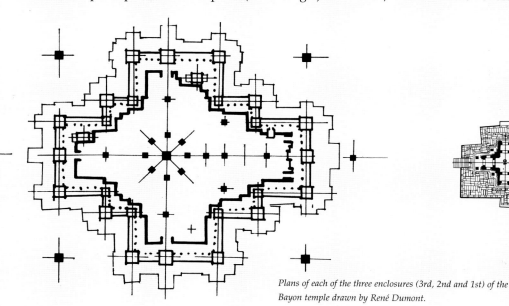

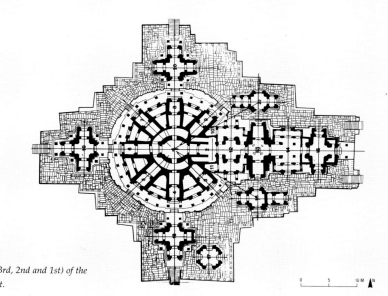

Plans of each of the three enclosures (3rd, 2nd and 1st) of the Bayon temple drawn by René Dumont.

Buddha incarnated as the king, along the lines of a *Devaraja*, as some modern authors have mistakenly supposed.

In the south chamber of the central massif, and in the sanctuaries standing in front of this chamber to the south, past kings were venerated, in particular the king's own ancestors: the "god of Phimai," who was housed in one of these sanctuaries, is to be identified with one of his ancestors. On the west side there is a statue of Vishnu, honored here with the name of Harivarmeshvara, which recalls the name of a Cham king of Vijaya. This suggests that Vishnu was installed here during a period when Jayavarman VII believed he had firm control of that kingdom. To the north there must have been a sanctuary dedicated to Shiva, but the inscriptions and statues have all disappeared.

The new look of the royal palace: the royal square and the terraces

As we saw, Jayavarman VII installed himself in the old royal palace of Suryavarman I and that king's successors, and no doubt he had to restore or reconstruct the buildings; however, nothing remains of them except a few tiles. With regard to what does remain, it seems that he refurbished the interior pools; in particular, the "large pool," which measures 125 meters by 45 meters, was lined with stone steps, the first three of which were delicately sculpted with pairs of *garuda*, then with naga, and finally with fish. A large stele, bearing a Sanskrit poem praising one of the deceased wives of

The Royal Terraces, Angkor Thom.
King Jayavarman VII had these terraces built. This section is supported by alternating lions and *garuda* functioning as atlantes. In the background is the old entrance pavilion to the royal palace of King Suryavarman I. The photograph, taken in July 1989, shows the monument overgrown with vegetation.
Photo: Matthieu Ravaux

153

The Terrace of the Leper King, Angkor Thom:
gods and goddesses on the inner wall.
Photo: Guy Nafilyan

Below: The terrace of the Leper King, Angkor Thom:
naga and divinities on the inner wall.
Photo: Guy Nafilyan

The Royal Terraces, Angkor Thom.
The elephants to the south of the central stairway.
Photo: Guy Nafilyan

Terrace of the Leper King, Angkor Thom.
Seen from the south side of the Royal Terrace, one of whose flights of steps guarded by lions can be seen in the foreground. Among these many images is one of the "Leper King" flanked by two divinities.
Photo: Guy Nafilyan

Jayavarman VII who must have had her own sanctuary there, proves, if proof were needed, that he by no means abandoned the old temple of the Phimeanakas, even though this was dedicated to Shiva.

But the most striking evidence of his occupation of the royal palace is found in the sumptuous manner in which he laid out the square in front of the palace on its east side. First of all, he had the famous Terrace of Elephants built, partly concealing the palace's former east gopura and extending northwards the east gopura of the Baphuon temple. The terrace, 300 meters long, takes its name from its sculpted frieze of elephants. Lightweight shelters made of wood probably stood on it, the same type as those depicted in the bas-reliefs. This is where the king came to show himself to his people; he must also have used it as a viewing platform during feasts, when great spectacles were mounted in the royal square.

Opposite this terrace, and in a way closing off the square, is Prasat Suor Prat, a series of 12 sanctuary towers built of sandstone and laterite, the "towers of the tightrope dancers," as the Khmers have called them; their real purpose is still a mystery. These towers, which really are quite crudely built, must have been erected not by Jayavarman VII but by one of his successors.

North of the Terrace of Elephants is the Terrace of the Leper King. The name comes from a legendary king thought by the Khmers to be represented by a statue placed at the top of the terrace; in fact, this statue is of Yama, god of the underworld: this was the site of royal cremations. The sides of the terrace are magnificently sculpted with a multitude of figures, gods, or spirits carrying swords and charming goddesses, arranged in six or seven rows; the

155

bottom row depicts a variety of sea creatures. When this wall was being uncovered it was realized that, set back two meters, was another row of sculptures, with the space in between having been filled with laterite rubble. This is an indication of one of the many alterations that were carried out, this one being simply for the purpose of increasing the terrace's surface area.

The "houses with fire"

Decoration on the pool of the royal palace, Angkor Thom.
Various monsters inhabit these waters. Here the artist has dreamed up a fish with the head of a horse.
Photo: Claude Jacques

The inscription at the temple of Preah Khan at Angkor refers to the existence of 121 "houses with fire" built at regular intervals, it seems, along the principal routes across the Khmer empire. People have too readily jumped to the conclusion that these "houses" were simply *dharmashala*, travelers' halts. It is true that these are well-known features of Indian culture and that until recent times they were seen in Cambodian villages and regularly used by visitors. Nonetheless, the "houses with fire" were in fact sandstone sanctuaries; a number of them may have been identified. They were not a creation of Jayavarman VII because there is evidence to show that this type of sanctuary existed back in the time of Suryavarman I. We do not know what kinds of ceremony might have been carried out in them, but the inscriptions state that fire played an important role in Khmer temples and that it had its own guardians.

However, the most interesting fact about these "houses with fire," indicated briefly by the inscription, concerns their geographical distribution. The north of the empire apparently was very well provided with them, and it is difficult to understand why there were so few in the south, given Jayavarman VII's great interest in Champa in the southeast, which it seems he wanted to annex. Perhaps the routes leading in that direction had still to be established.

The organization of the hospitals

Fragment of a pediment.
A sick person in the arms of a man, and beside them a harpist. *Photo: Luc Ionesco*

The inscription at the temple of Ta Prohm tells us that there existed in the empire 102 "hospitals" or *arogyashala*, literally "houses of the sick." It seems their creation is not to be attributed to Jayavarman VII, since there are rare but undoubted traces of such establishments dating from the reign of Yashovarman I. On the other hand, it is clear that Jayavarman VII made an effort to organize these hospitals and to contribute to their good management.

Fortunately, nearly 20 stelae have been discovered bearing a long Sanskrit poem consisting in particular of a set of rules governing these hospitals. This gives a fairly precise idea of how they functioned. But whether they were real hospitals, housing sick people, or just dispensaries, we do not know.

As always, the nature of the stelae is religious first and foremost and their inscriptions are addressed above all to divinities (in this case, particularly to the healing Buddha Bhaishajyaguru) who were housed in the sanctuary which always existed alongside this type of establishment. The purpose of detailing the "regulations" here was to remind the gods of the king's good works. The passage containing the eulogy of the king, which is quite short, includes the following fine verse:

People's sickness of body became for him a sickness of the soul, so much more afflicting; for it is the suffering of their subjects that makes kings suffer, and not their own suffering.

This verse has often been cited as a perfect demonstration of the king's Buddhist compassion. In fact, it is nothing of the sort. It is simply an expression of how royalty was regarded in the Indian world: the king is his kingdom and it is therefore normal that he should feel in himself, in some way physiologically, every ailment that might manifest itself in the kingdom.

A close study of the various poems shows first of all that there existed four categories of hospital. The first included only the four hospitals situated not far from the gates of the capital, two of whose sanctuaries are fairly well preserved and are easily visible: Ta Prohm Kel to the south, almost opposite Angkor Wat, and the "hospital chapel" situated near the temple of Ta Keo, to the east. These hospitals were clearly the most important and the king assumed entire responsibility for the upkeep of the divinities there. The permanent staff comprised about 200 people.

The second category of hospital is poorly represented because all that has been found is a single stele, at the city of Phimai: it seems they were almost as important establishments as those in the first category, but the king was not responsible for the upkeep of their divinities. The difference between the last two categories was only in the number of employees: 98 people worked in the third, and 50 in the fourth.

What these hospital stelae tell us above all is that the king contributed to the care of the sick by donating, three times a year, a certain quantity of remedies, a list of which has come down to us. However, it must be pointed out that the quantities he gave were small and therefore symbolic; moreover, he donated only 36 different items, almost all of which have been identified, which represents only a tiny proportion of the entire Khmer pharmacopaea. It is also quite clear that the choice too must have had symbolic significance. A detailed pharmacological study of these medicines would reveal a great deal about the medicine of the era.

King Jayavarman VII.
Presumed statue of Jayavarman VII, found in the temple of Krol Romeas (Angkor). The king was probably meditating before the Buddha. Height 135 cm. National Museum of Phnom Penh.
Photo: Luc Ionesco, EFEO

Frenetic changes

The Khmers of all periods reworked the plans of their monuments whenever they deemed it necessary. But in the age of Jayavarman VII these renovations became the rule, to the point that the French scholar Philippe Sterne was able to perceive three periods in the construction and decoration of the temples, and Jacques Dumarçay even distinguished four in that of the Bayon temple. The history of the man and of his reign is not well enough known for us to explain the reason for these frenetic changes with anything other than guesswork. The evolution of the king's religious faith has been cited in particular as a reason; however, since we do not even know exactly how long his reign lasted, it cannot be ruled out that the later alterations were ordered by his successor, or by a subsequent successor.

Whatever the reason, Jayavarman VII will live forever, one hopes, through the architectural works which display not his megalomania, as is too often claimed, but a profound piety. This is how he appears in the fine statues of him meditating before the Buddha.

A gateway at Angkor.
This reconstruction, drawn by Louis Delaporte at the
end of the 19th century, is largely a product of the
artist's imagination.
(Récit de voyage *by Francis Garnier*)

CHAPTER 8

The Decline of Angkor

and its resurrection

There are few Khmer monuments dating from the 13th century onwards. The last known temple of the Angkor period is the Mangalartha, the only building erected by Jayavarman VIII during his long reign of more than 50 years. Angkor was gradually "abandoned," under the pressure of invasions by Thais, to be rediscovered in the 16th century and becoming for a time a center of pilgrimage. From the beginning of the 19th century Westerners—the French in particular—discovered the ruins of Angkor and began the process of restoring them.

O ver the centuries a curious association arose between the figure of the "Leper King," who belongs to distant legend, and the king Jayavarman VII. This idea was reinforced when a French doctor thought he recognized, on a bas-relief at the Bayon, signs of this terrible disease on the hands of a royal personage depicted there. It is easy to imagine how much speculation grew out of that diagnosis, including the idea that it was because the king suffered from leprosy that he

The Leper King.
A whole legend—and even a novel, by French writer Pierre Benoit—has been inspired by this statue of the Leper King, which in fact is a representation of Yama, the god of the underworld. The terrace was probably used for royal cremations.
Photo: Guy Nafilyan

was prompted to establish hospitals. There is no firm basis to any of this. The famous statue known as the Leper King, on the terrace named after it, in fact represents the god of the underworld, Yama. The signs of leprosy are just lichen on the statue's surface. This statue, anyway, is not a masterpiece of sculpture and very likely is of a later date than Jayavarman VII's reign.

Nothing is known of Jayavarman VII's death, which might have occurred about 1220. His successor was Indravarman II, mentioned in passing in an inscription dating from the end of the 13th century.

The date 1243 is associated with the name of Indravarman II, and it might have been the date of his death. Some 25 years had passed since the passing of Jayavarman VII; the paucity of documentation means it cannot be stated categorically that only one monarch reigned at Angkor for the whole of that period. At any rate, it is possible that some of the works attributed to the previous reign might belong to the age of this king, or kings. It becomes more difficult to establish a chronology for the history of Khmer art from the 13th century onwards, partly because we possess fewer facts about historical events to support any such chronology, and in particular there are fewer monuments. As for the statuary, it forms an ill-defined category called "post-Bayon."

A return to the cult of Shiva: Jayavarman VIII

Head of a divinity at Bakong.
Photo: Guy Nafilyan

The successor to Indravarman II was Jayavarman VIII, whose reign lasted more than 50 years. The most notable event in this period was the appearance of Kublai Khan's Mongols in Southeast Asia. It is possible that some of their troops, coming from the direction of Champa, might even have launched an attack on Cambodia in 1283, although without success. At any rate, the king deemed it prudent to pay tribute to the Great Khan in 1285 and in 1292.

It was during the reign of Jayavarman VIII that the Thais from the north of present-day Thailand, who had begun to throw off the Khmer yoke in the first half of the century, asserted their rights to their kingdoms—at Sukhothai at the expense of the Khmers, and at Chiang-Mai at the expense of a Mon dynasty. Before long they were to become a threat to the Khmer empire. At the same time, Lavo (now named Lopburi) also seems to have claimed its independence.

Unlike his predecessors, Jayavarman VIII was not a Buddhist. Nevertheless, he had no reason to want to abandon the well-fortified capital of Jayavarman VII. But he had no means of moving the state temple, since the city's layout was by now so restrictive. He therefore decided to transform the central sanctuary of the Bayon and to install the Hindu god Hari-Hara in the place of the Buddha. Presumably it was at this point that the statue of the Buddha installed by Jayavarman VII was broken into pieces and thrown down the "central well." This statue, 3.6 meters high, was retrieved in 1935 and ceremoniously placed on a nearby terrace. At the same time that the Buddha was deposed, the Buddhas engraved on the pillars were transformed, very crudely, into Hindu ascetics. Also, numerous Buddhas sculpted in decorative wall niches were hacked off, for example at Ta Prohm and at Preah Khan.

It was probably during his reign that the bas-reliefs in the Bayon's interior gallery were carved; they are clearly of Hindu inspiration, and relate as much to the cult of Shiva as to that of Vishnu. By no means all the scenes have been identified, but there are plenty of the themes favored by the Khmers that had been frequently illustrated elsewhere: the Churning of the Ocean of Milk, for example, or scenes from the great Indian epics, the *Mahabharata* and the *Ramayana*. There is even an illustration of the legend of the Leper King, just as it can still be read today in the *Royal Chronicles*, and another showing the construction of a temple, perhaps Angkor Wat.

The Mangalartha, the last known temple of the Angkor period, was also built in the reign of Jayavarman VIII. It was erected—or rather, altered, since recently it was discovered that it replaced an old sanctuary dating from the era of Yashovarman I—in honor of a Brahmin sage named Jayamangalartha who, born at the end of the 12th century, had lived for an amazing 104 years. The Mangalartha stands to the east of Angkor Thom, hidden between the causeway that leads to the Bayon and the one leading to the royal palace.

Finally, it was under this reign that some of the sanctuaries of Ta Prohm began to be used again. They had probably been abandoned for some time. Now construction work was carried out to raise the height of the interior courtyards: on the whole, this was a scheme of mediocre quality and it seems almost certain to have been the undertaking of a private individual.

A Chinese traveler's eyewitness account

Jayavarman VIII was forced to abdicate in 1295 by his son-in-law, who reigned under the name of Shrindravarman. Shortly after, in 1296 and 1297, an ambassador from China came to Angkor. One of his entourage was Zhou Daguan, the author of a famous account, *Report on the Customs of Cambodia*, which has been widely used as an aid to understanding the Khmers of that period. His testimony shows that the change of king must have been more dramatic an event than the inscriptions would have us believe. He wrote:

> The new prince is the son-in-law of the old sovereign. Originally he was in charge of leading the troops. The father-in-law loved his daughter; the daughter stole his golden sword and took it to her husband. The king's son was consequently deprived of the succession. He plotted to raise the troops, but the new prince heard about it, cut off his toes and consigned him to a dark chamber.

The "golden sword" is without doubt the famous Preah Khan, the sword that was the safeguard of the empire; a copy was carefully preserved until quite recently by the Brahmins of the royal palace of Phnom Penh.

Niches from which images of the Buddha have been cut out, the temple of Preah Khan.
During the reign of Jayavarman VIII, almost all figures of the Buddha were systematically removed. This example of iconoclastic folly was most unusual.
Photo: Guy Nafilyan

It is largely due to Zhou Daguan's account that we can envisage, to a certain extent, what life was like in the city of Angkor Thom. The Chinese visitor gives a lengthy eyewitness report of royal ceremonies.

> When the prince goes out, he is preceded by an escort of soldiers; then come the standards, the pennants, and music. Between three and five hundred palace maidens, dressed in fabrics decorated with foliage, and with flowers in their chignons, hold candles, and form a troop of their own; even in full daylight their candles are lit. Then come other palace maidens carrying the royal gold and silver utensils and a whole series of ornaments, all of very unusual design and whose purpose I do not know. Then came palace maidens holding spears and shields; they are the palace's private guard, and they too form a troop of their own. Afterwards come carts drawn by goats and carts drawn by horses, all of them decorated with gold. The ministers and the princes are all mounted on elephants; their innumerable red parasols can be seen from afar. After them come the king's wives and concubines, in palanquins, in carts, on horses, on elephants; certainly they have more than one hundred parasols flecked with gold. Behind them, there is the king, standing up on an elephant and holding in his hand the precious sword. The elephant's tusks are likewise sheathed in gold. There are more than twenty white parasols flecked with gold and with gold handles. Many elephants crowd around him, and here too there are troops to protect him.

> ... This shows that although it is a kingdom of barbarians, these people leave no doubt as to what a prince is. (*Report on the Customs of Cambodia* by Zhou Daguan, translated from the French of Paul Pelliot.)

However, there are many indications to show that this report does not entirely warrant the unquestioning trust that has been all too readily placed in it. There was a colony of Chinese people living at Angkor and they were the source of most of Zhou Daguan's information. More often than not, it seems, the events he reported, and which he claimed to have witnessed in person, were in fact stories that circulated within this group. He accepted their anecdotes unreservedly, since they were about these "barbarians." Thus he recounts this "extraordinary" incident:

> In the city, near the East gate, there was a barbarian who fornicated with his younger sister. They clung together with their skin and their flesh never separating and after three days with no nourishment, both died. My compatriot Mr Sie, who has spent thirty-five years in this country, states that he has seen this happen twice. If this is the case, the people of this country must know how to use the supernatural powers of the holy Buddha.

Likewise, it is odd that people have simply accepted without comment the chapter concerning the nights spent by the king on the top of the Phimeanakas, which clearly is based on a well-known legend:

> There is a golden tower, on the top of which lies the king. All the natives claim that in the tower there is a spirit that is a nine-headed serpent, master of the land of the whole kingdom. It appears every night in the form of a woman. The sovereign first lies with her, then unites with her.

It is easy to recognize here the legend of Soma as daughter of the king of the naga of the region. Moreover, the "master of the land of the whole kingdom" must be the *Devaraja* (the god king) and consequently there seems to have been an amalgamation of legends.

Long ago it was noticed that Zhou Daguan made a number of glaring errors concerning the geography of the capital, notably on the subject of the reservoirs. In spite of all this, though, his account still represents an invaluable document, with its variety of lively descriptions of the capital city and of the interior of the country, even if we do need to be rather more skeptical than we were with regard to the strict accuracy of the information. At the same time, the imaginative aspect of the anecdotes can be appreciated for its own sake, and it does give some idea both of how the Khmers lived and of the rather frightening impression they gave to foreigners.

Lastly, it is interesting to note that Zhou Daguan refers to the temple of Angkor Wat as the "tomb of Lou Pan." Lou Pan is an artisan in ancient Chinese legend. Clearly, already in this era the Khmers confused Vishnuloka, the posthumous name of King Suryavarman II, and Vishvakarman, an artisan god to whom is sometimes attributed the building of Angkor Wat. The latter name apparently stuck in the minds of the Chinese, and they linked it to their own legends. But this Chinese name for Angkor Wat would have remained totally inexplicable, like Funan and Chenla, had we not known the Khmer legends that clarify it.

The last, little-known kings

Shrindravarman was a Buddhist, but not of the same sect as Jayavarman VII. He was responsible for the earliest Pali inscription found in Cambodia, thus clearly marking the official adoption of the Buddhist "Lesser Vehicle," which probably came into this country under the influence of Thai kingdoms. The inscription bears the date 1309, two years after Shrindravarman had abdicated in favor of a prince of his line named Shrindrajayavarman, who reigned for 20 years without leaving any other trace.

In 1327 a new king, Jayavarma-Parameshvara, ascended the throne. His name is known to us through the very last Sanskrit inscription discovered at Angkor, not far from the northeast corner of the Angkor Wat moat. What he did during his reign, and when he died, are not known.

The different versions of the *Royal Chronicles*—the most important among the rare "historical" documents available to us now—all agree in giving 1431 as the date when the Khmer kings, under threat from the Thais, abandoned Angkor and went off to establish themselves in the Phnom Penh region. However, this date is far from certain and there is even some doubt about whether the kings abandoned Angkor at all: we do not have to believe these documents just because they are the only ones we have.

In fact, it is difficult to trust the *Royal Chronicles* in connection with this period of Khmer history. They were compiled in the 19th century on the basis of unpublished documents, and endeavor to produce a coherent history of the Khmers. Recent research by an American scholar, Michael Vickery, shows clearly that certain chapters had to be contrived when as was the case for this period, there was a lack of sources. Moreover, as Vickery has noted, given that the stories that describe the beginnings of the Khmer nation up to the 15th century are unanimously regarded as legends, it would be surprising if the chronicles became "historical" just when there were scarcely any more inscriptions to provide information.

The West's discovery of Angkor

About 1550 or 1551, as the king of Cambodia went on elephant hunts in the very dense forests which exist all over this kingdom, his people, when beating through the undergrowth, came upon some imposing buildings whose interiors were overgrown with luxuriant vegetation which they were unable to cut back sufficiently to penetrate any further. And when this was reported to the king, he went to the place himself; seeing the extent and the height of the external walls, he wanted to see inside, so he ordered immediately that all the undergrowth was cut down and burned. (Diogo do Couto, quoted by Bernard-Philippe Groslier in *Angkor et le Cambodge au XVIe siècle d'après les sources portugaises et espagnoles.*)

This is how, according to the Portuguese traveler and historian Diogo do Couto, writing at the end of the 16th century, the Khmers rediscovered their former capital. This rediscovery, which is related in varying degrees of detail in a number of Spanish and Portuguese accounts of the period, supports the frequently made assertion that the Khmers knew nothing about the origin of these ruins. One of them, for example, wrote: "It is astonishing that no natives of this kingdom live there, and that only wild and fierce animals inhabit this place. And these people traditionally believe that this city must have been built by foreigners."

The Spanish and Portuguese began to wonder about who really built Angkor, and came up with some quite extraordinary suggestions, such as Alexander the Great or the Roman emperor Trajan, and some even went as far as to imagine that this was the "fantastic city of Plato's Atlantis or that of his Republic." These ludicrous theories certainly did not come from the Khmers themselves, but they would not have been dreamt up had the latter not insisted on their ignorance of their own past, and in particular of these ruins.

In fact, this was not the case at all, as proved by some inscriptions dating from more or less the same time and carved on stone at Angkor Wat itself: they express the wish that a young king should govern Cambodia "like the ancient line of kings who built the great capital Indrapattha [Angkor Thom] and the noble Vishnuloka [Angkor Wat], as well as all the great strongholds throughout the Cambodian territory." It was in about the middle of the 16th century that the Khmer kings became interested in Angkor again. Between 1546 and 1564, Ang Chan, using artists who were clearly influenced by the Siamese art of Ayutthaya, had the 600 square meters or so of bas-reliefs carved in the north gallery (eastern portion) and in the east gallery (northern portion), which had not been decorated in the 12th century.

Ang Chan's grandson, Satha, lived at Angkor, probably even within the enclosure of Angkor Wat, but perhaps only for certain periods at a time. This king, an inscription states, "had 'the temple' restored to its true state as of old." This restoration work was rather clumsy in parts—such as when round columns were taken from the bottom of the temple and re-used in the courtyards of the top level, where they now stand rather awkwardly in the midst of square pillars. It was perhaps he who was responsible for transforming the central sanctuary of the temple into a sort of stupa, by sealing off the four doorways and sculpting the stones used for this purpose

Decorated praying man.
This magnificent 16th-century wooden statue was found at Angkor Wat. Overall height 92cm.
National Museum, Phnom Penh.
Photo: Luc Ionesco, EFEO

with large standing Buddhas. A number of magnificent statues in wood also must date from this period, notably the justly famous praying figure, discovered at Angkor Wat.

But Angkor Wat was not the only center of interest. Several sanctuaries at Angkor Thom were also altered and bas-reliefs were carved at the north end of the Terrace of Elephants, in the Preah Pithu, and at the monument without a name, known simply as "486"; other terraces were also built in this era. There was a certain taste for monumental sculpture: examples include the clothed Buddha at Tep Pranam, the reclining Buddha at the Baphuon, occupying the whole length of the west gallery of the third enclosure, and the seated Buddha of Phnom Bakheng, that seems to have been left unfinished. Phnom Kulen again became, if it had ever ceased to be, an important religious center and it was here that the great reclining Buddha was carved in rock at Preah Thom, in 1586. Its caves sheltered hermits, as in former times.

Economic renewal

However, Satha was not content with just restoring Angkor Wat and other temples. Most probably he tried to revive the whole region, in particular by ordering hydraulic works on a considerable scale. We know from Diogo do Couto that the canal system within Angkor Thom was functioning and that therefore it was being maintained. Moreover, the Eastern Baray to the east, Jayaviravarman's walls and those of Jayavarman VII's city, together with the Western Baray to the west, formed a long barricade that effectively closed off Angkor to the north for a length of some 20 kilometers, and it is likely that this caused serious flooding during the rainy season. It was no doubt in this era that a breach was made in Jayaviravarman's wall in order to allow the Siem Reap river to flow through. This river, which possibly had been diverted much earlier into the canals that irrigated the whole region north of the Eastern Baray, was by then flowing permanently along an old canal bed excavated between this reservoir and Angkor Thom. A bridge had to be built over this canal, the Spean Thma ("stone bridge"). It was made out of blocks of sandstone, many of which bore carved sculptures, having been taken from a post-Angkor temple, and this helps to date the bridge. However, the river here failed to stay within the banks of the canal, which certainly must have been designed for a much smaller and less forceful flow of water than it now had to take. Instead, the river deviated from the paved bed that had been laid under the piers of the bridge, and created a new, deep bed to the east of the bridge.

Spean Thma.
A bridge on the Siem Reap river, between the Gate of Victories at Angkor Thom and the temple of Ta Keo. The stones used for this bridge were taken from a sanctuary dating from the 13th century, so the bridge must have been built at the end of the 16th century, when Angkor was again occupied by the country's kings. *Spean thma* means simply "stone bridge."
Photo: Claude Jacques

Angkor Wat, center of pilgrimage in the 16th century

Not only did the sanctuary of Angkor Wat attract the interest of the Khmer kings, it seems that in the 16th century it enjoyed great renown as a holy place—yet the Spanish and Portuguese visitors were obviously unaware of this fact, too. It is known that at that time Angkor Wat was referred to in distant places as the *Jetavana*, the name of an important site connected with the life of the Buddha, near Shravasti in India. A map of Angkor Wat has even been found, drawn by a Japanese merchant at the beginning of the 17th century; this merchant had probably traveled from Ayutthaya, capital of Siam, attracted by the place's fame, and the map's legend indicates that he thought he was actually in India.

Subsequently Angkor Wat's great fame faded somewhat, but there is no reason to suppose that it has ever been completely forgotten. On the contrary, there is a later clue suggesting the great importance that the Khmers still attached to it. Queen Ang Mei, who was taken prisoner by the Vietnamese in about 1840, during a particularly dark period in Khmer history, had used the outline of the three famous towers of Angkor Wat on her personal seal.

The West's second discovery of Angkor

Dancers at the temple of Thommanon.
The presence of dancers, seen here in the temple of Thommanon, and who previously appeared at Angkor Wat, symbolizes the beginnings of a renaissance for Angkor.
Photo: Guy Nafilyan

Opposite
A pillar at Angkor Wat attacked by the fearsome thyo-bacillus which causes this disease of stone.
In some places, more than one-third is already lost.
Photo: Guy Nafilyan

The West, however, knew nothing at all about the Khmer ruins, having taken no notice of the reports by Spanish and Portuguese travelers. No mention was made of these in accounts written by the French who came to Ayutthaya at the end of the 17th century.

The first European to report the existence of the monuments of Angkor in the 19th century was not the famous botanist Henri Mouhot, as is often stated, but a French missionary, Father Bouillevaux, who was established at Battambang—at that time under Thai jurisdiction—and who in his memoirs, published in 1874, expressed a certain pique at having been thus supplanted.

> Before continuing, we wish to protest against certain examples of exaggeration and charlatanism. There are people who claim to have made important discoveries in Cambodia and elsewhere, but the majority of these fine discoveries have been known about for a very long time. Thus, for example, the pagoda of Angcor and the ruins of Angcor-Thôm were not found, as is said, by Mouhot, for the very good reason that they have never been either forgotten or lost. Previous missionaries knew them, and refer to them briefly. The Portuguese travelers of the 16th century visited them, and finally, certain 13th-century Chinese chroniclers mention them in their accounts, in a more or less clear fashion. Mouhot saw Angkor after several others, and in particular, after I did. His journey enjoyed great publicity and so he made this country known to many readers. The leaders of the Mekhong expedition, M. de Lagrée in particular, have made a special study of these monuments, and have given interesting descriptions of them. That is true… But let us not exaggerate any of this... (C.E. Bouillevaux, *Voyage dans l'Indochine* (1848-1856).)

It has to be said, however, that, although Father Bouillevaux did report at the time on the existence of these ruins, they had not interested him very much. For this reason it must be acknowledged that the part played by Henri Mouhot, from his journey of exploration in 1858 until his death in 1861, was of much greater significance than that of the missionary.

From that time on, explorers and then archaeologists continued to work on the monuments, seeking to uncover the secrets of the civilization that had created them. There is certainly still much work to be done, but we have come a long way. Let us hope that, in the near future, after the cataclysmic events the country has lived through, all the wonders of Angkor can be freely visited and revisited. This will, it is hoped, signal the rebirth of the Khmer people.

APPENDIX

ANGKOR AND THE ÉCOLE FRANÇAISE D'EXTRÊME-ORIENT

A 19th-century French mission among Khmer ruins. Engraving from *Voyage au Cambodge. L'architecture khmère* by Louis Delaporte (published by Delagrave, Paris 1880).

The name Angkor is inseparable from that of the École française d'Extrême-Orient, so closely have they been linked ever since the learned institution was established. It is not very easy, however, to assess the body of work that has been accomplished over the years. One has to turn to the descriptions written at the end of the last century and to the old photographs in order to see the Angkor monuments as they were, mostly hidden in the forest, buried or partly buried under masses of earth, and always covered with dense vegetation. It is also important to remember that for a long time archaeological missions had to operate with very little finance and very few men, and their living conditions were far from luxurious.

An archaeological commission for Indochina had been set up by the French government in 1898 at the instigation of French scholars; in January 1900 the commission became the École française d'Extrême-Orient. Of course, Khmer archaeology was not the institution's only field of research, but it has always been an important part of its work.

In 1863 Cambodia, threatened with being overrun by its two neighbors, Siam and the empire of Annam,

became a French protectorate. The Khmers' past history had become known during the 1860s, in Europe in particular, thanks to Henri Mouhot's expedition, which was sponsored by the Royal Geographical Society of London, and subsequently to the Mekong mission, which was led by Doudart de Lagrée, and whose object was to find a route into China along the great Mekong river. The reports that were published aroused keen interest in this previously little-known civilization and the new learned institution was able to benefit from the explorers' findings and also from scholarly research that was being carried out in Paris. However, at that time Angkor was under Siamese control and all that the École française d'Extrême-Orient could do was to send one or two relatively small study missions there. The most important of these was the one led by Dufour and Carpeaux, sent to study the Bayon temple and its bas-reliefs (Carpeaux, son of the sculptor Jean Baptiste Carpeaux, died at Angkor).

The first inventory of the monuments

Under the terms of the Franco-Siamese Treaty of 1907, the provinces of Battambang, Sisophon and Siem-Reap were returned to Cambodia. The way was finally clear for the École française d'Extrême-Orient to move in. Almost immediately, Commander Lunet de Lajonquière was sent on a mission to complete his monumental *Inventaire des monuments du Cambodge*, which he had started in 1900. At the same time it was decided to create the post of conservator of the monuments at Angkor; the first holder of this post, Jean Commaille, was a civil servant with a passion for Khmer art. He was officially appointed on 14 July 1908, having been at Angkor since the previous December to start the necessary work of clearing away undergrowth.

The very first monument that Jean Commaille tackled was Angkor Wat. The monument was in a particularly good state of preservation. For many centuries it had been held in high regard and so had been constantly occupied and relatively well maintained by the occupants of the Buddhist pagoda, which was inopportunely erected on the actual causeway, right in front of the monument. This pagoda had to be relocated, and the many trees hiding the temple were felled. It was also necessary to remove great quantities of earth that had been carried there by the wind but above all by people, for some purpose that is now inexplicable. The earth had accumulated on either side of the causeway, on the cruciform terrace—where it filled the four decorative pools—and on the courtyard of the second tier. Such accumulations of earth were also found elsewhere: for example, 20,000 cubic meters of earth had to be removed from the foot of the Terrace of Elephants.

Jean Commaille then turned to the Angkor Thom complex, and more precisely to the Bayon temple. There, too, the approach avenues and the area around the temples had first to be cleared of undergrowth, but also a number of towers that were in danger of collapsing had to be strengthened, as well as was possible. Together with this pioneering work, studies were made of the monuments, in as minute a detail as was then possible. At the same time, the idea of tourism began to be considered and, with this in mind, roadways were established inside the area now designated the "Angkor park," and in fact it is these roadways that are still in use today.

On 29 April 1916 Jean Commaille was murdered by thieves on the road from Siem-Reap to Angkor Wat. Today his remains lie at the foot of the Bayon temple, at a spot marked by a small memorial.

The work of Henri Marchal and Georges Trouvé

Commaille was replaced by Henri Marchal, an architect who was the inspector of civil buildings in Indochina. He had been in the region since 1905 and had already been involved with the Khmer monuments on several occasions. It is difficult to summarize this man's life in a few lines or to describe his total devotion to the Angkor temples, which he was never able to leave for good. He spent time at all the sites in the Angkor group, and at many others, tirelessly trying to fathom their secrets, making sketches, checking their condition. In addition to the work he carried out to reinforce numerous monuments—which has sometimes been criticized without allowances being made for the modest means at his disposal—he wrote several books and very many articles. These are still essential reading for an understanding of the Angkor monuments.

The last project he was in charge of before his retirement, and also his most spectacular, was the restoration, using the anastylosis method that had just been learned from the Dutch at Java, of the delightful temple of Banteay Srei. This was the temple that the French writer André Malraux had helped to make known when he plundered its sculptures some years earlier.

Although Marchal retired in July 1933, it was not until December 1937 that he left Cambodia for France—for good, he thought. In fact, at the end of the Second World War, he was invited to take part in an archaeological project at Pondicherry, and he accordingly went there in 1946. In 1948, following a serious accident that had occurred at Angkor Wat, he was persuaded to take charge again of the Conservation des Monuments d'Angkor for a few months. This was a period when Angkor was in an unsafe zone where few people were willing to go. Already aged 72, he was never to leave his adopted country again. He died at Siem-Reap, near his beloved monuments, on April 12 1970, at the age of 94, shortly before the outbreak of the cataclysmic events that were to engulf Cambodia with the installation of the Khmer Rouge regime.

In 1931 a young architect, Georges Trouvé, had become Marchal's deputy, and naturally took over as head of the Angkor Conservation when Marchal was due to retire. Trouvé was extraordinarily gifted and in the space of a few years accomplished some magnificent work of prospecting and making finds, especially around the Eastern Baray. However, one achievement has to be singled out: his discovery and extrication of Prasat Ak Yum, the first known temple-mountain, which had been almost entirely buried under the south embankment of the Western Baray.

Among his other works are the extrication of the temple of Pre Rup, begun by Henri Marchal, the extrication and restoration of the temple of Preah Ko in the Roluos group, and the excavations at the Bayon, which led to his discovery of the statue of the Buddha.

His accidental death at the age of 33, on 18 July 1935, was an incalculable loss for Khmer archaeology.

Archaeological research

In 1926 the young Philippe Sterne had called into question the whole existing chronology of the art of Angkor and this acted as a spur to further research. The scholar George Cœdès, Director of the École française d'Extrême-Orient, established a definitive chronological framework for the art of the Bayon temple. The archaeologist Victor Goloubew successfully showed that it was definitely not the Bayon temple that marked the center of the first city of Angkor, but Phnom Bakheng. Subsequently, together with Henri Marchal, he tried to find the boundaries of this city, carrying out numerous surveys, the first systematic surveys to have been made in this region. These did not always produce decisive results, but at least they did bring to light within the Angkor Thom enclosure a quantity of civil works that predated the construction of Jayavarman VII's capital city. At the same time, Goloubew and Marchal discovered a large part of the constructions that surrounded the ancient site of Phnom Bakheng, in particular the great avenue which led eastwards as far as the river. These investigations certainly would have been worth pursuing. Victor Goloubew was in fact the pioneer of aerial archaeological reconnaissance in Cambodia.

A little later, Pierre Dupont, a new member of the École, together with Philippe Stern undertook some investigations at Phnom Kulen in an attempt to learn about the beginnings of the Khmer empire.

After the death of Georges Trouvé, the architect Jacques Lagisquet was seconded to head the Conservation des Monuments d'Angkor for an interim period. He stayed in the post for over a year, until the arrival of Maurice Glaize, who got down to work at the end of 1936 and continued until 1945. Among his many projects at various monuments, Glaize carried out two quite remarkable restoration projects: Banteay Samre and, above all, the temple of Bakong, whose central sanctuary was completely in ruins. Most of it had fallen to the bottom of the pyramid, and the monks, wanting to build some wooden shrines on the top terrace, had cleared away all the fallen stones; patiently, stone by stone, Maurice Glaize managed to complete the feat of entirely rebuilding this tower.

The effects of the Second World War were of course felt at Angkor, but Glaize continued with his activities: it was during this period that he restored, most notably, the temple of Neak Pean and some of the sanctuaries at Preah Khan. The post-war period was in fact more difficult: Glaize had to return to France in 1945 and it was hard to replace him. There was a succession of conservators, all more or less transient and therefore unable to achieve any important work. Jacques Lagisquet, who had headed the Conservation in 1936, returned to the job for a time, and was followed in 1948 by the indefatigable Henri Marchal. Jean Boisselier, Conservator of the National Museum at Phnom Penh, took over the job for an interim period on various occasions, and in particular carried out the restoration of the terrace of the Sras Srang pool.

Assistance given to restoration of the monuments

Eventually the architect Jean Laur was appointed head of the Conservation in 1954, with the assistance of René Dumont for three years. In 1955, the French army made a major gift of civil engineering equipment to the Conservation des Monuments d'Angkor. This made it possible to undertake work on a much larger scale, a scale that would have been unthinkable before. For a long time, restoring the imposing temple of the Baphuon had been regarded as an essential task, but until then, makeshift repairs were all that could be done because of the lack of adequate technical means. The new equipment also meant that more projects could be started up simultaneously and so, as well as various projects at Neak Pean, Preah Khan, Pre Rup and others, restoration of the temple of Thommanon and of the south causeway at Angkor Thom was undertaken.

In 1956 the government of Cambodia signed a ten-year agreement with the École française d'Extrême-Orient entrusting the conservation of the Angkor monuments and of the National Museum to the French institution, as well as giving it exclusive rights of archaeological exploration on Cambodian territory.

In October 1959 Bernard-Philippe Groslier took charge of the Conservation des Monuments d'Angkor,

and he was to be the last French conservator. During his period in office several generous grants were made by both Khmer and French authorities.

Assisted first by Guy Nafilyan, then by Jacques Dumarçay, he continued working on the projects started by his predecessor: the south approach causeway at Angkor Thom and the temple of Thommanon. He completed work at these sites but unfortunately he did not have time to complete the huge restoration scheme at the Baphuon temple. However, he did carry out some major work on the west causeway at Angkor Wat, where it crosses the moat, and on the western banks of the Sras Srang pool.

He also completely restored Prasat Kravan, a particularly tricky task since this temple is brick-built and contains bas-reliefs sculpted in brick. He had the five towers rebuilt to a level as high as was possible without resorting to unreliable guesswork; he cleared the terrace where these towers stood, and which had been completely buried; then discovered the foundations of the east gopura and an ancillary building, which enabled the original layout to be worked out. He also uncovered several small brick temples standing to the north of Phnom Bakheng.

However, like all his predecessors, he was not content with just reconstructing the monuments. He had already done some excavations at the site of the royal palace of Angkor Thom in 1952 and again in 1957. In 1962 he excavated the area surrounding the southern group of Sambor Prei Kuk and a prehistoric site at Mimot in the province of Kompong Cham; then, in 1946, at Angkor itself, the western side of the Sras Srang pool. In 1969 and 1970 he extricated the area around the Terrace of the Leper King, discovering some interesting reliefs on the north side of the terrace. He also had some complete surveys made of the great complexes at Angkor: Angkor Wat, under the direction of Guy Nafilyan, and the Bayon temple, Phnom Bakheng and Ta Keo, under the direction of Jacques Dumarçay.

In 1966 a new agreement was signed, under whose terms, while the École française d'Extrême-Orient was to continue playing an important part, the royal Khmer government began to assume again the central role in conserving the country's historic monuments.

From March 1970, following the overthrow of Prince Sihanouk and the dreadful war that followed, Bernard-Philippe Groslier had the difficult task of closing down the various works in progress for an indefinite period. It was necessary to do this in such a way that work could be halted without endangering the monuments. The French team from the École, and all the Khmer workers from the Conservation, displayed admirable courage in achieving this goal. As far as possible the most interesting archaeological objects were taken to the National Museum at Phnom Penh where they would be safer, and others were given effective protection.

In this way the École française d'Extrême-Orient left the monuments of Angkor that they had looked after for more than 60 years.

Claude Jacques

Restoration of the Baphuon temple: realigning columns, the east causeway.
Photo: EFEO

THE ORIENTATION OF THE TEMPLES

The Khmer temple, as a general rule, has its main entrance opening to the east, and its axis follows an east–west alignment, reflecting the universe's solar cycle.

However, certain temples, and not least the important, depart from this rule. Koh Ker and the great Preah Khan in Kompong Svay, for example, open to the northeast and, in particular, Angkor Wat opens to the west.

Topographical conditions have been cited as the reason for these exceptions, but the fact that Angkor Wat faces the setting sun, for example, has nothing at all to do with the lie of the land, which here is absolutely flat, and is certainly not just by chance. It must, instead, be something to do with the idea of death—we still cannot be sure—or perhaps with the cult of Vishnu.

In Khmer architecture the orientation of temples is of fundamental importance, and is based on theology, cosmology, and astronomy rather than topographical considerations.

Also, their layout has been precisely described in numerous Indian treatises on architecture (*Mayamata, Manasara, Kamikagama, Ajitagama* and others). Only one of these treatises has been published in French translation: the *Mayamata*, translated, annotated and edited by Bruno Dagens. I shall draw on this work in explaining the method by which a temple's orientation was determined (it is interesting to note that the Roman architect Vitruvius uses more or less the same method to determine the cardinal points):

• first of all a flat, square space must be established, measuring one "fathom" (1.78 meters) on each side, and made level using the "water method"

• a post (which acts a gnomon or *sanku*) one cubit long (about 50 centimeters) is fixed vertically at the center of this space

• taking this gnomon as the center, a circle is drawn, its diameter being double the height of the gnomon, i.e. with a radius of one cubit (fig. 1)

1

• the point where the shadow of the gnomon touches the circle in the morning is marked (fig. 2)

2

• the point where the shadow of the gnomon touches the circle in the evening is marked (fig. 3)

3

• these two reference points are joined by a straight line, and this gives us the east-west direction (fig. 4)

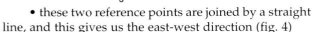

4

• taking these same two reference points as centers, two arcs of a circle are drawn; these two arcs intersect and form the shape of a fish (*matsya* in Sanskrit), which gives us the north–south direction.

5

The distance between the east-west line and the parallel line that passes through the center of the original circle varies according to the seasons; it is greatest at the solstices. This variation might explain what is referred to as the lateral displacement off the temple axis: the central sanctuary is scarcely ever situated in the exact geometric center of the enclosures that surround it. Unfortunately, we do not have sufficient knowledge at present to verify this hypothesis.

The same method governs the layout of temples that are clearly oriented towards the north, south, or west.

On the other hand, we currently have no definite theories to explain why some temples face towards the intermediate points of the compass. It has been suggested that in these cases in particular, the orientation was in fact determined by material reasons such as topography—for example the surface contours of the site. This is very unlikely, as we have already seen, because religious considerations, founded on mythology (relating to the divinities belonging to the temple or to the locality and so on) or on cosmology (astronomical and astrological positions and directions) were certainly of much greater importance. The choice of area and precise site was itself determined by a prior study in which soothsayers, priests, architects, and certainly also the benefactors all played a part. But this does not mean, of course, that topographical considerations were not intelligently taken into account. Further study of the relevant texts is needed and it is to be hoped that a close study of the inscriptions will fill the gaps in our knowledge of Khmer civilization.

René Dumont

THE SANCTUARY:
The typical Khmer building

A square sanctuary with pilasters and a single doorway in a projecting structure.

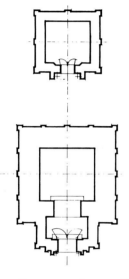

Square sanctuary, with projecting chamber forming a vestibule.

Plans drawn by René Dumont

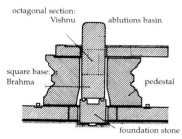

cylindrical summit: Shiva

octagonal section: Vishnu — ablutions basin

square base: Brahma — pedestal

foundation stone

A lingam. *Photo by Guy Nafilyan and drawing of vertical section based on one drawn by Maurice Glaize*

The sanctuary is the central building of the Khmer temple, at once a shelter for the temple's divinity and a center of the cosmological representation.

There are two typical layouts:

• the simple, square sanctuary, facing in four directions

• the composite sanctuary, which has in addition to the above layout an antechamber that gives it an axis along a single direction.

Architecture

The sanctuary comprises at least a main body, cubic in shape, set on a foundation with one or several levels, and topped by a superstructure. From the bottom upwards, it consists of the following:

A stone FOUNDATION: built of sandstone or laterite, this separates the temple from the ground and forms a kind of insulating course. Apart from the steps that make up the first flight, there is no decoration here.

BASE: this is really the pedestal of the temple, varying in height, and with powerful molding which, in the classical era, is rigorously symmetrical on either side of a central torus, or ring. This torus, varying in sectional profile, is often decorated with lotus petals that always point upwards.

Sometimes the base comprises two or more levels, forming a tiered pyramid. This is the type of temple that Philippe Stern defines as a "temple-mountain."

PLATFORM: the base carries the platform (which some authors call a bahut or plinth) on which the sanctuary (or each sanctuary) stands; the platform is also molded and has a stairway of several steps.

The SANCTUARY is generally square in plan and approximately (or in some cases exactly) cubic in volume. More than a chamber surrounded by walls, it is a mass of masonry in which there is a cavity, the cella, which houses the central idol, the divinity. This cavity is called *garbha griha* in Sanskrit: the hollow of the matrix. The inside walls usually have no decoration.

The central idol can be simply a statue of the divinity placed on a pedestal; but since the majority of temples are Shivaite, most often this idol is a lingam, or phallus. The lingam rests on a cubic stone, which has 17 cavities hollowed out of its top surface: one large central cavity surrounded by 16 small ones. These cavities contained small quantities of various substances, precious metals, semiprecious stones, seeds... this is the "semen" (bija) of the divinity, and thus of the temple. The lingam, planted in its pedestal, received liquids for ablutions which, having run down the lingam, were collected on a stone slab into which a shallow basin and an overflow lip had been cut. From there the liquids ran along a channel hollowed out of a stone that was set

into the paving of the cella, passed through the wall and from a kind of spout spread out into the ground outside. This ritual arrangement is not universal but is found frequently, particularly in the earliest Khmer architecture.

The cella was closed in at the top either by a wooden ceiling or a canopy that separated the interior arrangements of the cella from the upper part of the edifice, and so concealed the often rather crude inner structure just above the cella.

The SUPERSTRUCTURE is the "covering" of the sanctuary. It consists of an ensemble of tiers, diminishing in size from bottom up (three, four or five tiers, but rarely more). Each of these tiers (or rather, false tiers) more or less reproduces the parts of the body of the sanctuary, on a much smaller scale vertically, and markedly less so horizontally.

On top of these tiers, a motif similar in shape to a vase, or a lotus flower, crowns the sanctuary. There are indications to suggest that a metallic point (or trident?) topped the sanctuary's silhouette.

Inside, it can be seen that the construction of these diminishing tiers was achieved by means of horizontal levels of brick or stone, according to which was used in the building, each one placed further out of plumb, and either forming a continuous sloping line, or else a broken line composed of sloping and vertical surfaces. This produces either a concave pyramid with a very sharply angled profile, or else a succession of drums, square in section, joined together by shafts. In the early period, the interior surfaces were generally very well finished, the bricks given a smooth and even polished finish. This tradition was carried on for a certain time, but in the last period of Khmer art, the inner surfaces of the corbeled vaults were no longer finished and instead consisted of rough blocks of masonry. This unrefined appearance was concealed by the wooden ceilings.

The sanctuary's façade

Philippe Stern and his school were able to establish a chronology of Khmer architecture by studying the ways in which the shapes of the façades changed over time. This led to an important revision of the existing chronology of Khmer monuments. We will not go back over the various points that are now well established, nor over the method that Stern called the "evolution of motifs method," because they are explained in works written by Stern himself, by Gilberte de Coral-Rémusat and Jean Boisselier, and by scholars whom they influenced.

The study of Khmer art has concentrated above all on classifying the forms of architectural decoration, which include:

• the ensemble of elements framing the door, which I shall call the portal

• the actual mural decorations, comprising niches housing the figures, and all the decorations on the wall surfaces framing the portals

• the profile of the molding of the bases and the decoration on these moldings

• the profiles of the cornices and bases, both of the main body of the sanctuary and of the diminishing tiers.

The main element of the sanctuary façade is the portal, which comprises:

1. The door frame, an ensemble of interlocking moldings.

2. The two decorated columns, one on either side of the door; the type of decoration on these columns, and the number of elements in the decorations, are an important aid to dating the structure.

3. The "decorated" lintel, the most important element, because often the age of the monument can be determined solely through a study of the motifs used on the lintel.

This ensemble, comprising door frame, lintel and columns, is in turn framed by:

4. The pilasters, which have a base (in many cases the same as that of the whole monument) and a capital, generally representing the cornice of the body of the sanctuary, which is the contour of the base stood upright: between base and capital, on the flat surface of the pilaster, there is distinctive and often very ornate decoration.

It should be noted that there is no contour and no decoration on the sides facing the door: the pilasters' inside surfaces are always cut cleanly, and left bare.

5. Above this ensemble is the pediment, which comprises two parts:

• The arch of the pediment, which assimilated Indian influences in the early centuries and is one of the most characteristic motifs in Khmer art. The evolution of the Khmer pediment over the centuries follows a clear line of development.

• The tympanum of the pediment, decorated either with plant motifs, with or without figures, or else with actual bas-reliefs, some of them masterpieces of Khmer sculpture. They include above all the tympanums at Banteay Srei, but also those of Preah Vihear at Angkor Wat, of Banteay Samre, or of Beng Mealea.

6. Finally, there is another very important decorative element on the portal: the false door. Even though the true doors with their wooden leaves have long since disappeared, the custom of representing false doorways on three sides of the sanctuary means that the design and decoration of doors have been preserved.

Buildings that are not sanctuaries copy the latter's decoration. Their doorways are similar, as also are many of their pediments. However, their superstructures are different and the galleries are covered with corbeled vaults, creating an image of roofs of decorated concave tiles.

There are various types of window in the annexes of the sanctuary (but never in the main body of the sanctuary itself) and in all the other types of building:

• windows with bars: the stone bars over the openings are carefully turned

• windows without bars, particularly in the entrance porches.

However there are also the very distinctive false windows, which can be:

• blind windows, with the wall lying behind real stone bars (sometimes referred to as balusters), as carefully finished and set as if they were protecting a real opening

• blind windows with semi-bars cut in the masonry. To save time, the Khmers subsequently invented:

• windows with partial bars: the upper part of the window is flat and decorated with small flowers and has a draw cord engraved in the stone

• and finally, windows with only an imitation curtain decorated with small flowers and draw cord.

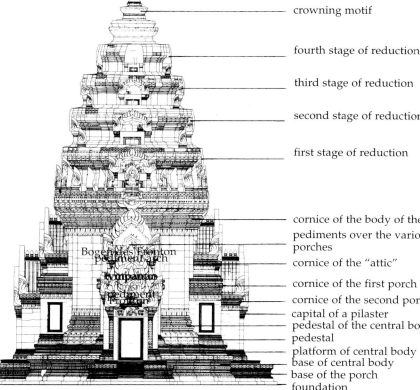

crowning motif

fourth stage of reduction

third stage of reduction

second stage of reduction

first stage of reduction

cornice of the body of the sanctuary
pediments over the various porches
cornice of the "attic"
cornice of the first porch
cornice of the second porch
capital of a pilaster
pedestal of the central body
pedestal
platform of central body
base of central body
base of the porch
foundation

Central sanctuary of Phimai, south side.
Drawing by Pierre Richard, EFEO

This humorous aspect of Khmer decoration is yet another indication of the nature of Khmer architecture as "image." The statue is the image of the god, in the center of temple that represents the cosmos, and where a window was needed as part of the overall design, it was enough—during the period of feverish construction under Jayavarman VII—simply to carve the image of a window.

The antechamber must have been intended for special rituals, or perhaps it housed the mythical "mount" of the central god, for example a statue of the bull Nandi.

The central sanctuary of Banteay Srei, one of the finest examples of Khmer architecture, belongs to this category, as does the central sanctuary of Preah Vihear. But the best image is that of Prasat Khna Seng Keo, an 11th-century temple, in the style of the Baphuon, studied by Henri Parmentier in his *Art khmer classique*. The ground plan of the sanctuary is very clear, with its double annexes on the north, west and south sides and, on the east, linked by a cylindrical chamber with false windows (but with real stone bars) to the antechamber (called *mukhasala* or *mandapa*, according to various authors).

This antechamber is cruciform in plan and is covered by a groin vault over its central crossing. It also has a false story, a kind of simply shaped attic, which can be clearly seen in section.

The architectural composition of the sanctuary with an antechamber is found frequently in Khmer art, and the finest example is that of Wat Ek in Battambang province, of which, unfortunately, we do not have a good detailed description. It is all the more regrettable that, while all the other examples relate to "level" temples, or those with a linear layout, such as Wat Phu and Preah Vihear, the Wat Ek sanctuary is placed on high tiers and is the only temple-mountain with an antechamber.

René Dumont

THE STYLES OF KHMER ART

The evolution of style in art follows the same course as the life of human beings and of all living things: youth, maturity, old age. An artistic tradition displays different characteristics as it passes from one period of its "life" to the next, even when religious or social rules constrain the artist to such an extent that it seems the only kind of creative activity possible is to copy previous models. Khmer art provides one of the clearest examples of stylistic evolution.

At one time it was seen as falling into two main periods: primitive Khmer art and classical Khmer art. Subsequently, when the term "primitive" came to be regarded as pejorative, "classical" was replaced by "Angkor" and the history of Khmer art was then divided into three periods: pre-Angkor, Angkor, and post-Angkor. The latter relates to everything dating from after Angkor, in other words from about the 14th century up to modern times, and will not be considered here, not because it is uninteresting, but because it has only just begun to be studied.

The main periods were subdivided either by century, for example 10th-century Khmer art, or by ruler, for example the art of Indravarman, Yashovarman, or the various kings named Jayavarman (principally Jayavarman II, IV, V and VII). This emulated the system used in the West for designating chronological periods, but though it works well for European history, where the chronology of kings and institutions is firmly established, it does not adapt well to a history that is still being written, and that is constantly being modified as new discoveries are made.

Khmer art evolved in response to four principal types of innovatory influence:
• invention (though, as the French scholar Gilberte de Coral-Rémusat has observed, "the creative spark was quite rare")
• the contribution of art from outside (principally India, but also Indonesia and Champa)
• borrowings from styles of the past, a consciously "historical" style in which not only was the immediately preceding style copied, but much older themes were sought out and reintroduced, though with such definite modifications that there was a clear distinction between the original and the new version
• the imitation of different techniques, the best known being the imitation of decorations on light wooden constructions; the quality of the decoration in the Preah Ko style owes much to the copying of decorations in lime mortar, which are often inaccurately referred to as "stucco" decorations.

Having studied a number of architectural and decorative characteristics, Philippe Stern and Gilberte de Coral-Rémusat compiled a list of 13 styles, each of them named after the most important or best-known monument displaying the relevant characteristics. With regard to sculpture, Jean Boisselier and Pierre Dupont suggested adding two more styles: the Phnom Da style, as first in the list, and then that of Prasat Andet, in between the Prei Kmeng and Kompong Preah styles. Finally, Philippe Stern himself subdivided the latter style into three periods. (The style of Pre Rup [961] and of Banteay Srei [967] have been regarded by some

authors as one and the same, given their closeness in time, but because the art of Banteay Srei is of such outstanding quality, I prefer to regard it as a style on its own, even though it is the sole example.)

Altogether, then, we now have a list of 15 styles in Khmer art:
• Phnom Da, from the 6th century to the early 7th century
• Sambor Prei Kuk, first half of 7th century
• Prei Kmeng, 7th century, about 635 to 700
• Prasat Andet, almost contemporary with Prei Kmeng
• Kompong Preah, essentially 8th century
• Kulen, 9th century, about 825 to 875
• Preah Ko, late 9th century
• Bakheng, late 9th century, early 10th
• Koh Ker, first half of 10th century, about 921 to 944
• Pre Rup, mid-10th century
• Banteay Srei, 967
• The Khleangs, late 10th century, early 11th
• Baphuon, mid- to late 11th century
• Angkor Wat, 12th century, about 1100 to 1175
• Bayon, late 12th century, early 13th century, about 1177 to 1230. This style lasts through three periods, as defined by Philippe Sterne in his great work *Les Monuments khmers du style du Bayon et Jayavarman VII*.

These numerous subdivisions should not be seen as a strict compartmentalization of Khmer art but on the contrary as elements of a continuous development with wide fluctuations. Also, there is inevitably some overlapping, especially between styles of the earliest era, and local artistic traditions sometimes must have had an influence, whether archaic or innovatory. The subject of local artistic schools has been referred to by some authors, and it would be worth investigating their possible influence.

The styles listed above can be grouped together in wider time spans corresponding to the three ages of Angkor civilization.

First the early age, when pre-Khmer or pre-Ankor art was developing out of various elements from India, introduced through texts and models brought by travelers. This art is referred to as primitive, but right from the outset it produced some masterpieces of astonishing architectural and sculptural perfection.

The following styles belong to this early period:
• Phnom Da, with some wonderful statues
• Sambor Prei Kuk, with sculpture of the same quality and extremely elaborate architectural compositions
• Prei Kmeng, together with Prasat Andet; the sculpture includes some masterpieces such as the Hari-Hara at Prasat Andet, but the architectural remains are fewer and of poorer quality
• Kompong Preah, which has been described as lacking in quality, yet it has some lintels that are beautiful in the simplicity of their composition and quality of their carving.

The next period has to be considered on its own. It is represented by the Kulen style, which corresponds roughly to the exceptionally long reign of Jayavarman II, from 802 to 850, with his four successive capital cities (Indrapura, Hariharalaya, Amarendrapura, Mahendraparvata) and his numerous foundations, particularly at Phnom Kulen. This style, and this period, are characterized by intense activity and a burgeoning of experiments and new solutions, drawing inspiration from both the past and from features copied from the art of foreign countries, mainly Champa and Indonesia. What is perhaps the first temple-mountain to have been built, at Krus Aram Rong Chen, belongs to this period.

Angkorian art proper, dating from the 9th century to the 13th, can be subdivided into three periods:

• a pre-classical period, grouping the styles of Preah Ko, Bakheng and Pre Rup, from the 9th century to the middle of the 10th, leaving aside Banteay Srei and its particular style (which is both the culmination of the early development stage and at the same time an example of the perfection that a work of art can attain, transcending all notions of classicism)

• a classical period, from the middle of the 10th century to the middle of the 13th, including the styles of the Khleangs, the Baphuon temple, and Angkor Wat

• a post-classical period. This term is inadequate, and it would be better to describe it as the era and style of the Bayon, since the style of the Bayon is to Khmer art what late Gothic is to the Middle Ages, and the Baroque or the Rococo to the Neo-classical age. One is reluctant to describe these three periods as periods of artistic "decadence."

The Sambor Prei Kuk Style

Leaving aside the style of Phnom Da, which has been designated only for the purpose of classifying its sculptures, which are in fact very fine, it is the style of Sambor Prei Kuk which marks the beginning of Khmer art in the 7th century, in all three artistic domains: architecture, sculpture and decoration.

A very important ensemble of monuments at Sambor Prei Kuk, in the province of Kompong Thom, comprises several groups of temples, one of which, the central group, is of a later date than the others. The other groups—south and north, and not counting the temples that stand alone—all belong to the 7th century. Beside these two early groups, north and south, a huge reservoir has been discovered through an aerial survey, proving that hydraulic systems (for agricultural purposes, but based on symbolic principles) had already been developed by that date.

The south group, around an important central sanctuary with a rectangular ground plan, consists of five secondary sanctuaries, which unusually are octagonal in plan. In front of the central sanctuary, standing alone but linked to it by a causeway raised on small pillars which were discovered during excavations, there is a special sanctuary housing a stone platform that once supported a statue of the bull Nandi. An enclosure formed by a very thick wall surrounds this ensemble. This wall has a decoration, left unfinished, consisting of large circular medallions carved in the brick. The enclosure is entered through gopura, which have collapsed.

The north group likewise is enclosed by a wall, but with simple doorways. Here the central sanctuary is square in plan, with two successive annexes on each of the four sides and with four doorways, which was exceptional for the period. The sanctuary is raised above the rest of the group, standing on a terrace at whose corners there were formerly four very small temples; this composition foreshadows the temple-mountain.

Lintel at Sambor Prei Kuk, Prasat Sandam.
Photo: René Dumont

The decorative elements of this style are very characteristic. Lintels in the Sambor Prei Kuk style comprise:

• A horizontal element: an arch, flat in profile and formed by two or four carved arcades; it has a large medallion in the center and, sometimes, two smaller ones in its "quarters" (lintels were often divided into four sections.

• At both ends a *makara* (a sea monster with a trunk) faces inwards, standing up on two feet, its tail raised in the shape of highly decorative volutes. These facing *makara* carry small riders on their backs and from their mouths they spit out small lions, at the same time as "swallowing" the end of the arch. This positioning of *makara*, facing inwards, gave rise to the term "converging movement," used to convey the style that is typical of lintels of this period. Garlands and pendants hang from the arch, and small leaves stand up above it. The *makara* are placed on what Philippe Stern called "consoles." These in fact are the abacuses of the columns—or rather, representations of them because, as can be seen, this is really the image of an arch resting on two columns, framing the entrance doorway to the sanctuary.

The columns of this style are very simple. Frequently small, they are round (cylindrical and turned) and they have a capital, a middle ring, and a base. Among the series of moldings on the capital is a fairly large torus (convex molding) called a "bulb" or turban. It is reminiscent of Indian columns and pillars, which themselves were inspired by capitals at Persepolis in ancient Persia. As a result of misunderstanding or ignorance, this "bulb" is also found in the molding of the base, where it does not belong at all. Beneath the last molding on the capital, there are garlands alternating with pendants; small triangular leaves hang in the garlands.

Much of the rest of the decoration has disappeared, but nevertheless it is possible to see that the pediments were in the shape of an upside-down U and the tympanum contained an image of buildings sculpted in progressive diminution: "flying palaces."

The exterior wall decoration is also made up of other, larger images of "flying palaces," many of them showing the personages who are housed in the interior. All this decoration carved in brick was at one time coated with limewash.

In this era most of the buildings were of brick, except for their lintels, columns, and doorframes, which were all of stone. There were also a few buildings that were entirely of stone: sandstone, or even vacuole basalt, known for its hardness.

The Prei Kmeng Style

The style of Prei Kmeng, which spans the second half of the 7th century, survives only in some ruined temples; these are fairly numerous, however, and though not of great importance in themselves, are noteworthy for their lintels and columns.

The lintel in this style comprises, horizontally, either two or four arcades forming an arch that is flat in profile, or else a horizontal band which curves inwards at either end. In the center, sometimes in the quarters, and at the ends, clusters of plant motifs positioned vertically produce what has been termed a "static movement." Sometimes figures are superimposed on these clusters of plant motifs.

The columns are the same as those of the previous style, except that they have moldings, in particular beneath the garlands and pendants, and the decoration inside the garlands is more varied.

Kulen style. Lintel at Damrei Krap.
Photo: René Dumont

The Kompong Preah Style

The style of Kompong Preah is best represented, as far as architecture is concerned, by Prasat Phum Prasat and Prasat Kompong Preah. The towers here are still built of brick, but neither has any "flying palaces."

The lintels are the most characteristic element in this style. Described as unremarkable, they are simple in design, but of great quality because of the richness of their sculpted reliefs. The decoration consists of a simple and magnificent roll of foliage with horizontal branches, resting at either end on a leaf scroll, with upright leaves above and large upturned leaves below. The central motif also consists of plant motifs, but closer inspection reveals the face of a monster, where later the head of a *kala* or *rahu* appears. The "consoles" or abacuses are still clearly defined. Modifications to this roll of foliage would later give rise to a whole host of lintel decorations based on leafy branches, in other words, of the type found on practically all lintels in Khmer art.

The columns, always cylindrical, are ornate, with bands encircling them, especially in the form of a continuous succession of small flowers whose horizontal petals touch each other. The garlands and pendants under the capital are replaced by upturned leaves.

The pediments, which in the temple of Kompong Preah are very well preserved, are in the shape of an upside-down U and their tympanums contain the images of three buildings in progressive diminution.

Kompong Preah style. Lintel at Phum Prasat.
Photo: René Dumont

The Kulen Style

The style of Kulen corresponds broadly to the exceptionally long reign of Jayavarman II (802-850). This king, who had four different capital cities, the precise locations of which are unknown, was responsible for numerous foundations spread over a wide area. However, the most important and at present the best-known group is on the plateau of Phnom Kulen, northeast of what was later to become Angkor.

It was a period teeming with new projects, some innovatory, some inspired by the past. Some were based on foreign ideas: for example, on the plateau of Phnom Kulen, there are two temples that display more of Cham art than of Khmer art.

The architecture of the Prasat Damrei Krap ensemble belongs to the Champa tradition. Only the main "portal," on the principal façade, with its columns, lintel, pediment, and pilasters, is a product of Khmer art. The lintel seems to have been inspired by the Sambor Prei Kuk model but with some fundamental differences:

• the arch is replaced by a roll of foliage
• the *makara* at the ends, facing inwards, have four feet (instead of two)
• the pendants and garlands are enormous and contain a leaf scroll.

The horizontal element of the other lintels at Phnom Kulen is sometimes a roll of foliage derived from the Kompong Preah model, or sometimes the arch with four carved arcades like that at Sambor Prei Kuk, and sometimes a hybrid version combining the two types. In the center, there is always a motif showing a figure: *kala*, *garuda*, or some other class of supernatural being.

To sum up, all the elements of earlier styles are to be found in this one, but used in a different way, which distinguishes them from their predecessors. At the same time, this style shows early signs of what was later to become the most common type of decoration on Khmer lintels. As Gilberte de Coral-Rémusat wrote:

A new type of movement, the beginnings of which are seen in the Kompong Preah style, takes shape and becomes firmly established in that of Kulen; this is divergent dynamism, radiating outwards from the lintel's central motif. The motifs at either end of the lintel open outwards and the secondary motifs follow in the same direction. This divergent dynamism continued to be a characteristic of lintels right to the end of Khmer civilization.

During this same period, the column also undergoes noticeable changes. At first there are the usual round columns, but also some surprising square columns, which are found only in the Kulen style. Then octagonal columns make their first appearance; these are to become the absolute norm, apart from a few rare examples of a return to the round column (at the Bakong and at Banteay Srei).

The Preah Ko Style

After the Kulen style comes the beginning of Angkor art proper. This comprises several styles: the pre-classical styles of Preah Ko, Phnom Bakheng, Koh Ker and Pre Rup; and the classical styles of Banteay Srei, the Khleangs, the Baphuon, and Angkor Wat.

The style of Preah Ko, which lasted for the duration of Indravarman's reign, includes a series of foundations which have been precisely dated: the Indratataka reservoir built in 877; Preah Ko, the temple-monastery built on the level, in 879; and above all the Bakong temple, the first temple-mountain built of sandstone, in 881. Certain decorative elements of this era are of a quality that is sometimes equaled but rarely surpassed—the lintels in the Preah Ko style are the most beautiful in the whole of Khmer art.

In the Roluos group—Preah Ko, Bakong, and Lolei (893)—all the elements of Angkor Khmer art are already present: temple built on the level, temple-mountain, concentric enclosures with their gopura (entrance pavilions), libraries, long halls (which foreshadow the galleries), moats, and pools. There are lintels, columns, pilasters, pediments, *devata* in niches, *dvarapala*, and even an example of a large bas-relief. All these elements now start to evolve, more or less step-by-step.

The lintel is the most notable element in the Preah Ko style, where it appears in its most complete form. Starting from this type, the lintel was to evolve above all through the progressive disappearance of its components (see diagram).

If the design of the lintel is simplified, and reduced to a diagram, its parts can be enumerated as follows:
1. Horizontal element (arch or branch of foliage)
2. Central element
3. End elements
4. Quarter divisions (not always present)
5. Upper elements (above the branch)
6. Lower elements (under the branch)
7. "Consoles," or abacuses
8. A lower band linking the abacuses
9. An upper band

For a description of the lintels at Preah Ko, I again turn to Gilberte de Coral-Rémusat: "The horizontal branch of foliage, which is sometimes straight and sometimes wavy, now becomes a definitive element, at the expense of the arch; it opens outwards, either in *makara* heads, or in naga heads, either in scrolls of up-turned foliage or, more rarely, in some other motif dictated by the artist's imagination. Under the branch, the scrolls of foliage from now on appear on their own; the garlands have disappeared, the pendants are still sometimes there but, more often, they too have disappeared."

The evolution—and the variation—of each of these elements helps to date the construction:

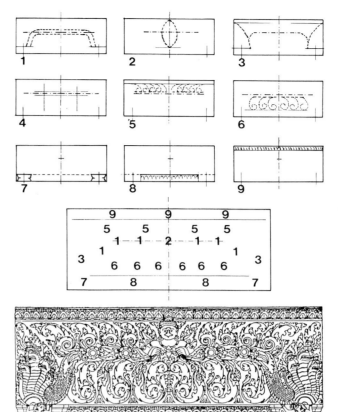

1. The branch of foliage is in reality a "metamorphosis" of the whole lotus plant: rhizome, stems, roots, leaves in various stages of growth, and sometimes flowers and fruits as well. This branch tends to move downwards progressively, sometimes its middle part being bent down, sometimes the whole branch being moved down and, in the final period of Khmer art, the lintel that Phillipe Sterne called "without branch" is in reality a lintel where the branch has reached the bottom and is represented by a succession of leaf scrolls, the up-turned leaves having become volutes.

A schematic representation of the decorative elements of lintel. Typical example of the Preah Ko style (element no. 4, divisions into four, is not found in this style).
Drawings and photo by René Dumont

177

2. The choice of motifs that enliven the central motif is varied: *kala* or *rahu*, *garuda*, *Indra* on the three-headed elephant, various divinities, the lotus, and sometimes complete scenes.

3. The end motifs—*makara*, naga, foliage—hardly follow the downward movement, because they always rest on the columns, initially with pseudo-abacuses in between, and later a simple shelf projecting from the lower decorative band. Finally, the lintel of the last period rests directly on the tops of the columns.

4. The quarter divisions appear and disappear from one period to another, but only rarely are they an accurate indication of the lintel's date.

5. The leaves above the branch follow the general movement of the whole composition, to the point where, together with the leaf scroll at the bottom of the lintel, they constitute the most important part of the decoration.

6. The upturned leaves under the roll of foliage appear always to be similar, but the artists' skill has created them in extraordinary variety, despite the apparent uniformity of their general outline. The principal variation in the Angkor Wat style and in that of the Bayon temple concerns what Stern called the "thong branch, with repeated breaks," where the central branch merges and intermingles with the upturned leaves.

7. The "consoles," or pseudo-abacuses of the columns gradually become less important as the centuries pass: they are well defined as abacuses at Sambor Prei Kuk and in the styles that followed, up to the Preah Ko style; at the end of the 9th century, at the Bakheng and at Koh Ker, they become less obvious. In the Pre Rup style, they have become no more than a shelf under the central motif. This lower band subsequently disappears entirely.

8. The band linking the abacuses depends upon their presence. It can be completely bare and smooth when the abacuses are strongly defined, but as the latter begin to be erased, it gains in importance. Equilibrium is reached when a single continuous decorative band runs under the whole length of the lintel with shelves resting directly over the two columns, and another shelf in the middle, as if supporting the central motif. This lower band subsequently disappears completely.

9. The upper band, bare or decorated, makes a line enclosing the whole composition. Although practically a permanent feature, only the Preah Ko style gives it prominence. Its presence seems to be linked to a tenth element: the decorative band superimposed above the lintel. This band which, at Preah Ko, seems attached to the lintel, becomes the lower element of the pediment.

In the Preah Ko style, the columns are still cylindrical. However, except for some at Banteay Srei, from now on they are to become octagonal. It was soon realized that cutting the unseen surface was unnecessary, so the columns are actually seven-sided, while still appearing to be eight-sided.

The "bulb" still appears in the capitals of the columns and, curiously, often in the base as well. The number of ribs increases, as does the number of leaves on each face of the octagon. Sometimes there are pendants but in certain cases these point upwards: this paradox indicates a misunderstanding of the original model from which they were copied.

The pediments are in the shape of an upside-down U and are sometimes formed by three curved sections. They are very high. The trend is towards the shape of a dentated arch with several curves.

The Bakheng and Koh Ker Styles

The style of the Bakheng (late 9th, early 10th century) coincides with one of the most important events in the history of the Khmer kingdom: the foundation by King Yashovarman of the first city of Angkor, under the name Yashodharapura. In the middle of the new city, on a natural hill, the king was to erect a temple-mountain in the form of a tiered pyramid, in the middle of an immense square four kilometers a side. Earlier he had excavated, or rather, constructed, an immense reservoir, the Yashodharatataka, seven kilometers long by 1,800 meters wide. Among many other of this king's foundations there was Lolei, the temple dedicated to his ancestors which he erected in 893, in the middle of the reservoir built by his predecessor.

The style of this period is displayed in grandiose architectural creations, chief among them Phnom Bakheng, but the decoration has become meagre, and in particular there are fewer reliefs carved in sandstone.

The style of Koh Ker belongs to the first half of the 10th century. It developed, under the reign of Jayavarman IV, from about 921 to 944, a long way from Angkor: about 100 kilometers to the northeast in a region which today is arid and unfertile, where the king built an enormous group of monuments.

In both these styles, the lintels have become much more poorly decorated, having lost the small figures that proliferated on them during the Preah Ko style. However, at Koh Ker, a certain liveliness returns, with quite significant scenes forming the central motif. The middle of the branch is bent, initiating the general movement downwards. Often the two central scrolls of leaves pointing downwards are tied with a cord. This feature is characteristic of the 10th century and continues into the beginning of the 11th century.

On the columns, the number of rings and leaves continues to multiply. The small leaves on the corner get bigger, and then there are one leaf and two identical half-leaves on each face of the column.

The sides of the pediments, still in the shape of an inverted U but with multiple segments, at the Bakheng temple have begun to curve, but it is in the Koh Ker style that multi-curved pediments, so characteristic of Khmer art, first appear. Also at Koh Ker, the first triangular pediments are found, a translation in stone of the wooden pediments of the gallery roofs (tiles on timber frames). This form is also sometimes found on the entrance pavilions, but never on the sanctuaries.

Lintel at Prasat Kraham (Koh Ker group).
Photo: Guy Nafilyan

The Pre Rup Style

The Pre Rup style (second half of 10th century) marks the return of the royal seat to the city of Yashodharapura, that is, to Angkor, the creation of an "Eastern city" and a return to the past in terms of certain architectural and decorative features. However, there is also a definite move forwards, displayed in particular in the two great temples in this style, the Eastern Mebon (953) and Pre Rup itself (961).

The return to the past is displayed in copies of lintels in the Roluos group, but above all in the fact that the sanctuaries of these two temples are built of brick and that they were originally covered with decorations modeled in lime mortar as at Roluos (Bakong and Preah Ko). There are traces of these decorations at Pre Rup, in the form of silhouettes of *devata*, made out of a multitude of mortar pellets.

The discovery of what appeared to be two temple-mountains built close to each other during the same reign caused surprise. In fact, the Eastern Mebon is a temple-island, in the middle of the huge reservoir constructed by Yashovarman. In part, it has the character of a temple dedicated to the founder's ancestors, just as Prasat Lolei was erected by Yashovarman in honor of his ancestors in the middle of the reservoir excavated by Indravarman.

However, the Eastern Mebon, given the quincunx arrangement of its towers, might have added to the confusion because, with only two platforms, it stands considerably lower than Pre Rup. The latter is the last example of a temple-mountain without continuous galleries. It still has the long halls surrounding the pyramid, almost joining up with the first enclosure.

The Banteay Srei Style

The style of Banteay Srei (967) might seem to be a rather specious category since only six years separate it from Pre Rup; moreover, only two or three temples have been identified in this style. But what a style! Even if it were the sole example, Banteay Srei would justify naming a style of its own. First, it should be noted that it is not a royal temple: started during the reign of Rajendravarman and completed in that of Jayavarman V, it is actually the project of the latter king's guru, or religious tutor, a Brahmin called Yajnavaraha.

The Banteay Srei style is distinguished above all by its beauty and its perfection, which arouse the whole-hearted admiration of anyone lucky enough to see it.

LINTELS. The lintels of Banteay Srei are the successors of those of Pre Rup and the Eastern Mebon, but they also copy those of Lolei, Preah Ko, and the Bakong temple, themselves copied from lintels of a more distant past. But the "consoles" (abacuses) on top of the columns, such important elements in the Preah Ko style, have now disappeared.

Another element of the composition, which reappears at Banteay Srei, is the division of the lintel into quarters; there are three examples at least, and they hark back to an earlier time, that of the Sambor Prei Kuk and the Prei Kmeng styles. But the three examples are marked by heads of monsters holding a pendant or by elephant heads, derived from the central motif on the lintels at the Lolei temple.

Finally, there are plant motifs that Gilberte de Coral-Rémusat calls "flowerets" replacing the small multi-curved arches, and which are in fact the metamorphosis of a lotus more mythical than realistic.

COLUMNS. A marked return to the past is seen in the reappearance, for the last time, of cylindrical columns. They exit alongside octagonal columns.

In this style there are no longer rings marking the shafts at one-eighth intervals, giving the columns their characteristic plain appearance. A rather odd detail is that the decor of garlands and pendants is used randomly either on the upper or lower part of the column.

PEDIMENTS. The pediment is one of the most important elements in the art of Banteay Srei. The three types of pediment had already been used at Koh Ker: the pediment in the shape of an upside-down U, divided into three sections and with a dentated outline; the multi-curved pediment; and the triangular pediment. They are also all found at Banteay Srei, where they display the perfection typical of this style.

The three main sanctuaries have upside-down U pediments, divided into three sections and with slightly

Devata at Pre Rup.
Photo: René Dumont

Lintel at Banteay Srei showing quarter divisions.
Photo: René Dumont

Triangular pediment at Banteay Srei.
Photo: René Dumont

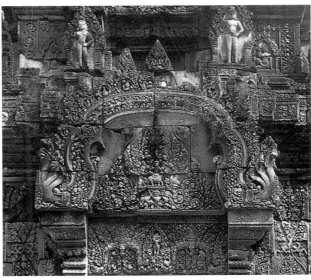

Pediment in the form of an inverted and dentated U, Banteay Srei.
Photo: René Dumont

curved outline. The little point of the dentations is strongly marked. The decoration inside the tympanums depicts plant motifs surrounding a figure or a small scene in the middle. At either end of the pediment's arch, magnificent naga are displayed.

But it is on the secondary buildings, the gopura and above all the libraries, that the finest example of multi-curved pediments, so typical of Khmer art, are to be found. The triple pediments of the libraries, their tiered structure, their contours, the detail of their decoration and the bas-reliefs that fill the tympanums of the outer pediments are of a quality unmatched except by the lintels in the Preah Ko style and the bas-reliefs at Angkor Wat, and by one or two lintels in this style.

Multi-curved pediment at Banteay Srei.
Photo: René Dumont

PILASTERS. To do justice to the beauty and variety of the pilasters at Banteay Srei would require a whole book—as would a description of the whole range of Khmer decoration with the astonishing metamorphoses of *kala*, *makara*, lion and naga, and above all the lotus, a constant element, in the most amazing variations.

The Khleangs Style

This style (end of the 10th century and the first part of the 11th) takes its name from two fairly unimportant buildings, which form two ensembles of galleries on the Royal Square at Angkor Thom, and have no sanctuaries. Their style, however, covers important and very varied examples of monuments: Ta Keo, Phimeanakas, at the Royal Palace, Chau Srei Vibol (Wat Trach), far from the capital on the ancient route to the east, Preah Vihear, in the north of the country, right on the border with Thailand, and Phnom Chisor, some 60 kilometers southeast of Phnom Penh.

The architecture of this period is very important because of subsequent experiments regarding, in particular, the construction of galleries and the way in which they were vaulted. Ta Keo, a temple-mountain, provides the first example of a surrounding gallery, raised on one of the tiers of the pyramid. It had been tentatively vaulted in brick, and the vault did not last. At the Phimeanakas temple, a surrounding gallery on the upper plateau of the tiered pyramid was vaulted in sandstone for the first time, but the gallery is extremely narrow.

Two temples at least, Ta Keo and Preah Vihear, are genuine masterpieces. Ta Keo could be regarded even as the prototype of the temple-mountain with surrounding gallery. As for Preah Vihear, a temple with ground plan built on a linear pattern, on the side of a natural hill

Walls decorated with bas-reliefs at the Baphuon temple.
Photo: René Dumont

right up to the summit, is certainly the most elegant of Khmer temples, in particular because of its triangular pediments. They were to be the last of their kind because subsequently all the galleries were vaulted in stone.

There is little development in the lintels, which seem rather monotonous and of inferior quality compared with their predecessors. In the center, the head of a *kala* normally has a tongue of leaves, already found at Banteay Srei. The bending of the horizontal branch is more pronounced here, without touching the bottom of the lintel. The quarter division is frequently found, but with "flowerets" instead of heads of monsters.

The columns start to evolve again, with a multiplication of groups of rings, so there are fewer bare areas and consequently fewer small triangular leaves, which end up resembling the teeth of a saw rather than leaves.

THE PEDIMENTS. In the Khleangs style, the naga-head ends seem to lose the head of the *makara*—traditionally appearing to devour (or spit out) the body of the naga—so that the sinuous contour of the arch seems to represent the body of the naga itself. But the combination *makara*-naga will reappear at Angkor Wat and at the Bayon. This arch contour becomes bulging in shape (as, faintly, at Banteay Srei), to imitate better the body of the naga.

The triangular pediments, one of the essential features that make the silhouetted shapes at Preah Vihear so elegant, are seen here for the last time.

The Baphuon Style

In the whole history of Khmer architecture one monument, the Baphuon temple, marks a pinnacle of daring construction. But it was to be at a very high cost:

almost all of the high retaining walls at this, the steepest of the temple-mountains, have collapsed.

As for the decoration, there has been little development from the preceding style and is worth noting only for some of its details: the central *kala* no longer has a leafy tongue and has normal jaws again, though its snout is scooped in a curious concave shape.

There is one innovation, however, which is at the same time a return to the past: the reappearance of lintels depicting scenes, while the tympanums of the pediments are again decorated with plant motifs. These consciously historical lintels have scenes that derive from those at Sambor Prei Kuk and Prei Kmeng. But while formerly the scene was shown beneath the arch, here it fills the entire surface of the lintel.

The columns hardly differ at all from the preceding style. The main feature of the pediments, as already seen at the Khleangs, is the suppression of the *kala* head at the ends of the pediment and the transformation of the simple arch into a curving, bulging shape evoking the serpentine body of the naga.

The sculpture of the Baphuon style is notable both for the statuary that, as always in a period of innovation, becomes more lifelike, more graceful, almost feminine, and for the important bas-relief wall decorations arranged in panels.

The Angkor Wat Style

The Angkor Wat style (12th century) includes temples that are important in terms of both their size and the quality of their architecture and decoration. It represents the highest point of classical Khmer art; to borrow the words with which the French art historian Henri Focillon described European art of the Middle Ages, closely contemporary with this Khmer art: "the point where there is the greatest harmony between the various parts... a brief moment when artistic forms are at their peak."

Belonging to this period are Preah Palilay, Preah Pithu, Thommanon, Chau Say Tevoda and, away from Angkor, in Thailand, Phimai and many others. Above all, there are the two gigantic monuments of Beng Mealea and Angkor Wat, covering more or less the same surface area, but the former is built on the flat while the second is in the form of a pyramid.

All architectural features are here, in complete form: at the Bayon temple, there is a tentative experiment with the layout radiating out from the central massif; Angkor Wat, with its terraces and its pyramid, its entrance pavilions, its sanctuary towers and its galleries, some surrounding the whole and some aligned on the monument's axes, and its libraries, represents the most complete and most accomplished example of Khmer architecture.

The architectural elements and decoration—lintels, columns, pediments, pilasters, false doors—continue the previous models. But an additional type appears— the "lintel without branch"—the result of the branch of foliage having steadily descended until it vanished behind the leaf scrolls at the bottom, themselves surmounted by a decoration of plant motifs.

There are also some lintels "with repeatedly broken branches," a prototype of which was seen at Banteay Srei whose origins, even older, are to be found in the horizontal branches formed by the bodies of intertwined naga found on certain lintels at Preah Ko.

The columns continue to evolve, the number of rings increasing to ten or 12. Sometimes it is difficult to distinguish a hierarchical pattern here. The bare parts are smaller and the leaves have become a saw-tooth pattern. In the courtyard of the second enclosure, there are polygonal columns with 20 visible faces (and not just 16 as some have stated).

The pediments retain the bulging arch of the previous style but it is once again decorated, as when it had a plain outline. The arch still follows the pattern of five curves and counter-curves with ends turning upwards. There is also the motif of the *kala*-head spitting out a naga, though perhaps these are the traditional *makara* with very atrophied trunks.

Where the pediments of the preceding style contained tympanums decorated with plant motifs placed above lintels depicting scenes, they now have scenes from the *Ramayana* and the *Mahabharata*.

The sculpture is extremely important. There are some very fine statues in the round, generally with a cold, hieratic air. The art of bas-relief, appearing also on the pediments found on all the temples, reaches its peak of perfection on the interior walls of the third enclosure, on the galleries, and on the corner pavilions: altogether these bas-reliefs cover more than 700 meters. The only wall decorations depicting scenes were those on the upper level of the Bakong and the reliefs sculpted in brick inside the sanctuaries at Prasat Kravan, in addition to the sole example of painted mural decoration in the sanctuaries at Prasat Neang Khmau, representing the same themes. There were also the small panels, in the previous style, at the Baphuon temple and at Prasat Khna Seng Keo.

At Angkor Wat, we have a display of complete mastery of mural decoration, in the composition and carving of the succession of scenes of battles between Pandavas and Kauravas (from the *Mahabharata*), of royal parades or scenes of heaven and hell, and in the extraordinary composition of the Churning of the Ocean of Milk by gods and demons, depicted in a single scene 45 meters long.

The Bayon Style

The Bayon style covers a surprisingly large number of buildings, so large that certain authors refuse to admit that one reign could have been long enough for so many works to have been conceived and built. Nevertheless, even if Jayavarman VII's immediate predecessors and successors erected temples and statues in the same style, it is clear that it was this king who was directly responsible for the principal foundations, including Ta Prohm, Preah Khan, and the Bayon temple in his city of Angkor Thom.

Unfortunately, the consequence of so much activity is the poor quality of the construction, often of the decoration, and sometimes of the sculpture: it would have been necessary to employ all available manpower, competent or otherwise, to carry out all these projects, and architects, sculptors, and stone dressers cannot become skilled overnight.

Nevertheless, this period is important not only for the countless number of temples and images created, but also for some works in particular that are of very high quality.

The most important, best-known and most impressive creation is the tower of faces, an innovation in both architectural and sculptural terms. Given the great difficulties associated with creating sculpture on a gigantic scale, it has to be acknowledged that the Khmers of this era created, at the Bayon temple and elsewhere, the most beautiful giant sculptures which, moreover, are imbued with a symbolic significance that makes them deeply spiritual.

Another innovation is the city wall at Angkor Thom, measuring altogether 12 kilometers (three kilometers a side). It is the first example of a defensive wall, creating a veritable fortress—but at the same time it is important not to lose sight of the wall's magical role as boundary of the microcosm represented by the royal city.

A third great innovation, despite its poor execution, is the Bayon temple itself, in its complex layout. Above all there is the central sanctuary, which, described as circular, essentially radiates outwards—the radiation of the bodhisattva Lokeshvara, projecting his divine mercy over the city, the kingdom, the world, and the whole universe in the eight directions of the monument's ground plan and the ten spatial directions.

The architecture of the temples is on such a huge scale, with so many buildings, that it is impossible to deal with them here, and instead I shall limit myself to examining only the usual elements of their principal motifs. A study in greater depth is to be found in the book *Le Cambodge* by Jean Boisselier and above all in the magnificent work by Philippe Sterne, *Les Monuments du style due Bayon et Jayavarman VII.*

There are two main types of lintel:

• the lintel with "thong-type" branch that has repeated breaks (which already appeared sporadically at Angkor Wat), in which the central branch moves down to the bottom of the lintel, then moves up again, interlaced with another piece of itself: the branch thus covers the whole bottom half of the lintel

Lintel at Preah Khan.
Photo: René Dumont

Lintel without branch, at the Baphuon temple.
Photo: René Dumont

• the lintel without branch: in fact, it is the branch itself which, having descended to the bottom of the lintel, turns into a succession of leaf scrolls surmounted by triangular curved leaves, turning either inwards or outwards.

The other lintels are of various designs but mostly they derive from the preceding style. They are easily distinguished by the clumsy way they have been executed compared with the skillful way the Angkor Wat examples were made.

The columns here are no more than a pile of moldings, with very little order in their arrangement—like a pile of somewhat chipped plates!

The pediments, still in the usual multi-curved shape, show the same elements as at Angkor Wat but less skillfully done and more simplified: *kala* or *makara* atrophied at the ends, an arch whose profile is most often bulging in shape and with less skilful decoration. The tympanums still have scenes carved on them, including in particular a large Lokeshvara surrounded by praying figures.

The motifs used by Stern to trace the evolution of this style also include the *devata* on mural decorations, which were already frequently found at Angkor Wat, and here become the norm, but with coiffures, garments, and gestures that fall into definite types, which enables them to be classified. There are also the great *garuda*, *devata* and *asura*; balustrades formed by naga; and the corner motifs represented by the sanctuary towers. All these additional motifs belong to the Bayon style and provide a guide to the study of this style's development.

The Pediments

It would be impossible to deal with all the elements of Khmer decoration—pilasters, false doors, *devata* and *dvarapala* with or without niches or arcades—but a few words on the Khmer pediment are essential. If Khmer architecture, despite the various influences on it, sometimes obvious, sometimes more subtle, displays numerous features that differentiate it from other architectural traditions of the same family, there is one that distinguishes it above all: the pediment.

The Khmer pediment, after a period of gestation lasting from the 7th to the 10th century, reaches its full expression on the libraries and on certain gopura at Bantea Srei (967). Its shape will alter only very slightly, in some details or in the decoration of its tympanum.

As usual, the original model was Indian. The first pediments are shaped like a horseshoe or an inverted U. The precursors were the horseshoe shapes found in Indian grottoes and temples, and also the arches of the *kudu*, a kind of dormer window, or the image of one. This inverted U can be wider or higher, but above all its shape divides and becomes a three-curved arch, as a result of the superimposition of two inverted U arches, a narrower upon a wider. A reminder of this—the remainder of angles jutting out from the triple-segmented arch—still exists as a point sticking up out of the curving outline of the arch, even though it is no longer at the point where the superimposed arches intersect but is now almost at the top.

THE MULTI-CURVED PEDIMENT

From Banteay Srei on, the general design of the Khmer multi-curved pediment, or simply the Khmer pediment, comprises elements that are unchanging in

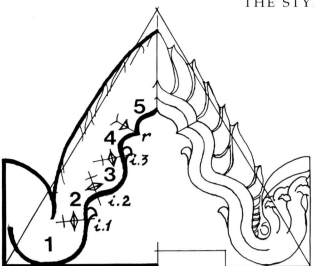

• then three-curved pediments, formed out of two superimposed Us, with the curves of the sides more accentuated

• then, mainly starting with Banteay Srei (967), the multi-curved pediment appears, to subsequently become the predominant form, with this constant formula of five curves on each side of the arch, always with the pointed projection not far from the top.

There are other features marking the pediment's evolution to be found in the detail of the decoration, in the arch's outline, which can be either flat or bulging, and in the decoration of the tympanums, showing either plant motifs or scenes.

THE TRIANGULAR PEDIMENT

An important variant is: the triangular pediment—derived from the normal timber-framed form—which appears, made of stone, in the Koh Ker group (between 921 and 944). It seems that a wooden structure, forming a gable, has been replaced by a heavy sandstone structure, placed on the end walls of the galleries or of the gopura. Triangular pediments are also found on pairs of pilasters, as at Banteay Srei (the gopura of the second enclosure). At Preah Vihear, where triangular pediments make their last appearance, they are placed either on gable-end walls or on reinforced pillars.

There is little variation in the decorative composition of the triangular pediment. Two sloping slides form an approximately equilateral triangle. They represent the planks that closed the tile-and-timber roof, and they are narrower at the bottom than at the top. Both are slightly curved, following the line of the roof. Their decoration consists of longitudinal molding, with beading and various motifs. Flowerets are spaced round the decoration and, in the lower part, the moldings rise in the shape of a double volute, which is often very elegant. At the point where the side of the triangle rests on the pillar (or on the corner of the wall), there is always a motif indicating the lower jaw of the *makara* (seen on the lintels or the pediments). Both the volutes and the jaw are a reminder that this is a stylized *makara* transformed into decorative plant motifs. These plant motifs are also found along the outer surface of the pediment's sloping side, in the form of triangular leaves shaped like flames, and also in the decoration at the top, above the lozenge shape, in the form of a decoration carved inside an almond shape. The finest example of this type of pediment is without doubt that of the east gopura of the second enclosure at Banteay Srei.

The triangular pediment appears on galleries that have tiled roofs and disappears when galleries with corbeled vaults become widespread; when galleries became continuous structures with corner pavilions, there was no justification for this type of pediment. In any case, it is used only on edifices of secondary importance, never on the actual sanctuaries.

For other elements in the evolution of Khmer architecture, the reader should turn to the works of Gilberte de Coral-Rémusat, Philippe Stern, and Jean Boisselier. The decoration of the pilasters, for example, is fascinating, with its leaf scrolls, some of which recall those found in Renaissance architecture. Then there are the windows with "balusters" or stone bars, which evolve into the rather witty form of the false window.

number and arrangement. The variations lie in the dimensions, the ratio of height to length of the base, and the details.

The Khmer pediment comprises an arch consisting of two curving sides, forming undulating lines, with points of inward and outward flexion. This arch frames a tympanum that in some cases contains either images of buildings in progressive diminution, or more often, decoration depicting plant motifs, with or without figures, or sometimes complete scenes based on subjects derived from various religious or epic texts (the *Ramayana* above all). On the outer surface of this arch, decorative foliage in the shape of flames constitute a kind of large curvilinear triangle. However, the fundamental element of the whole is the outline of the arch.

Each side comprises a succession of five alternating inward and outward curves. The first, resting on the pilaster, is convex (1). A flexion point (i.1) on the vertical line reverses the direction of the curve, which becomes concave (2). When the line becomes horizontal, a new flexion point (i.2) moves the curve into a convex shape again (3). Then, after another flexion point (i.3) close to the vertical line, the curve becomes convex again (4). Here there is a jutting feature (r) in the shape of a curved point. Then the curve is concave again (5), at last reaching the top of the arch where a final small inflexion is marked by a small point facing inwards.

In fact, these five curves have merely followed the line of the double U-shaped arch, pushing the sharp angles outwards.

On the arch's inner surface, at the level of the vertical flexion points (i.1 and i.3), there are nearly always two spurs depicting a leaf just opening.

The outer curve (1) is finished off with a vertical line and a curve, the whole describing a kind of curvilinear triangle (perhaps we can think of it as a semi-heart upside down); this too is typical of Khmer art. It forms the end of the pediment in which innumerable naga were to be carved, and also *makara, kala,* leafy motifs etc.

The general shape of the pediment is finished off with a series of decorative, triangular leaves on the arch's outer surface, added on to the overall large curvilinear triangle.

The evolution of the Khmer pediment can therefore be summed up as follows:

• first, pediments in the shape of an inverted U, in the early stages of rather stiff appearance but becoming more supple as the sides of the arch begin to curve

René Dumont

Map of the
Angkor Area

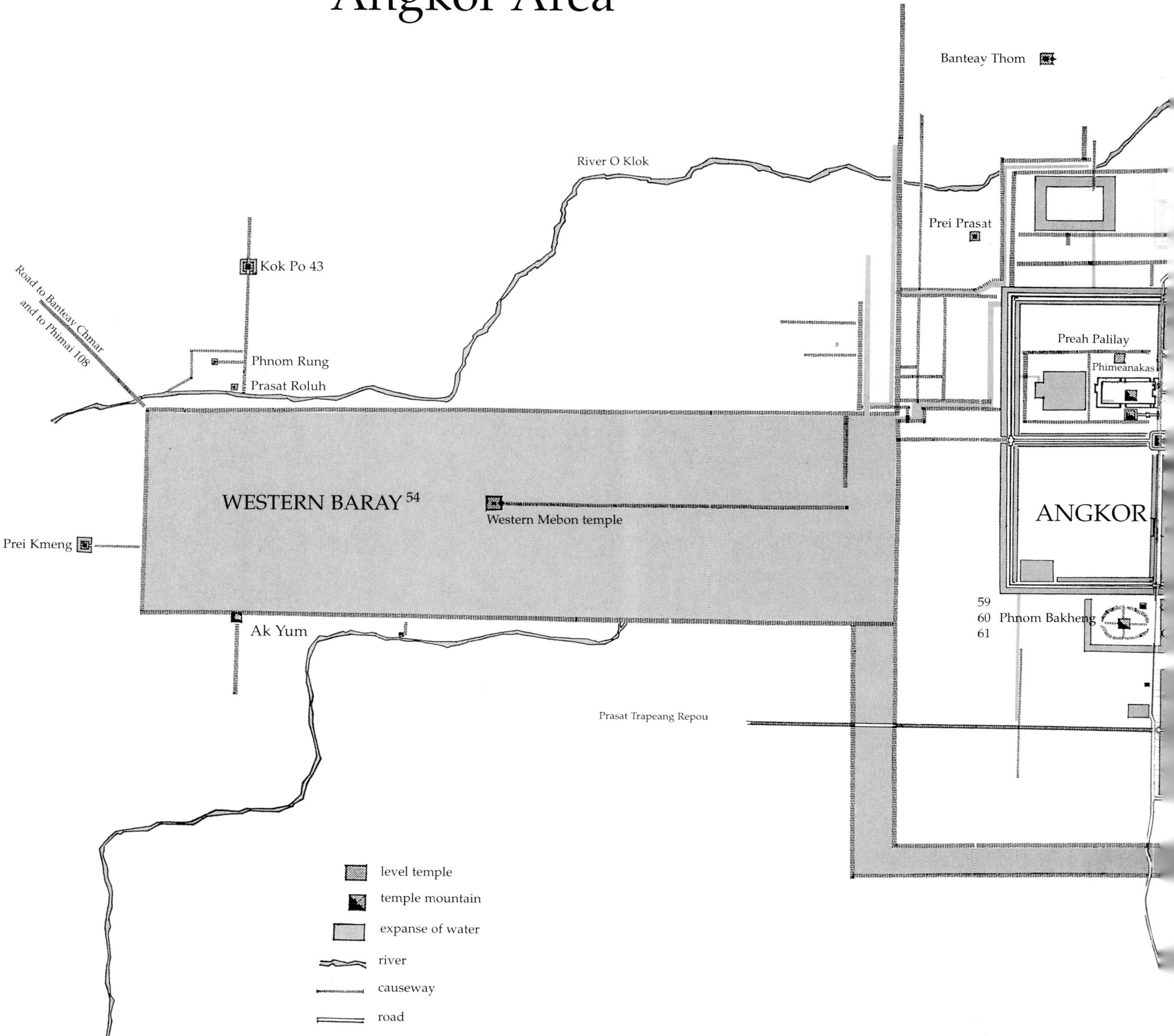

Banteay Thom

River O Klok

Prei Prasat

Kok Po 43

Road to Banteav Chmar
and to Phimai 108

Phnom Rung

Prasat Roluh

Preah Palilay

Phimeanakas

WESTERN BARAY 54

Western Mebon temple

ANGKOR

Prei Kmeng

59
60 Phnom Bakheng
61

Ak Yum

Prasat Trapeang Repou

level temple

temple mountain

expanse of water

river

causeway

road

The numbers refer to the pages with an illustration.

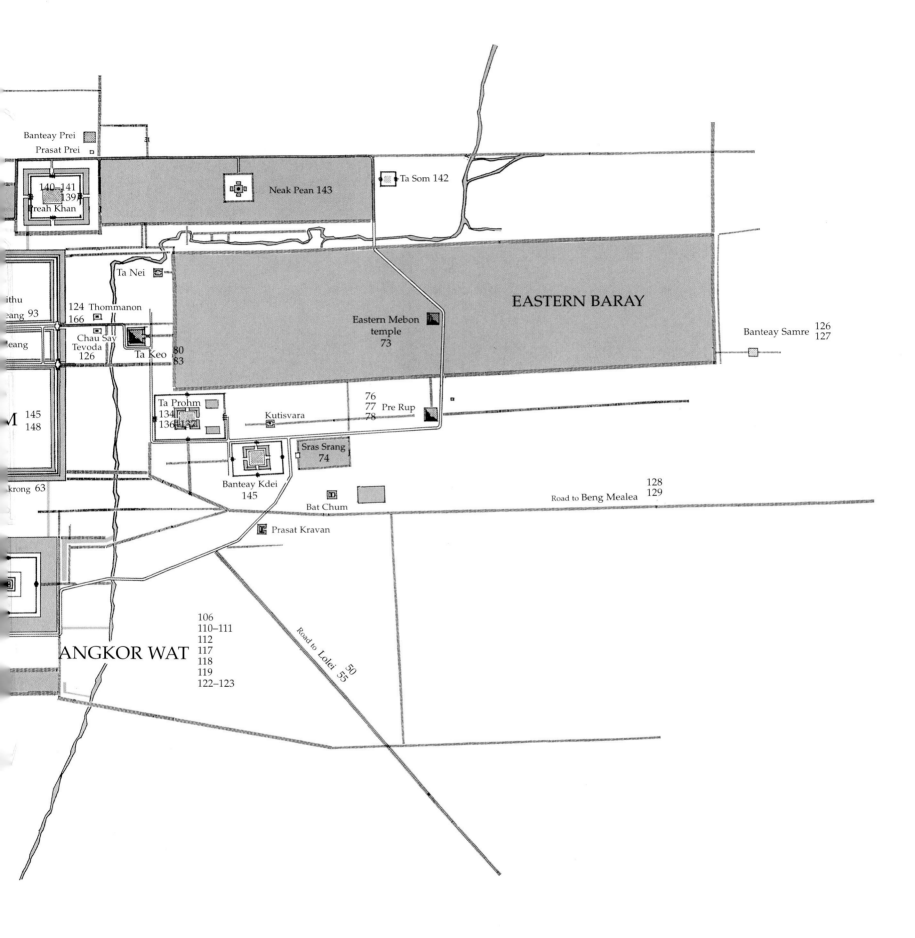

Banteay Prei
Prasat Prei

140–141
139
Preah Khan

Ta Som 142

Neak Pean 143

EASTERN BARAY

Ta Nei

ithu
eang 93

124 Thommanon
166

Eastern Mebon
temple
73

Banteay Samre   126
127

Chau Say
Tevoda
126

Ta Keo   80
83

M   145
148

Ta Prohm
134
136 137

Kutisvara

76
77 Pre Rup
78

Sras Srang
74

krong 63

Banteay Kdei
145

Bat Chum

128
129
Road to Beng Mealea

Prasat Kravan

106
110–111
112
117
118
119
122–123

ANGKOR WAT

Road to Lolei 50
55

CHRONOLOGY

DATES	In the World		In Cambodia	
	Events	*Architecture*	*Events*	*Architecture*
511	Death of Clovis, king of the Franks.			
514			Death of Jayavarman (of Funan). Rudravarman comes to power in south of Cambodia.	
537		Santa Sophia in Constantinople completed. Kondo (Golden Hall) built in Horoyu-ji, Japan.		
590–604	Pontificate of Gregory the Great.			
593			Mahendravarman comes to power in Bhavapura/Sambor Prei Kuk.	
600			Ishanavarman I comes to power.	
615				Southern group of Sambor Prei Kuk.
618	Beginning of Tang Dynasty in China.			
622	Flight of Mohammed to Medina: the Hegira.			
628			Death of Ishanavarman and the collapse of the Khmer empire.	
632	Death of Mohammed.			
655			Jayavarman I comes to power.	The temple of Ak Yum.
c. 670		St Laurence, Bradford-on-Avon, built.		
700	The epic *Beowulf* composed		Death of Jayavarman I and collapse of the Khmer empire.	
708		Temple of Horoyu-ji in Japan built.		The Lompong Preat styles at Prei Kmeng.
711	Arab invasion of Spain.			
713			Queen Jayadevi reigns in Angkor region.	
715		Great Mosque of Damascus built.		
731	Bede completes his *Ecclesiastical History*.	Temple of Borobudur in Java built.		
768	Charlemagne becomes king of the Franks.	Kailasa temple at Ellora built, India.		
790			Consecration of Jayavarman II as king of Indrapura.	
800	Charlemagne crowned emperor.	Chapel of Charlemagne, Aachen, built.		
802			Consecration of Jayavarman II as *chakravartin*, "emperor of the world."	The Kulen style.
814	Death of Charlemagne.			
842	The Oaths of Strasbourg.		Jayavarman III	
877	Death of Emperor Charles the Bald.		Indravarman I becomes "supreme king" of the Khmers.	
880				Consecration of the Preah Ko temple.
881				Consecration of the state temple of Bakong.
886	King Alfred drives the Danes from London.			
889			Yashovarman I becomes "supreme king" of the Khmers.	
893				Consecration of the Lolei temple.
905	The Caliph regains Syria and Egypt.			Consecration of the Phnom Bakheng temple.
907	Fall of the Tang Dynasty in China.			Temple of Baksei Camkrong built.
915	Saracens driven from their last base in Italy, on the Garigliano.		Harshavarman I	
915–917		The first Abbey of Cluny, France, built.	Ishanavarman II	
928			Jayavarman IV, king of Koh Ker, becomes "supreme king" of the Khmers.	Consecration of the state temple of Koh Ker.
932	Birth of the Persian poet Firdausi.			
944			Rajendravarman becomes "supreme king" of the Khmers.	
946	King Edmund of England murdered.			
948				Reconsecration of the Baksei Camkrong temple.
953				Consecration of the Eastern Mebon temple.
960	Sung Dynasty founded in China.			
961				Consecration of the state temple of Pre Rup.
967				Consecration of the Banteay Srei temple.
ca. 968			Jayavarman V, son of Rajendravarman, becomes "supreme king" of the Khmers.	
982	Eric the Red begins colonization of Greenland.			
987				
1000			Death of Jayavarman V. He has built his state temple at Ta Keo.	Ta Keo temple built.
1001			Udayadityavarman I	
1002			Suryavarman I and Jayaviravarman are both	
1006–19		The Church of St-Philibert in Tournus, France.	consecrated "supreme king" of the Khmers in the same year and there is a struggle for power.	

	In the World		In Cambodia	
DATES	Events	Architecture	Events	Architecture
1011			Suryavarman I is finally defeated.	Royal Palace of Angkor Thom at Phimeanakas.
1016	Canute become sole king of England.			
1023–24		The Abbey of Mont-St-Michel.		
1042–66	Edward the Confessor is king of England.			
1050			Udayadityavarman II becomes "supreme king" of the Khmers. He builds the Baphuon as his state temple.	The state temple of Baphuon built.
1063		St. Mark's in Venice begun.		
1066	Battle of Hastings.			
1080			Harshavarman III	The Phimai temple.
1085	The *Domesday Book* begun.		Jayavarman VI, of the Mahidharapura dynasty, becomes "supreme king" of the Khmers.	
1093		Durham Cathedral begun.		
1095	The First Crusade launched by Pope Urban II at Clermont.			
1099	Capture of Jerusalem by the Crusaders.			
1113			Suryavarman becomes "supreme king" of the Khmers.	
1115		St. Bernard founds Clairvaux, France.		
c. 1140				The state temple of Angkor Wat built.
1144		The choir of St-Denis in France consecrated.		
c. 1150				The temples of Beng Mealea, Banteay Samre, Chau Say Tevoda, Thommanon built.
1150			Yashovarman II	
1152–1190	Reign of Emperor Frederick Barbarossa.			
1163		Notre Dame Cathedral in Paris begun.		
1165			Death of Yashovarman II.	
1170	St. Thomas á Becket murdered.		Tribhuvanadityavarman comes to power.	
1177			Sack of Angkor by Cham king Jaya-Indravarman IV.	
1180		Wells Cathedral begun.		
1180–1223	Philippe Auguste is king of France.			
1181			Jayavarman VII becomes "supreme king" after defeating the Cham king Jaya-Indravarman IV.	The walls of Angkor Thom. The state temple of Bayon. The temple of Ta Prohm. The "hospitals."
1186				
1191				The temple of Preah Khan.
1194		Chartres Cathedral begun.		
1204	Constantinople is sacked by Crusaders.			
1210		Reims Cathedral begun.		
1216–72	Henry III is king of England.			
1220			Death of Jayavarman VII	
1226	Death of St. Francis of Assisi.			
1227	Death of Gengis Khan.			
1243			Jayavarman VIII; centre of the Bayon becomes a sanctuary to Shiva.	
1248		Cologne Cathedral begun.		
1279	Fall of the Sung Dynasty in China.			
1281	Fleet sent by Kublai Khan to invade Japan destroyed by typhoon.			
1283	Teutonic Knights complete their colonization of Prussia.			
1287	Fall of Pagan to Kublai Khan's Mongols.			
1295				Consecration of the temple of Mangalartha.
1296		Florence Cathedral begun.		
1309	Pope Clement V moves to Avignon.			
1337	Hundred Years War begins.			
1348	The Great Plague in Europe.			
1350			Ayutthaya, capital of Siam, founded.	
1368	Beginning of the Ming Dynasty in China.			
1378–1417	Great Schism.			
1415	Battle of Agincourt.			
1431	Death of Joan of Arc.		Traditional date for the fall of Angkor to Thai forces.	
1453	Fall of Constantinople to the Turks.		The Portuguese Dominican Gaspar da Cruz tried unsuccessfully to be established at the court of Ang Chan at Lovek.	
1455–85	War of the Roses.			
1509–1547	Henry VIII is king of England.			
1555			First description of Angkor by a European, the Portuguese traveler Diogo de Couto.	
End of the 16th century				

GLOSSARY

acroteria (Greek, "highest") In architecture, small statues or ornamental plaques set on the highest point of a pediment, at the corners of a roof etc.

anasytlosis A method of reconstructing a ruined structure by carefully piecing together its original parts.

ashrama (Sanskrit, "hermitage") A form of monastery or retreat for those at the end of their active life who want to prepare for the afterlife.

atlantes (Greek, "Atlas") In architecture, supports in the form of carved figures. Unlike caryatids, atlantes are usually built into a wall.

angkor (Cambodian Sanskrit) A Khmer form of the Sanskrit work *nagara*, meaning "city" or "capital." The word is also found in the form *nokor*.

apsaras (Sanskrit) In Hinduism, female celestial dancers. They are noted in particular for literally dancing in attendance on kings, gods, and those who have died a hero's death in battle.

avatar (Sanskrit, "descent") In Hinduism, an incarnation of a deity; in particular, the various incarnations in human and animal form of Vishnu. Krishna and Rama are well-known avatars of Vishnu.

arogyashala (Sanskrit, "house of the sick") Hospitals. It is not known whether these were true hospitals, where the sick could stay, or merely dispensaries where they could obtain medical attention and advice.

banteay (Khmer, "fortress") The word is found in the name of several temples that were likened to fortresses because of their enclosure walls.

baray (Sanskrit) A reservoir. Sometimes very large, their primary function was as part of a vast irrigation system in which rivers, canals, and dikes were utilized. They also had an important religious symbolism.

bodhisattva (Sanskrit, "one who is enlightened") In Buddhism, a spiritual being who, out of compassion, forgoes the final stage of spiritual enlightenment in order to help others.

Brahma (Sanskrit) In Hinduism, the creator of the universe, the eternal spirit from which all being originates and to which all returns. In classical Hindu thought, Brahma forms a trinity with Vishnu and Shiva, a concept reflected in the structure of the lingam (see below).

Brahmin (Sanskrit) A Hindu priest, a member of the highest Hindu caste.

Buddha (Sanskrit, "the enlightened one") In Buddhism, one who has attained complete spiritual illumination. The Buddha, Siddharta Gautama, who lived in the 6th century B.C., was the first of the Buddhas.

cella, *pl. cellae* (Latin) The central inner chamber of a temple, usually the "holy of holies."

chakravartin (Sanskrit, "one who turns the wheel [of the Law]") Supreme king of kings. A title used by ancient emperors of India and adopted by the Khmer king Jayavarman II when he had completed his conquests.

Champa An Indianized state that flourished in what is now south and central Vietnam from the 2nd to the 15th centuries.

Chenla (Chinese) The Chinese name for the early Cambodian kingdom that succeeded Fu-nan (see below) and preceded the Khmer era. It flourished from the 6th to the 8th centuries.

Churning of the Ocean of Milk In Hindu mythology, the story of how the gods and demons came together to churn the great Ocean of Milk in order to create the elixir of immortality. The snake Vasuki, which had wrapped itself around Mount Mandara, was pulled back and forth as the rope by the gods and demons, the mountain being the churn.

dentated (Latin, "tooth") In architecture, having a form characterized by a series of recesses and curves.

devaraja (Sanskrit, "the god who is king") A translation into Sanskrit of the Cambodian phrase *Kamrateng Jagat ta Raja*, which refers to the deity charged with protecting the country's well-being. The cult of the *devaraja* (who was seen as the spiritual equivalent of the *chakravartin*) was introduced to Cambodia by Jayavarman II at the beginning of the 9th century.

devata (Sanskrit) A general term for divinities.

dharmashala (Sanskrit, "room of the Law") A place set aside for travelers to rest in. Such travelers' halts were once to be found in every Khmer village, the care of visitors being a part of Hindu and Buddhist morality.

dvarapala (Sanskrit, "guardian of the doorway") Divinities placed at sanctuary doorways or entrances to keep evil spirits from entering.

Fu-nan (Chinese) The Chinese name for the Indianized kingdom that preceded Angkor. Situated in the south of present-day Cambodia. It was succeeded by Chenla (see above). It was in existence as early as the 1st century and reached its high point in the 5th century.

Ganesha (Sanskrit) In Hinduism, the elephant-headed god of wisdom and fertility, the son of Shiva.

garuda (Sanskrit) In Hinduism, a mythical creature with the beak, wings, and claws of an eagle, but the arms and torso of a man. A *garuda* serves as the mount of the god Vishnu.

gopura (Sanskrit) Gateway pavilion in a temple. Often elaborately decorated, they had an important symbolic function as the points of entrance to a sacred area.

guru (Sanskrit, "master") A spiritual teacher or guide.

Hari-Hara (Sanskrit) A Hindu deity who combines the characteristics of both Vishnu (Hari) and Shiva (Hara), a synthesis that resulted from the merging of two major cults. Images of Hari-Hara have Shiva's attributes on the right and Vishnu's on the left.

Indra (Sanskrit, "king") The principal god in the Vedic Hindu pantheon, associated with war and storm. One of the main guardian deities of the horizon, his special role was as protector of the East. He is usually shown mounted on a three-headed elephant.

kala (Sanskrit, "black, death") A monster shown with a grinning face and bulging eyes. Appearing over a doorway, they act as door guardians keeping evil out of temples.

karma (Sanskrit, "act, deed") In Buddhism and Hinduism, the sum of our actions during the successive stages of existence, seen as determining our fate in future incarnations.

kompong (Khmer) A town or village on the banks of a river or lake.

Krishna (Sanskrit, "the black one") In Hinduism, one of the principal incarnations of the god Vishnu. Usually depicted as a handsome, blue-skinned youth playing a flute, Krishna is one of the most popular figures in Hindu mythology, his amorous adventures often illustrated.

Lakshmi (Sanskrit) The Hindu goddess of beauty and good fortune, also known as Shru. The wife of Shiva, she was born as a result of the Churning of the Ocean of Milk (see above).

laterite (Latin, "brick tile") A soil found in hot, damp climates that becomes very hard when exposed to air and so can be cut into blocks and used for building. It was used extensively in Cambodia.

Lesser Vehicle One of the major Buddhist sects, also known as Theravada or Hinayana Buddhism. By the 15th century it had largely replaced Mahayana (see below) in Cambodia and other parts of Southeast Asia. It marked a return to the simplicity, austerity, and piety of earlier forms of Buddhist belief and practice.

lingam (Sanskrit, "phallus") In Hinduism, a stylized phallus that represents the god Shiva as cosmic creator and pillar of the world. Typically a lingam has three sections, the lower sections representing Brahma and Vishnu.

Lokeshvara (Sanskrit, "Lord of the World") In Asian Buddhism, the familiar form of the name Avalokiteshvara, one of the best-known and best-loved bodhisattva (see above). As Lokeshvara is the "Lord who looks down with compassion" on all creation, he is often depicted with several faces looking in different directions.

Mahabharata (Sanskrit, "great story") One of the two great Indian epics, it recounts the wars between two families struggling for dominance of north India. Its best-known section is the Bhagavad Gita, in which the god Krishna acts as spiritual guide to Arjuna. See also Ramayana.

Mahayana (Sanskrit, "Greater Vehicle") One of the major sects of Buddhism. Developing in the 1st century in India, it is best known for its concept of the bodhisattva (see above). It spread quickly and was the dominant form of Buddhism in Cambodia during the 12th and 13th centuries. It was gradually replaced by Hinayana Buddhism (see Lesser Vehicle above).

makara (Sanskrit) In Khmer mythology, a mythical water monster that has the body of a crocodile and, usually, the trunk of an elephant. In Khmer temples they are usually depicted around doorways.

Meru (Sanskrit) In Hindu mythology, the cosmic mountain at the center of the universe, home of the gods. In Khmer temples the central sanctuary is a representation of Mount Meru.

naga (Sanskrit) In Khmer mythology, a mythical water creature that usually takes the form of a many-headed cobra. The naga was seen both as the progenitor of the Khmer race and the protector of the kingdom's riches.

Nandi (Sanskrit) In Hinduism, the sacred bull that acts as the mount of the god Shiva.

pala (Sanskrit) Guardian.

phnom (Khmer) Mountain, hill.

prasat, or **prasada** (Sanskrit) A sanctuary in the form of a tower. In Khmer architecture the *prasat* is a representation of the cosmic Mount Meru, which stands at the center of the universe.

preah (Khmer, "holy") A word prefixed to the name of a sacred person or thing; a mark of spiritual distinction.

rahu (Sanskrit) A demon usually shown devouring the Moon.

Rama (Sanskrit) In Hinduism, an incarnation of the god Vishnu. Originally he was a folk hero, and only gradually became regarded as an avatar of Vishnu. His many adventures are recounted in the epic *Ramayana*.

Ramayana (Sanskrit, "the story of Rama") One of the two great Indian epics, which was very popular in Southeast Asia. It is an account of the exploits of Rama, the ninth incarnation of the god Vishnu. The Cambodian version was known as the Reamker. See also Mahabharata.

sampot Cambodian garment worn on the lower part of the body. It consists of a length of material wrapped around the waist and then drawn up between the legs to form a loose pair of pants.

shaka (Sanskrit) An Indian era used in Khmer inscriptions. It begins 78 years behind the Western system.

shastra (Sanskrit) A text or treatise.

Shiva (Sanskrit, "auspicious") The Hindi god of destruction: Shiva the Destroyer. He is also linked to creation, however, his central symbol being the lingam (see above). He is usually shown dancing, his dance representing the cosmic rhythm of creation and destruction.

spean (Khmer) Bridge.

stele, *pl. stelae* (Greek, "block of stone") An upright slab of stone on which a text has been inscribed.

stung (Khmer) River.

stupa (Sanskrit, "crown of the head") A Buddhist shrine in the form of a large dome, usually containing religious relics.

thom (Khmer) Great.

wat (Thai) Shrine or temple.

Vishnu (Sanskrit) The Hindu god who acts as "Preserver of the Universe." He forms a trinity with Brahma (Creator) and Shiva (Destroyer). Considered the embodiment of compassion, he is best known through his ten incarnations, notably Rama and Krishna.

Yama (Sanskrit) In Hinduism, the god of the justice who presides over the Underworld. He is usually shown riding a buffalo and with eight arms, several of them wielding clubs.

yogin (Sanskrit, "yoke, union") Someone who practices yoga, a Hindu spiritual discipline that seeks spiritual enlightenment through the austere training of mind and body. A spiritual guide or teacher.

yoni (Sanskrit, "womb") In Hinduism, the emblem of the female genitals, symbolizing the feminine principle.

BIBLIOGRAPHY

BOISSELIER, Jean: *Le Cambodge* (Manuel d'archéologie d'Extrême-Orient, première partie, tome I), Paris, 1966.
BOISSELIER, Jean: *Tendances de l'art khmer*, Paris, 1956.

CŒDÈS, George: *Histoire des États hindouisés d'Indochine et d'Indonésie*, 3e édition, éd. de Brocard, Paris, 1964.

DAGENS, Bruno: *Angkor, la forêt de pierre*, Gallimard, Paris, 1989.
DELAPORTE, Louis: *Voyage au Cambodge. L'architecture khmère*, Delagrave, Paris, 1880.
DUMARÇAY, Jacques, le Bayon (I: *Histoire architecturale du temple. Atlas et notices des planches*, 1967; II: *Textes et planches*, 1973), EFEO n° 3.
DUMARÇAY, Jacques: *Ta Kev (étude architecturale du temple)*, EFEO n° 6.
DUMARÇAY, Jacques: *Phnom Bakheng (étude architecturale du temple)*, Paris, 1972 EFEO n° 7

FINOT, Louis, GOLOUBEW Victor et CŒDÈS George: *Le Temple d'Angkor Vat*, 5 vol., Paris, 1929–1932. EFEO n° 2
FINOT Louis, GOLOUBEW, Victor et PARMENTIER Henri: *Le Temple d'Içvarapura (Banteay Srei)*, Paris, 1926. EFEO n° 1,

GITEAU, Madelaine: *Histoire du Cambodge*, éd. Marcel Didier, Paris, 1957.
GLAIZE, Maurice: *Les Monuments du groupe d'Angkor. Guide*, dernière éd. Maisonneuve, Paris, 1963.
GROSLIER, Bernard-Philippe: *Angkor, hommes et pierres*, Albin Michel, Paris, 1956.
GROSLIER, Bernard-Philippe: *Indochine, carrefour des arts*, L'art dans le monde, Albin Michel, Paris, 1961.
GROSLIER, Bernard-Philippe: *Indochine*, Mundi, Paris, 1966.

LUNET DE LAJONQUIERE: *Inventaire descriptif des monuments du Cambodge*, pub. de l'EFEO, vol. IV, VIII et IX, Paris, 1902–1911.

NAFILYAN, Guy: *Angkor Vat*, EFEO, 1969.

STERN, Philippe: *Les Monuments du style khmer du Bayon et Jayavarman VII*, PUF, Paris, 1965.

TITLES IN ENGLISH:

CHANDLER, David, *A History of Cambodia*, Westview Press, Boulder, California, 1983. Revised edition Colorado and Oxford, 1992.
CŒDES, George, *Angkor: An Introduction*, trans. Emily Floyd Gardiner, Oxford University Press, New York and Hong Kong, 1963.

FREEMAN, Michael and WARNER, Roger, *Angkor: The Hidden Glories*, Houghton Mifflin, Boston, 1990.

GITEAU, Madeleine, *Khmer Sculpture and the Angkor Civilization*, Abrams, New York/Thames and Hudson, London, 1965.
GROSLIER, Philippe and ARTHAUD, Jacques, *Angkor, Art and Civilization*, Praeger, New York/Thames and Hudson, London, 1966.

MOUHOT, M. Henri, *Travels in the Central Parts of Indo-China (Siam), Cambodia, and Laos, During the Years 1858, 1859, and 1860* (English translation), John Murray, London, 1864 (reprinted White Lotus, Bangkok, 1986).

RAWSON, Philip, *The Art of South East Asia: Cambodia, Vietnam, Thailand, Laos, Burma, Java, Bali*, Thames and Hudson, London, 1967 (Asia Books, Bangkok, 1990).

ZHOU, Daguan, *The Customs of Cambodia*, trans. by Paul Pelliot, The Siam Society, Bangkok, 1992.

INDEX

This index contains all proper names, qualified as follows:
B: *baray*; C: city, province or kingdom; D: divinity; E: exalted personage;
G: term in mythical geography; M: monarch; P: prince or princess;
S: archaeological site or temple.
Small capital letters: modern author; italics: book title.
An * is used to refer to captions.
When a placename does not refer to a location in Cambodia, the name of
the country is given in parentheses.